U. S. Nonproliferation Export Controls

Theory, Description and Analysis

Edited by

Gary K. Bertsch
Richard T. Cupitt
Takehiko Yamamoto

University Press of America, Inc.
Lanham • New York • London

Copyright © 1996 by
University Press of America,® Inc.
4720 Boston Way
Lanham, Maryland 20706

3 Henrietta Street
London, WC2E 8LU England

Library of Congress Cataloging-in-Publication Data

U.S. and Japanese nonproliferation export controls / edited by Gary K.
Bertsch, Richard T. Cupitt, Takehiko Yamamoto.
p.   cm.
Includes bibliographical references and index.
1. Nuclear nonproliferation--International cooperation. 2. Export
controls--United States. 3. Export controls--Japan. I. Bertsch, Gary
K. II. Cupitt, Richard T. III. Yamamoto, Takehiko.
JX1974.73.U14   1996   327.1'74--dc20   95-43591 CIP

ISBN 0-7618-0191-X (cloth: alk: ppr.)
ISBN 0-7618-0192-8 (pbk: alk: ppr.)

In Memory of Dean Rusk (1909-1994)

Dean Rusk served from 1961-1969 as Secretary of State in the Kennedy and Johnson Administrations. Subsequently, from 1970 until his death on December 20, 1994, he served as a Professor of International Law at the University of Georgia. Professor Rusk provided the inspiration for the formation of the Center for East-West Trade Policy. He was a strong supporter of the Center and participated in many projects and activities. In *As I Saw It,* Dean Rusk included a "Message to the Young" which reads in part:

Your generation will discover in the decades ahead whether mankind can organize a durable peace in a world in which thousands of megatons are lying around in the hands of frail human beings. A world in which collective security--what my generation used to try to curb the obscenity of war--is withering away, and we are not even discussing what shall take its place.

As secretary of state, I was required to study in great detail the full effects of a nuclear war. Few others have done so. Throughout history it has been possible for us to pick ourselves out of the death and destruction of war and start over again. We will not have that chance after World War III. In that conflagration-if one occurs-this earth may no longer sustain the human race. And so mankind has reached this point: We must prevent war before it occurs....

Can we live together, different races of people, their different religions and cultures, to share this planet peacefully and overcome that terrible difference between "we" and "they" which has crowded the human story with so much senseless tragedy? Will nations restrain their extravagant notions of sovereignty and join hands to find answers which no one nation can find alone? Will we in our personal lives find more satisfaction in the delights of the mind and spirit and ease our pressure upon material resources? Your generation will discover these things.

-Dean Rusk (as told to his son, Richard Rusk,)
As I Saw It, (New York: W.W. Norton and Company, 1990.)

July 1996

To

Rick,

with respect & best wishes!

Gary

iii

Contents

Trends in National Policies

The Asian-Pacific Region and Export Controls

Issues on the Horizon

Conclusion

Foreword

The post-Cold War era has involved not only the loss of focus provided by a single overriding policy objective, but has also brought with it a growing awareness of opportunities and risks, some new and some partly overshadowed in the past. Among these has been the problem of nuclear proliferation.

According to a White Paper prepared by the Clinton Administration for the Forum on the Role of Science and Technology in Promoting National Security and Global Stability (Washington, D.C., March 29-30, 1995), controlling the spread of material and technology is the first pillar of U.S. nonproliferation policy.

From across the Pacific, in early 1995, Japanese Foreign Minister Yohei Kono stated that the proliferation of weapons of mass destruction and conventional weapons "constitute a major threat to global peace..." and that "Japan must play a leading role" in this issue.

As this is written, the United States, Japan and representatives from more than one hundred and seventy other countries are meeting in New York to review the Nuclear Non-Proliferation Treaty (NPT). No matter the outcome of this review, recent experience in Iraq and elsewhere has shown that effective export controls remain a key element in any workable non-proliferation strategy. Without them the flow of enriched fuel and other crucial technology into undesirable channels can simply not be halted or delayed. This indeed captures the essence of many of the discussions surrounding the decision whether or not to extend the NPT indefinitely. The project leading to this book continues and deepens the University of Georgia's Center for East-West Trade Policy's "Export Controls in the 1990s" program. The overall research program was initiated with a grant from the Pew Charitable Trusts in 1990. The project has been designed to explore and promote changes in export control policies that reflect the changes in the global security environment, including disintegration of the Soviet Union, regime changes in Eastern Europe, and the rise of "sporadic militarism" in the Third World. One product of that initial grant was a set of case studies on national export control. Our difficulty in finding an expert on Japanese export controls for that study, along with "research and dialogue" initiatives recommended by an international group of export controls specialists at a workshop held at the University of Georgia in October 1991, helped direct our interests towards developing a collaborative research project between Japanese and U.S. researchers on export control issues.

As it matured, the project has acquired several layers of objectives, some related specifically to nonproliferation export controls, some related to the broader benefits of U.S.-Japanese collaboration on social scientific, policy-oriented research. From specific to general, these objectives are:

•To formulate a series of U.S.-Japanese nonproliferation export control policy recommendations

•To promote export control policies and multilateral export controls that curb weapons proliferation and enhance international security, with minimal disruption to peaceful international trade

•To promote greater understanding of U.S. and Japanese interests and goals surrounding export controls

•To promote and disseminate the results of joint U.S.-Japanese social scientific, policy-relevant research that can lay the groundwork for future research in this and other areas of public policy

•To develop a cadre of U.S. and Japanese nonproliferation export control scholars; (this may entail encouraging younger scholars to specialize in this area)

•To promote ongoing dialogue among U.S. and Japanese export control communities

•To promote ongoing research between American and Japanese researchers

The chapters in this volume served as background for the successful March 27-28, 1995 workshop in Athens. With input from more than two dozen scholars, business leaders, and government policy-makers from the United States and Japan over a three year period, a number of new ideas emerged that will form the basis for additional policy recommendations. As both U.S. and Japanese export control policy remains in flux in the middle of 1995, this work can be influential as new strategies take shape. Recommendations from that workshop are being sent to the policy-making communities in Japan and the United States.

Martin J. Hillenbrand
May 1995

Preface

The Gulf War proved how dangerous the world can be if the indiscriminate transfer of weapons is allowed to proceed. Both the United States and Japan should work vigorously toward establishing a new regime for controlling arms exports and the transfer of military technologies, especially to Third World countries that pose obvious risks.

Jimmy Carter and Yasuhiro Nakasone[1]

Trends and Issues

The sale of conventional and unconventional weapons, and the materials and technology to produce them, represents a grave threat to global security in the 1990s and beyond.[2] Weapons today are more sophisticated, have greater killing power, and are more widely produced than ever before. Left uncontrolled there is reason to believe that conventional and unconventional weapons will continue to spread and fuel new arms races in various areas of confrontation around the globe.[3] Most nations of the world could become more heavily armed and the likelihood for destructive conflicts could grow even higher.

There are various trends that make the contemporary threat of weapons proliferation very real. First, the end of the Cold War may increase rather than decrease the spread of weapons.[4] During the Cold War period the United States and Soviet Union had considerable influence on the weapons acquisition programs of their allied and client states. The superpowers were also inclined to ensure the security of these states and this worked to increase perceptions of security and reduce the demand for weapons in many of the states. Today the superpowers are losing some influence, and may reduce their security guarantees. This makes their former clients and allies less certain about their own security. This can work to increase the demand for weapons.

Second, there are more and more countries with the capacity to produce and export sophisticated weapons and dual-use technology

(technology which can be used for both weapons and non-weapons, civilian applications). Most countries in East Asia now produce weapons and some are emerging as major arms exporters.[5] Some have even developed or explored various options in the nuclear and chemical areas. China possesses a fully developed nuclear capability, North Korea was until recently pursuing such a capability, and South Korea and Taiwan are reported to have engaged in nuclear weapons related research.[6] Furthermore, China, Taiwan, and the two Koreas have engaged in the development of chemical weapons and ballistic missiles capable of delivering nuclear or chemical weapons to the territory of their principal adversary.[7]

Third, the production and sale of weaponry is big business in today's world. All states are rightly concerned with economic growth and welfare, and few states will deny themselves the earnings weapons and dual-use exports can generate. The United States is the biggest producer and exporter of arms and accounted for over 50 percent of global arms transfers and related services over the last decade. President Bush's decision to sell 150 F-16 aircraft to Taiwan during the heat of the 1992 U.S. presidential campaign demonstrated the lack of resolve of a rich and powerful country (i.e., a country that many feel can afford to resist arms exports) in restraining its weapons trade. The United States is also grappling with the difficult problem of managing its dual-use exports. U.S. policy is dedicated to controlling dual-use technology exports that might go into the weapons systems of perceived adversaries. But U.S. policy is also dedicated to eliminating unnecessary restraints on dual-use exports. How it manages these two often competing policy objectives remains a difficult and complicated challenge.[8]

Fourth, the slow pace of converting military to civilian production in the world's leading weapons producers suggests that weapons production and exports will continue. If countries like the United States, Russia, France, China, and others continue to produce large quantities of weapons in their relatively secure environments, one can assume that they intend to export significant portions of these quantities. As long as there is a surplus of weapons and dual-use technologies in the global economy, there will be strong pressures to export them.

Fifth, the disintegration of the Soviet Union raises the possibility of an expanded proliferation of weapons and weapons related materials and technologies. Many of the newly independent states (NIS) of the former Soviet Union have inherited massive weapons industries, bulging stockpiles, and considerable weapons technology and know-how. Questions are being raised about the accounting and control of nuclear and other weapons of mass destruction (WMD). At the same time, the new post-Soviet governments are weak and unstable, and are losing control of much of what goes on within their borders. A "sell anything" mentality exists at all levels within the societies as individuals, military industrial enterprises, and governments are forced to generate income to deal with growing economic hardship. Organized crime and corruption permeates all aspects of the economic and political systems. Porous borders and the lack of effective customs control make it possible to move illegal weapons transfers from one country to another. With nascent export control systems, weak intelligence and political cooperation among states in the region, the opportunities for selling off the post-Soviet arsenals are considerable.

Other Responses

Although this book is about governmental efforts to control the export of weapons and weapons related materials and technologies, we should recognize that export controls are not the only policy instruments available. Export controls will be most successful when pursued in conjunction with a variety of "supply" and "demand-side" strategies. For example, if more is done to reduce the demand for weapons and related materials and technologies, export controls will not have to be imposed as often. Fewer uses of export controls will allow more governmental attention to fewer cases. This in turn may result in more effective export controls.

What are some of the "demand-side" strategies that will make countries feel more secure and help reduce demand? First, confidence building measures are useful in reducing the demand for weapons. Such measures can make countries feel more secure and less inclined to pursue security through weapons imports. In the absence of confidence building, the future consequences of arms racing and proliferation are likely to be both dangerous and costly. This in turn will place tremendous pressures on national and international export control efforts.

Second, diplomacy and security assurances can help reduce the demand for weapons. Diplomatic approaches can buy time while other approaches such as export controls can be implemented and improved. Diplomatic efforts should be pursued within any bilateral, regional, or multilateral fora in which security, arms control, and disarmament issues (for example, U.S., Russian, and Chinese theater and tactical nuclear weapons in the Northeast Asian region) can be discussed.

Third, while many taxpayers resist foreign economic and technical aid as luxuries a nation can ill afford, aid and assistance to reduce the demand for weapons can actually be a cost-saving measure. The United States is currently investing considerable sums in North Korea and in the four nuclear republics of the former Soviet Union. If the United States can help Belarus, Kazakhstan, Russia, and Ukraine denuclearize and secure and not proliferate their weapons programs, then it will be able to spend less for U.S. defense later on. Economic inducements to get North Korea to comply with its NPT/IAEA obligations may be cheaper than defending against a nuclear armed and exporting North Korea.

There are also various strategies to restrict and reduce the supply of conventional and unconventional weapons and the materials and technology to produce them. One way to limit the supply of weapons is to get businesses and states to stop producing them. The oversupply of weapons is a major cause of their proliferation. The export of weapons and weapons related goods and technologies is lucrative business in much of the world today. Weapons producing enterprises have to be convinced that they can profit by producing alternative goods and services. Because converting from military to civilian production is costly, governments must provide incentives for conversion. Thus far, there is little successful conversion in the world.[9] This fact, along with continuing demand, means that incredible pressures are being placed on export control systems.

Export Control

Export control has been and remains a key means of slowing weapons proliferation. Through history, governments have imposed controls on their militarily related and strategic exports to keep them from adding to the arsenals of perceived adversaries.[10] Export controls remain a central element in national and international efforts to restrain the spread of weapons in the 1990s.[11]

Countries that produce weapons and weapons related goods and technologies are being asked to control their export. This responsibility to control the spread of weapons is greatly complicated because many weapons related goods and technologies (e.g., computers or nuclear energy technology) are "dual-use" items and, can be used for both civilian and weapons purposes. The challenge is to control the export of these goods and technologies when they are intended for purposes of weapons production and facilitate their export when they are used for peaceful commercial purposes.

International cooperation on nonproliferation export control is a supply-side strategy of considerable importance.[12] If one country denies an export to a suspicious, weapons-oriented end-user in a rogue nation, other countries must cooperate and also control the export for the strategy to be effective. Because there are many producers (companies and countries) of weapons related goods and technologies, one company or country that undercuts or ignores international norms and agreements and sells controlled weapons or weapons technology to proscribed end-users can defeat the purpose of export controls. Weapons producing and exporting countries must cooperate closely to impede the export of weapons and weapons related transfer to countries that will use them in ways that threaten the security of other countries.

Japan and the United States have cooperated closely on export controls during the post-World War II period. The United States, Japan, and key allies worked together in the Coordinating Committee for Multilateral Export Controls (COCOM) to control the export of munitions, nuclear items, and militarily critical industrial goods and technologies to the Soviet Union and other communist destinations. They began to cooperate in other, newer multilateral export control arrangements. Both were founding members of the Australia Group (AG), the Missile Technology Control Regime (MTCR), the Nuclear Suppliers Group (NSG), and the fledgling Supercomputer Regime. Taking that cooperation as a basis, this book examines the prospects for coordinating U.S. and Japanese export control policies in the post Cold War period.

The Project and Book

In 1992, faculty at The University of Georgia in the United States and Waseda University in Japan organized a joint research and service project to examine the opportunities for Japanese-American export control cooperation in the post Cold War period. The project examined:

•how Japanese and U.S. policymakers viewed export controls;

•their understanding of the relationships between export controls, military security, and economic growth;

•the interests and preferences of various private and governmental "players" in the national export control policymaking communities,

•the basis for bilateral and international cooperation to control the proliferation of weapons of mass destruction;

•the policy implications of these and related research issues; and, future research and policy agendas in this issue area.

Through support from The Japan Foundation Center for Global Partnership and the Japan-U.S. Friendship Commission, The University of Georgia and Waseda University faculty organized an international research team to examine these and related issues of export controls in the 1990s. The chapters that follow represent a part of that research.

The chapters in Part I frame the issues and examine the environment in which export controls will be pursued in the 1990s and beyond. The chapters in Part II examine the historical legacy surrounding U.S. and Japanese export controls and these two countries' export control cooperation. Part III addresses key policy trends in Japan and the United States and has chapters examining U.S. and Japanese policy, policy change and reform, and the perspectives and roles of various actors within the business and governmental communities. Part IV examines export control issues within the broader Asia-Pacific region, raising the challenges of export controls in the Koreas, China, and the former Soviet Union. Part V examines a number of issues on the horizon and Part VI identifies findings, recommendations, and prospects for the future.

Notes

1. Jimmy Carter and Yasuhiro Nakasone, "Ensuring in an Unsure World: The U.S.-Japan Global Partnership in the 1990's" (Tokyo: International Institute for Global Partnership, 1991): 2.

2. For descriptions and analyses of the problem, see: William E. Burrows and Robert Windrem, *Critical Mass.- The Dangerous Race for Superweapons in a Fragmenting World* (New York: Simon and Schuster, 1994); William D. Hartung, *And Weapons for All* (New York: Harper Collins, 1994); Elizabeth J. Kirk, W. Thomas Wander, and Brian Smith, eds., *Trends and Implications for Arms Control, Proliferation and International Security in the Changing Global Environment* (Washington, D.C.: American Association for the Advancement of Science, 1993); Michael Pugh, "Combating the Arms Proliferation Problem," *NATO Review* (February 1994); and, W. Thomas Wander and Eric H. Arnett, eds., *The Proliferation of Advanced Weaponry: Technology, Motivation, and Responses* (Washington, D.C.: American Association for the Advancement of Science, 1992).

3. See Michael T. Klare, "Growing Firepower in the Third World," *The Bulletin of the Atomic Scientists,* 46,4 (May, 1990), pp. 9-13, and, "The Next   Great Arms Race," *Foreign Affairs,* 72,3 (Summer, 1993), pp. 136-52.

4. For a discussion of this possibility in East and Southeast Asia, see Klare, "The Next Great Arms Race." Also, see Peter van Ham, *Managing Nonproliferation Regimes in the 1990s* (London, Pinter Publishers, 1993), pp. 58-69, and Andrew Pierre, "Conventional Arms Proliferation Today: Changed Dimensions, New Responses," in Kirk, Wander, and Smith, eds., *Trends and Implications for Arms Control, Proliferation, and International Security in the Changing Global Environment,* pp. 209-25.

5. Klare, pp. 145-48.

6. *Ibid.,* pp. 148-49.

7. *Ibid.,* p. 150.

8. See, for example, J. David Richardson, *Sizing Up US. Export Disincentives* (Washington, D.C.: Institute for International Economics, 1993); National Academy of Sciences, *Finding Common Ground.- US. Export Controls in a Changed Global Environment* (Washington, D.C.: National Academy Press, 1991); and, Gary Bertsch and Steven Elliott-Gower, eds., *Export Controls in Transition* (Durham, NC: Duke University Press, 1992).

9. See, for example, Igor Khripunov, "Delusions v. Conversion," *Bulletin of the Atomic Scientists,* 53,4 (1994), pp. 11-13.

10. See, for example, Carlo M. Cipolla, *Guns, Sails, and Empires. Technological Innovation and the Early Phases of European Expansion, 1400-1700* (New York: Pantheon Books, 1965).

11. See, for example, Kathleen Bailey and Robert Rudney, eds., *Proliferation and Export Controls* (New York: University Press of America, 1993).

12. See Gary Bertsch and Richard Cupitt, "Nonproliferation Export Controls in the 1990s: Enhancing International Cooperation," *Washington Quarterly 16* (Autumn, 1993), pp. 53-70; and Gary Bertsch, Richard Cupitt, and Steven Elliott-Gower, eds., *International Cooperation on Nonproliferation Export Controls* (Ann Arbor: University of Michigan Press, 1994).

Acknowledgements

This book is a product of a multinational, multiple year research project. Perhaps more than most research publications, this project reflects the talent and effort of many people. With their many significant contributions, they made this possible. We have been fortunate to receive direct financial support from the University of Georgia, the Japan Foundation Center for Global Partnership, and the United States-Japan Friendship Commission. Many individuals at each institution also gave their time and effort to assist us, but we would especially like to thank Director Eric Gangloff and Program Officer Margaret Mihori of the United States-Japan Friendship Commission, former Executive Director Minoru Kusuda, Assistant Director Takashi Ishida and Program Officer Christine Donis-Keller of the Japan Foundation Center for Global Partnership, Linda Allen, Paula Tolbert and Steve Elliot-Gower at the University of Georgia.

A number of other institutions assisted in this project, particularly Waseda University, the Center for Information on Strategic Technologies (CISTEC) and the International Institute for Policy Studies (IIPS). In addition to the many contributions of Michio Yoneta, a member of the research team, and Director General of the Research Department at CISTEC, we would like to extend our special thanks to Executive Managing Director Nobuyoshi Kakuma for his continued backing. We also appreciate the support of Dr.Eng. and former Ambassador Ryukichi Imai, a senior research fellow at IIPS. We are pleased to note that export controls have become one of the Institute's major research areas. As members of the research team, senior research fellows Jun-ichi Ozawa and Takeshi Ito of IIPS made direct contributions to both this book and the project workshops.

We wish to thank the many graduate and undergraduate assistants that helped during the course of this project including Shannon Drake, Olga Fantova, Seema Gahlaut, Suzette Grillot, Ann Hicks, Roger Herrin, Scott Jones, Laura Mobley and Ruth Wilkerson.

Special thanks needs to go to two graduate students at the

University of Georgia. Jonathan Benjamin-Alvarado took primary responsibility for assisting with preparing the manuscript as well as being an essential aide in our workshop activities. Shungo Kawanishi proved an invaluable graduate assistant, particularly at the workshops, in helping to bridge the cultural and language differences that might have hindered cooperation between the U.S. and Japanese participants in the project.

Special thanks to the office manager of the Center for International Trade and Security, Linda Haygood. Her assistance to our work can not be fully measured and is always appreciated.

We have had the special privilege of working with a group of excellent scholars and policy experts during the course of this project. In addition to those members of the research team already mentioned, we would like to include Professor Beverly Crawford, Professor Lewis Ortmeyer, Professor Thomas Shoenbaum, Professor Michael Mastanduno, Dr. Zachary Davis, Dr. Glennon Harrison, Dr. Cathleen Fisher, Mr. Dan Hoydysh, Professor Yuzo Murayama, Professor Hajime Izumi, Gakyushu Shidori, Susumu Hirai, Shuji Kurokawa, Professor Yoko Yasuhara, Dr. Elina Kirichenko, Dr. Igor Khripunov, Professor Jan Zielonka, Mr. Kenichi Suganuma, Ms. Keiko Yanai and Mr. Masao Hosokawa.

In addition to those mentioned above, we would also like to thank the many other members of the U.S. and Japanese governments and business communities that have helped our research efforts.

Finally, our families gave their support and understanding to our schedule of research , writing, conferences, workshops, and administration, and deserve our special consideration.

Chapter 1

Forging A New Consensus on Multilateral Non-Proliferation Export Controls: Three Lessons from the Cold War and Its Aftermath

Beverly Crawford

Introduction

The central problem exporters of dual-use high technologies face in the post-Soviet environment is that of achieving consensus on which technologies they should jointly restrict, to whom, and for how long. The death of COCOM in 1994 symbolizes that multilateral export control policies must be constructed upon a new basis; as Bertsch and Cupitt have written, "Nonproliferation, not containment is the dominant rationale for export control policy in the post-cold war era."[1] This rationale is underscored by North Korea's recent reluctance to permit the IAEA's nuclear inspections. Before the cold war ended, a number of multilateral non-proliferation regimes were working to restrict dual-use exports. Yet in the current environment of fierce global economic competition, with little consensus on the aims of dual-use non-proliferation to guide states' cooperative restrictions, their firms are tempted to export civilian goods with military significance to the highest bidder and evade enforcement attempts. The problems triggered by economic competition are compounded by the proliferation of new states with the potential to produce weapons of mass destruction. Many new states, in particular the NIS--including Russia itself--have not gained the strength to enforce market rational behavior in their societies, much less enforce export controls. Increased pressure for enforcement will only provide partial assurance of successful multilateral export control regimes. What is needed is a new basis for agreement among those states who wish to pursue some kind of harmonized and coordinated export control policy.

As the world's leaders in the development, production, and export of high technology goods, Japan and the United States must provide joint leadership in forging that agreement. In doing so, they should find it useful to analyze export control controversies of the past in order to avoid similar disputes in the future. Such analysis should help to build agreement on a solid, consensual foundation. Once general agreement is reached between these two leading states, other exporting states will have a higher incentive to follow.

While the body of COCOM is still warm and before a successor is chosen, analysts should perform a series of autopsies in order to discover the causes of its successes and failures. In this paper I shall attempt a first cut at this task. It is my argument that US and Japanese decision-makers charged with shaping consensus in new export control regimes that restrict dual-use technologies can learn from the experience of those who took on that responsibility during the cold war. The problem of multiple and conflicting policy goals arising from the growing prominence of dual-use technology emerged during the last half of the Cold War. And within COCOM, some policy solutions succeeded and other attempts failed. As the Urengoi pipeline dispute and the Toshiba incident of the 1980s suggest, COCOM members did not always agree on the scope and direction of export controls despite the fact that their rationale derived from a clear strategy of military containment. Members were not always able to enforce those controls uniformly, and export control policy often became symbolic currency in wider foreign policy disputes among allies. Similar problems of achieving agreement are likely to rear their heads again, particularly in an environment where threats may be multiple and their sources divergent. We therefore have much to learn from the cold war episode.

In this paper I suggest that the cold war experience and its aftermath offers three lessons for those charged with the task of selecting COCOM's successor: 1) Be wary of formulating a grand strategy or common security policy to guide export control; incremental, small steps focused on specific, time-bound strategies, targets and technologies will lead to more consensual agreement among technology suppliers and can build more lasting cooperation. 2) Engage in ongoing vulnerability assessments of specific technology exports. If suppliers agree that the export of certain commercial high technology goods have the potential to close the military technology gap between the exporter and importer and negate the effects of the exporter's advanced military systems, consensus on restriction will easier to reach. 3) Provide aid targeted to stabilize the legitimacy of new states. Reducing Western vulnerability to the "hemorrhaging" of weapons-related technology from the Newly Independent States of the former Soviet Union (NIS) to dangerous importers will not only be a function of their ability and willingness to construct export control laws and agreements. The legitimacy of these states and their ability to protect property rights and enforce market rational behavior must also be nourished by Western democracies. Weak, fragile, and unstable states in the region will feed incentives to sell technology abroad and weak states will have little enforcement capability.

In brief, the lessons for those who would forge a new consensus on export controls are these: be flexible about who is dangerous; be prudent about what is dangerous; and help shore up the wider legitimacy of new states. In the pages that follow, I examine each of these lessons in more detail.

Lesson One: Be wary of depending on a grand security strategy to guide multilateral export control policy.

The Western doctrine of Containment in the post-war period provided a stable guide to security policy. Some analysts even lament the passing of the cold war because it provided certainty about the source of military threat and provided for a straightforward and parsimonious military doctrine.[2] But with regard to multilateral export control of dual-use technologies and its corollary, "economic containment,"[3] the doctrine proved to be a blunt instrument and a weak foundation for multilateral agreement. Divergent interpretations among COCOM members of how the doctrine should be applied to economic relations with the Soviet bloc was a painful source of political conflict and sometimes contaminated other aspects of their relations.

The entire cold war period saw the airing of divergent definitions of Containment in East-West trade, primarily between the United States and the other allies. In the early days of deteriorating US-Soviet relations, the US attempted to use COCOM as an instrument of broad trade denial, bolstering that attempt with unilateral threats of aid termination to those countries that did not accept the US definition of economic containment and its application to export controls. Europeans, in particular, took a more restricted view of containment: to many European elites, Eastern Europe especially and even the Soviet Union were part of Europe in historical heritage and culture. Even in the darkest days of the cold war, European elites questioned the "essentialist" view prevailing in Washington, which held that the Soviet Union was an aggressive power, bent on destroying the West. In contrast, they saw the USSR as a formidable adversary, but nonetheless one that they could bargain with, even live with.[4]

Therefore, although these differences waxed and waned throughout the cold war, containment doctrine did provide a steady and essential guide to the control of those goods and technologies that had clear and dangerous military significance. Ironically, however, containment had just the opposite effect with regard to the control of dual-use technologies. Here, disagreements over the scope of economic containment actually obstructed consensus on common policies. In the 1970s and 1980s, US officials argued that the definition of "technology" should be expanded from simple machinery, equipment, and technical data to include knowledge skill, and information. The United States also pushed for COCOM control over joint ventures, turnkey plants, and long-ten-n technical training. European members and Japan argued that technology should continue to be narrowly defined as "machinery and transport equipment," and they refused to consider joint ventures, as such, as the target of control. In addition, they sharply opposed the extraterritorial application of American export controls.

Although containment doctrine gave the West a clear target for controlling military exports, it did not provide a basis for consensus on the commercial goods to be restricted. Without such consensus, two intractable problems emerged: 1) firms in member states, sensing disagreement, had fewer incentives to comply with the weakening the regime overall; 2) multilateral export control issues rules and were tempted to cheat, thus further impeding consensus and became politicized and were often used as instruments of leverage in negotiations on other foreign policy issues among the Western allies.

In particular the United States found itself coercing its partners into grudging acceptance of its position by issuing threats in other issue areas at stake in the relationship.

The Toshiba case of 1987 provides a good example of these problems, because, at first glance, it appears to be a clear cut case of straightforward cheating on a consensual agreement. The propeller milling equipment Toshiba Machine sold to the Soviets had unmistakable military significance and openly violated COCOM limits. A closer inspection of the case, however, reveals that more general disagreements about sales of dual-use technologies within COCOM and previous unpunished violations paved the way for the illegal sale. Toshiba machine officials remembered how their company had lost a similar milling equipment sale in 1974 to a French company because Japan's export control law had forbidden the sale. Apparently, French officials had not been so strict. Further investigation revealed increasing numbers of illegal sales by American, British, and Italian companies throughout the 1980s. Officials from Toshiba Machine felt they were unfairly singled out, and indeed it appears that they were singled out because of festering trade disputes between the US and Japan.

The conventional explanation blames lax enforcement for the illegal sale. But closer analysis suggests a deeper problem. During the 1980s,the debate over economic containment of dual-use technologies had become increasing heated. Firms in many COCOM member states sensed the intensity of disagreement among government authorities. Conflicts over what should or should not be controlled weakened the norms of restriction and led to the proliferation of regime violations, creating the milieu in which Toshiba Machine violated the rules. Company officials reasoned that if they did not make the sale, someone else would.

The lesson is that firms will be less tempted to cheat when their governments consensually agree to the regime principles and norms. Indeed, the basis for agreement existed on the control of clearly militarily significant technology, but that agreement was clouded by disputes over broadening dual-use controls. Clearly containment did not provide a sound basis for broad consensus.

Secondly, the Toshiba case and Japanese export controls became political currency in the hands of US decision makers in two arenas: First, with US politicians who had other bones to pick with Japan; second, with those negotiating cooperation agreements with Japan who needed leverage to extract bargaining concessions. American politicians blamed the sale for undermining America's anti-submarine warfare advances and threatening Western security at sea, and therefore they argued for sanctions against Toshiba's products in the US But it was later revealed that there was no direct link between the illegal sale of the equipment and the quieter submarines feared by the US Navy. The quieter submarines were launched well before the equipment was installed. But the issue became quickly politicized and congressional preference for sanctions against Toshiba steamrolled ahead before the real export control concerns could be investigated. US Administration officials promised to use their clout with Congress to halt sanctions against Toshiba if Japan would make concessions in negotiations over its participation in SDI research and enter into a joint venture with a U.S. firm to develop the FSX fighter plane. Many Japanese observers suggested that the sanctions against Toshiba for violating export control laws were simply a convenient way to protect American manufacturers of semiconductors in the US market.

In retrospect, what we have learned is that it was not consensus on the application of containment doctrine to dual-use export control that permitted the kind of agreement in COCOM needed to make enforcement efforts legitimate in the eyes of exporting firms. Nor was it the political and economic pressure that the United States exerted to coerce its allies to yield to its understanding of economic containment. *It was the consensus that existed with regard to the restriction of a much narrower band of clear militarily significant goods that gave COCOM its relatively long life.* Attempts to pursue broad strategies of economic containment with regard to dual-use technologies only clouded the agreement that existed. Ultimately we must accept that the logic of export control with regard to dual-use technologies fundamentally contradicts the logic of free trade. Any overarching security doctrine constructed for the post-cold war world is likely to be an equally blunt instrument with regard to trade restrictions. Rather than become a foundation for consensus, it is likely to exacerbate latent political and economic conflicts among coordinating states.

In the present period we are experiencing not only the proliferation and diffusion of technologies to build weapons of mass destruction, but the proliferation of new states with these technologies as well. When we attempt to control exports to specific destinations, we are facing a moving target. Consensus was difficult to reach in a relatively simple cold war environment, and the difficulties will be compounded in today's turbulent security milieu. It is for these reasons that export control regimes should be incremental and flexible, built "from the bottom up," rather than on the basis of a new grand strategy of Western or global security.

In this spirit of incrementalism, the typology of "supply-side export control strategies" developed by Gary Bertsch and Richard Cupitt can be an important first step in conceptualizing the scope and direction of non-proliferation export controls and therefore an important foundation upon which to build consensus.[5] It provides a flexible scheme for categorization of states and their position with regard to high technology exports. It also provides a set of sensible strategies that high technology exporters who have agreed to coordinate their export controls should pursue toward those states. Most important (and unlike the more rigid policies guided by containment strategy), the scheme allows for movement of states between categories: Over time, exporting states that coordinate their policies can watch for political and economic changes within the threatening states that could move them into the category of sensitive or even collaborating states. The case of China provides a good example of the importance of nuance in a categorization scheme. Were containment doctrine still to continue to guide export controls, the PRC would fall under the category of "threatening states." Recognizing that China's security policy does not currently threaten the coordinating states directly, Bertsch and Cupitt have placed it in the category of "sensitive" states, along with Israel, Brazil, and others. Such flexibility is required in the current tumultuous security environment.

The second virtue of the Bertsch-Cupitt scheme is that its range of dual-use technologies to be controlled is restricted to those that would contribute to the production and delivery of weapons of mass destruction. Although there will still be considerable debate over which technologies should be included, even within this narrow range, this specification will help suppliers avoid supplier conflicts such as that which erupted over construction of the Urengoi gas pipeline in 1982. At that time, US officials interpreted containment doctrine broadly to mean the restriction of any technologies that would contribute to Soviet economic strength and make the West more dependent on Soviet energy supplies. West European allies balked at such a broad definition, and a major dispute erupted as a result. In the current changing security environment, restricting the sale of dual-use technologies to specific weapons systems will certainly help to avoid similar disputes among technology suppliers.

One might also envision a typology of states categorized according to "demand side" considerations. In such a scheme, states would be categorized in accord with their incentives for acquiring weapons of mass destruction as well as their capabilities for doing so.[6] An understanding of the various incentives states have for acquiring such weapons can provide insight into those states' security policies. Knowing importers' security needs gives suppliers a range of policy strategies--including important confidence-building measures [7] that may weaken incentives to acquire the technology to produce weapons of mass destruction. Weakened incentives to produce weapons of mass destruction reduces the need for stringent export controls. What follows is a suggested typology of how incentives to produce dangerous weapons might be evaluated.

First, states tend to acquire production capability for those weapons when they face a powerful adversary who may also possess those weapons. Historically, the United States, the former Soviet Union, China, and India would fit this category. And all appear to see the weapons as having deterrent value. A newcomer to this category might be Pakistan, but it is not clear whether Pakistan's security strategy envisions these weapons as a deterrent.

Second, states may acquire these weapons as a badge of both domestic and international prestige: as former Great Powers, Britain and France saw nuclear weapons capability as a way to maintain their status in the face of the rising power of the United States after World War II. Brazil and Argentina may fit this category today. Nuclear weapons are the instrument of British and French deterrence strategy, and they would be likely to play a similar role in the policies of Brazil and Argentina.

Third, states who have no security guarantees from a nuclear power or states who are considered pariahs by the international community are likely to attempt to acquire weapons of mass destruction in order to assure their own security: Having no security guarantees, India also fits into this category, as well as Israel, Iraq, North Korea, and Libya. Preventative war rather than deterrence is likely to be the security strategy pursued by these states. Exporting states might consider offering alternative prestige incentives, security guarantees, or other incentives to those states likely to acquire weapons for these traditional reasons.

Devising incremental and limited strategies such as these is only the first step toward multilateral agreement on export control among technology suppliers. There will always be grounds to debate categorization schemes, no matter how narrow and limited they prove to be. Therefore the schemes should be viewed as a basis for discussion, rather than a set of rules written in stone. Even without the burden of a grand security strategy, agreement will be difficult, given variation among the coordinators in their perceptions of their own security requirements, economic needs, and judgments about security threats. It will therefore be essential to develop an objective standard for judging the extent to which high technology exports render them militarily vulnerable and thus directly jeopardize their military capabilities. It is to this issue that the discussion now turns.

Lesson Two: Engage in ongoing vulnerability assessments

In addition to the political clouds that containment doctrine cast on COCOM's attempts to reach agreement on dual-use technology restrictions, there were few objective standards that could be used as a basis for consensus on items in the "grey area" between pure commercial and pure military technology. Although export control policy was guided by the assumption that the West makes itself vulnerable when it trades with military rivals (or even economic competitors, who can quickly translate economic strength into military power), the assumption was never specified; nor was it systematically tested. Thus it was always unclear which specific items would render the West vulnerable if sold to an adversary, a potential adversary, or a trade competitor. Practitioners in this new export control environment should correct this error and engage in ongoing vulnerability assessments. Below I suggest four steps involved in such an analysis and illustrate these steps with a brief analysis of the vulnerability effects of Western technology transfer to the Soviet Union during the cold war.

Distinguish between Threats and Vulnerabilities

Any new framework for non-proliferation export controls should make a clear distinction between threats and vulnerabilities. Threats have to do with the intentions of importers that will harm a supplier state's national security. Do importers intend to attack, invade, or initiate an economic embargo to cut off vital resources? Or are they willing to negotiate the peaceful settlement of disputes, arms control agreements, and treaties to protect security? Here, the Bertsch-Cupitt

typology of states is important, for it is essential to assess the source of
a security threat and take measures to reduce our contribution to a
threatening state's incentive to endanger our security and capability to
carry out military threats against us.

The cold war's demise ended fears of attack, invasion, or economic
embargoes from a powerful Soviet Union, and generally reduced
perceptions of threat to Western states in the global military
environment. Peace appeared again to be divisible; ethnic and sectarian
wars did not seem likely to spill outside their borders. Indeed, the
Bertsch-Cupitt scheme indicates only four "threatening" states, all with
underdeveloped industrial capability.

Nonetheless, as threat perceptions have subsided to some extent,
arguments about "vulnerabilities" have intensified. Vulnerability
assessments focus not on intentions but rather on capabilities. The
globalization of production and exchange means that increasing numbers
of states may achieve military capabilities with civilian technologies,
whether those states are currently "threatening" or not. As Raymond
Vernon and Ethan Kapstein have argued, because sources of threat
change, there will always be a persistent national need to reduce
vulnerabilities by maintaining or increasing one's relative power
position in the international system and maintaining as much autonomy
as possible, despite changing threat perceptions. "Whatever the
contingencies and threats that defense planners foresee, their hope is to
maintain the largest possible measure of superiority over the enemy."[8]
Threats and vulnerabilities cannot always be easily distinguished from
one another, and although they are analytically separate, they should be
assessed together.

Assess the effects of commercial technology sales on military "gaps."

Vulnerability is heightened when the military capabilities of other
states--whether or not they are currently a threat-- increase relative to
one's own capabilities. The odds of heightened vulnerability increase
in an environment of global economic interdependence and free trade.
To the extent that others can build up their military capabilities with
advanced technologies available on the open market, supplier states
become vulnerable. In essence, this was the logic that led to the
Nuclear Non-Proliferation Treaty and the nonproliferation regime.

With regard to the export of dual-use technologies, a vulnerability analysis would assess which commercial technologies, if transferred to any state would endanger the supplier's security by closing the military gap between exporter and importer and, perhaps most importantly, negate the effects of the exporter's advanced military systems. Under this principle, technologies with military significance can be sold, but only if they do not close the military gap between the exporter and importer, and only if they do not negate either the defensive or offensive capabilities of the suppliers' military systems. According to this definition, for example, Toshiba's sale of milling equipment to produce quieter propellers for Soviet submarines had the potential to negate Western ASW capabilities.

On the whole, however, an assessment of Soviet imports of Western dual-use technologies during the cold war suggests low vulnerability effects, if measured by time lags in the development of weaponry similar to that of the West and by the size of the military technology gap. In light of massive Soviet illegal technology acquisition efforts (and lesser efforts to acquire technology through legal trade channels), we would expect the military technology gap between the West and the Soviet Union to have been closing. Yet throughout the cold war the West was years ahead of the USSR in its development of important military technologies. Historically, the Soviets had acquired foreign technology in early stages of weapons development, but it had taken time to modify that technology to Soviet specifications. Meanwhile, innovation in the West created new "gaps" that needed to be filled. Exports of dual-use technologies, whether legal or illegal, made little difference in the Soviet case.

In part, of course, this was due to the effectiveness of multilateral export controls. But recall that consensus on export control could only be reached on a narrow band of militarily significant technologies. The dual-use technologies that did find their way into the Soviet Union often through the Soviets' massive illegal acquisition of militarily significant technologies did little or nothing to make the West vulnerable. Therefore, an additional explanation for the Soviet's inability to close the military gap with Western dual-use technology is required.

One possible explanation rests on the Soviets' lack of capacity to absorb, diffuse, and adapt commercial technologies to military use. How well importing states are able to adapt dual-use technologies to military purposes depend largely on the strength of their military-industrial linkages and networks. An assessment of those linkages and networks is a third step in an overall vulnerability assessment.

Assess the strength of the importer's "commercial military-industrial" base

The increase in weapons' systems requiring dual-use technologies suggests that military strength increasingly rests on the civilian industrial base. But throughout the Cold War, Soviet capability for civilian technological innovation, diffusion, and adaptation lagged further and further behind that of the West. And since there were few backward and forward linkages among industries, few networks between engineers, scientists, and military technicians and a rigid divide between civilian and military industries, the Soviets had great difficulty adapting commercial western technology to military purposes.[9] This partly explains why the military technology gap remained large in favor of the West, despite the legal and increasingly illegal import of dual-use technologies.

In the current period, Third World country purchases of advanced Western technology are likely to go the way of Soviet purchases. The successful utilization of technology within any country depends on the extent to which its positive effects can be diffused throughout an industry, sector, or the economy as a whole. The success of commercial technology transfer depends on the nation's industrial structure and whether that structure provides for strong linkages among related industries through which the positive effects of innovation (whether domestic or imported) can spread. And the speed at which commercial innovation can be translated into weapons' systems seems to depend on the strength of the networks between scientists, engineers, and defense contractors in military and civilian industries and policy-makers in government. [10] Within a state that has a "commercial/military-industrial complex" these networks are both tight and stable. But in weak countries, these linkages do not exist, and the positive effects of commercial technology imports on military strength will be nil. Finally, if scarce resources are invested in military technology, third world states today, much like the Soviet Union during the cold war, will undercut their ability to innovate and develop economically, perpetuating their dependence on the international market. This does not mean, of course, that they cannot develop weapons of mass destruction with a weak industrial base. The cases of India and China and even Iraq suggest otherwise. But it is unlikely that they will be able to develop the sophisticated support and delivery systems necessary to make the weaponry wholly effective.[11] Indeed, the Gulf War demonstrated that this was the case with Iraq.

Assess business strategies for the sale of dual-use technologies

A third vulnerability assessment technique involves a careful examination of the business strategies of commercial exporters of dual-use technologies. Widespread publicity over the Toshiba case, Imhausen Chemie's sale of a chemical weapons plant to Libya, and the discovery that Iraq's 1991 invasion of Kuwait was assisted by military equipment and technology developed largely with illegal western assistance, have all bolstered recent calls for stepped up government enforcement of export controls. Given the potential gravity of the consequences of illegal exports, there is general agreement that such enforcement provisions are necessary. But practitioners must recognize that the vast majority of firms do not cheat and in fact have their own strategies for withholding high technology that could be adapted to military use.

Again, the Soviet case is illustrative. During the cold war, the pattern of business involvement combined with Western corporate strategy worked to ensure Soviet dependence on western technology rather than provide the means to build up the Soviet industrial base.[12] Western private investment was targeted primarily for extractive industries and commodity production, and most industrial cooperation agreements and joint ventures were in services and the marketing of Western imports. Investment targeted for manufacturing industries was largely confined to assembly operations, adding little value to the goods produced and intended for the Soviet market rather than for export. Component parts for Soviet plants were sourced in the West, inhibiting the creation of linkages between the joint venture and the rest of the economy. Corporate officials believed that transfer of obsolete technology through these ventures was sufficient to capture domestic market share. Contractual provisions ensured that the most advanced Western technologies were withheld from the Soviet economy. Technology transfer was used as a "hook" in order to get a foot into the Soviet market, and "core" technologies were rarely included in joint venture agreements.[13]

A knowledge of these business strategies in particular transactions involving questionable dual-use technologies is likely to be a useful contribution to an overall assessment of the contribution a particular technology transfer will make to the closing of the technology gap between importer and exporter and whether the transfer will negate the exporter's military advances.   In itself, however, an assessment of business strategies will be incomplete.   If they are to be a useful tool for forging multilateral consensus among coordinating states, and, most important, a tool to forge acceptance of export controls by exporting firms, vulnerability assessments must include specific information about technology gaps, information about the importer's diffusion and adaptation capabilities, as well as information about the strategies of corporations selling dual-use technologies.

The Policy Value of Vulnerability Assessments

Such vulnerability assessments would narrow the range of goods, even if exported to "threatening states" that would be controlled. Narrowing the range of controlled items increases the chances that consensus will be reached among supplier states on what should be controlled, particularly when suppliers cannot reach agreement on which states are "threatening" and which states are not threatening.   If the Soviet case provides an example, vulnerability assessments will show that extensive export controls beyond the restriction of military technology are seldom required and their costs in terms of reduced domestic innovative capability and restriction of constitutional freedoms at home far exceed the benefits.   The Cold War lesson is clear: enforcement of export controls is easiest when real agreement on restriction is reached, and real agreement is best reached when the scope and extent of vulnerability is clearly specified.

Despite vulnerability assessments, disagreements may persist

Vulnerability assessments will certainly not solve all the problems associated with achieving multilateral agreement on export control. They will be useless, for example, if suppliers believe that the proliferation of weapons of mass destruction can stabilize the international security environment.   Some analysts do argue that the proliferation of these weapons can make the international environment more secure.   For example, there are many scholars who believe that the more states that possess nuclear weapons, the less their adversaries are likely to launch attacks against them.   Nuclear weapons, and perhaps other weapons of mass destruction are said to equalize power among states; when power positions are clear and equal, neither side is likely to launch an attack. Nuclear, chemical, and biological weaponry are also believed by some to be an effective way of protecting the weak from the strong; strong states with aggressive ambitions are likely to behave with restraint toward smaller, weaker states who have weapons of mass destruction.[14] These views are still the domain of academic security analysts, but one should not be sanguine about their "proliferation" among practitioners, given the proper political circumstances.

Lesson Three: Assist New States to stabilize property rights on the basis of market rational behavior

The final lesson for those who would construct multilateral non-proliferation export control regimes comes from events in the Cold War's aftermath. In the NIS we are witnessing new vulnerabilities in old places, and the cold war experience did not prepare us for them. The central export control problem in former communist countries is the state's almost total loss of market control and inability to establish stable property rights on the basis of market rational behavior. With this loss of control, and with support of the dominant classical liberal economic ideology, military assets are being rapidly privatized, contrary to the interests of both the Russian state and Western governments. To the extent that these new states cannot establish market stability, the West can become vulnerable to the region's disintegration, turmoil, and potential economic collapse.[15] Within the Cold War logic, the prospect of the fragmentation of a powerful Soviet Union was a welcome scenario. A fragmented Soviet Union was a less powerful adversary whose threat to western security would be reduced. But in the aftermath of Communism, the threat is unintended chaos and new and fragile governments that have little capability to bring stability.

This turmoil directly impacts export control efforts. Fears of technology exodus from the former Soviet Union to dangerous Third World countries have replaced fears of technology exodus to the Soviet Union from the West. Uncertainty over control of economic forces and the disintegration of the Soviet state began to force thousands of Soviet scientists trained in building nuclear and chemical weapons to sell their expertise to states like North Korea or Iraq, thus increasing the military threat from those areas to the West and to the former Soviet Union itself.[16] In another example, a group of former party elites in Russia with good connections to the state bank--promising easy credit terms--

bought dual-use space technology and planned in early 1992 to sell it in global markets.[17] Although Yeltsin threatened to impose sanctions of such activity, it was entirely unclear whether his government had the power to do so.

In order to prevent this technology exodus from the former USSR to other dangerous countries, the Bush Administration initially provided $25 million to help finance international science and technology centers supporting former Soviet scientists and engineers so that they could redirect their talents to non-military endeavors.[18] But by mid-1994, these centers had not yet been established, and at the same time that the US provided funding for them, it blocked the purchase of missiles, rocket engines, satellites, space reactors, spacecraft and other aerospace technology from the former Soviet Union in order to force the decline of the Russian space and military industry so that it would pose no future threat to the US. Many argued that this embargo would further force former Soviet scientists to sell their knowledge to potential military rivals in the Third World.[19]

Before Russia and the other Newly Independent States can begin to enforce the export controls they have now established, the West must assist these new nations in strengthening their states and their science and technology infrastructure. We once feared both a strong state and scientific and technological advance in the region. Now, states must be strengthened or incidents like the above will proliferate. The current dominance of market logic, however, mitigates against strong states. It calls for "state shrinking" so that the domain of the market can expand. What those who call for state shrinking forget, however, is that is the state that must establish and protect legal and rational markets, and it is the state that must enforce new market-oriented laws. At the present time, market-oriented laws initiated by the central government of the Russian Federation are often ignored or opposed in regional and city governments; a weak central state has found it close to impossible to enforce market reforms.

If the coordinating states want these new states to cooperate in multilateral export control, they must be prepared to provide ample financial and technical assistance in these countries to strengthen the state in the ways discussed above. Assistance in strengthening export control laws in these states alone will not help, because the problems affecting export control are both deeper and more widespread than export controls themselves.

In an environment in which all technology supplying states are both under tremendous economic pressure and are unsure about the direction of post-Soviet political developments, obtaining more multilateral aid agreement to strengthen the state, the economy, and science and technology establishments in the NIS will be the most difficult task set forth in this essay. Raising export control issues to prominence in debates over economic aid will help. And clear vulnerability assessments will help to legitimize export control issues and place them on the aid agenda.

Conclusions

I have argued here that despite the new, uncertain, and tumultuous security environment of the post-cold war world, there are important lessons to be learned from the cold war experience for cooperation in multilateral non-proliferation export control regimes. The cold war taught us that--with regard to dual-use export controls-the construction of a grand strategy to guide joint decisions may actually do more harm than good. Because restricting dual-use technologies is highly controversial, it is best to pursue flexible and incremental decision-making procedures. Flexible typologies of states in their relation to the export of sensitive dual-use technologies, their own security strategies, and potential strategies to be pursued toward them may be an important beginning.

A second lesson from the cold war is that in lieu of grand political guidelines to guide export control, restrictions should be based on specific, case by case vulnerability analyses. The assessment should answer the following questions: 1) Does the potential sale of dual-use technology close the military gap between exporter and importer, negating the exporter's advanced weapons' systems? 2) Does the importing state possess the infrastructure, policy and technical networks, and industry linkages to adapt advanced civilian technology to military purposes? 3) What is the corporate strategy with regard to technology transfer in this case? Does the strategy provide for the withholding of key sensitive technologies? Certainly there are many more ways to refine a vulnerability analysis. These questions are merely suggestive and provide a first cut at the problem. But their answers can yield valuable data on the danger of any specific technology transfer to the exporting state's relative capabilities.

Finally, chaotic events in the former Soviet Union in the aftermath of the cold war have exposed entirely new export control problems, not evident in the cold war period. Extreme poverty and high temptation to engage in illegal trade in an environment with no legitimate state controls have led to the sale of many advanced technologies to "dangerous" states. To halt the "hemorrhaging" of high technology from the former Soviet Union will require more than tighter export controls. It will require financial and technical assistance to strengthen the state and shore up the economy to encourage the creation and protection of property rights. Without such broad assistance, the proliferation of new export control laws are likely to be unenforceable. Vulnerability assessments may raise the prominence of export control in aid debates, and help forge agreement on expanded multilateral assistance.

Notes

1. Gary K. Bertsch and Richard T. Cupitt, "Nonproliferation in the 1990s: Enhancing International Cooperation on Export Controls," *The Washington Quarterly*, Vol. 16, No. 4, pp. 53-70.

2. The best example is John J. Mearsheimer, "Back to the Future: Instability in Europe after the Cold War," *International Security* Vol. 15, No. I (Summer 1990), pp. 5-56.

3. See Michael Mastanduno, *Economic Containment: The Western Politics of East-West Trade* (Ithaca: Cornell University Press, 1992).

4. The term "essentialist" comes from Gail Lapidus and Alexander Dallin, "Reagan and the Americans: American Policy Toward the Soviet Union," in Kenneth A. Oye, Robert J. Lieber, and Donald Rothchild, eds., *Eagle Resurgent? The Reagan Era in American Foreign Policy* (Boston: Little, Brown, 1987). See also Strobe Talbott, *The Masters of the Game* (New York: Knopf, 1988).

5. "Nonproliferation in the 1990s: Enhancing International Cooperation on Export Controls," *The Washington Quarterly* Vol. 16, No 4, pp. 53-70.

6. This is Han S. Park's argument in "The Conundrum of North Korea's Bomb: An Unconventional Perspective," Paper prepared for the Workshop on Nonproliferation Export control: U.S. and Japanese Interests and Initiatives, April 5-6, 1994, Tokyo, Japan.

7. See Cathleen S. Fisher, "Reducing Demand and Controlling Supply: CBMs, Export Controls, and Integrated Strategies for Nonproliferation," paper prepared for delivery at the US-Japan Workshop on Non-Proliferation Export Controls" at Waseda University, Tokyo, April 5-6, 1994.

8. Raymond Vernon and Ethan Kapstein, "National Needs, Global Resources," *Daedalus* Vol 120, No. 4 (Fall 1991), P. 4.

9. Beverly Crawford, *Economic Vulnerability in International Relations* (New York: Columbia University Press, 1993), Chapter Four.

10. This argument is made persuasively by Philip Gummett and Judith Reppy, "Military Industrial Networks and Technical Change in the New Strategic Environment," *Government and Opposition* Vol 25, No. 3 (Summer, 1990), pp. 287-303.

11. See, for example, Future Security Environment Working Group, *The Future Security Environment* (Washington, D.C.: Commission on Integrated Long-Term Strategy, October 1988).

12. This argument about dependence was made by Timothy W. Luke, "Technology and Soviet Foreign Trade: On the Political Economy of an Underdeveloped Superpower," *International Studies Quarterly*, Vol. 29, 1985.

13. See Beverly Crawford *Economic Vulnerability in International Relations* Chapter Three.

14. See, for example, Kenneth Waltz, "The Case for Nuclear Proliferation," Steven Miller, "Western diplomacy and the Soviet nuclear legacy," in *Survival*, vol. 34, no. 3, (Autumn 1992); Barry R. Rosen, "The Security Dilemma and Ethnic Conflict," in *Survival* Vol. 35, no.1 (Spring 1993), pp. 27-47.

15. See "U.S.-NIS Dialogue on Nonproliferation Export Controls," Conference report, June 15-17, The Airlie Center, Virginia for specific country problems in the NIS.

16. See Eric Schmitt, "U.S. worries about spread of arms from Soviet sales," *The New York Times*, November 16, 1991, p. 5.

17. See "Russia to fight Private Sell-offs by Ex-Officials," *The New York Times*, February 29, 1992, p. 4.

18. The European Community and Russia also promised to assist in financing. See "Baker and Yeltsin Agree on U.S. Aid in Scrapping Arms," *New York Times*, February 18, 1992, pg. 1.

19. Opponents claimed that the acquisition of Moscow's best technology could save Washington and American industry many billions of dollars in development costs, ease Russia's economic woes, discourage the spread of Russian scientists to the third world, and help the US compete with foreign rivals. See "US Moves to Bar Americans Buying Soviet Technology," New *York Times*, March 1, 1992, pg. 1. In response to both of these moves, a

panel of 120 scientists and engineers from the National Academy of Sciences recommended that the United States provide $150 million to support Russia's scientific elite. The panel also called on the US to open its markets to Soviet high technology in order to create more revenue in the Soviet Union and discourage the exodus of Russian scientists, See "Panel Calls for Wider Help for Ex-Soviet Arms Experts," *New York Times,* March 14, 1992, pg. 3.

Chapter 2

An Emerging Export Control Regime In Asia Upon The Break-Up Of COCOM

Takehiko Yamamoto

1) *The term "strategic trade" is obsolete*

The high level meeting of COCOM (Co-ordinating Committee for the Export Control to the Communist Bloc), held on November 16, 1993 ascertained that COCOM would be dissolved by the end of March 1994 and that a new organization would be founded. This would be an organization whose purposes would be controlling conventional arms and dual-use technologies transfer to the developing countries that currently are, or could be in conflict. Therefore, COCOM, created in November 1949 when the Cold War was intensifying as a result of the Berlin Blockade, and the founding of the People's Republic of China, has ended its 44-year function for the moment, and will try to reorganize itself.

It is well known that COCOM was created informally (secretly) to control Western exports of military and militarily related goods and technology, which might have contributed to fulfilling the Soviet Union and other Communist countries' military potential, and that it exercised overwhelming influence as the "Technology Curtain" against the "Iron Curtain". COCOM has been the indispensable regime for the West to maintain its dominant position in militarily related technologies both nuclear and non-nuclear applications. That is to say: COCOM was established as an international regime for the West to compete in an

"Economic Cold War", which is an exception in international trade regimes. Therefore, trade relations with reference to COCOM control were called "strategic trade", and have been differentiated from general free trade relations. Consequently, it is natural that COCOM controls have been rapidly relaxed since 1990, following the US-Soviet summit talks held at Malta in December 1989. COCOM's objective was to fight the economic Cold War against the Soviet Union. One of the confronting military blocs disappeared on account of the dissolution of the Warsaw Treaty Organization (WTO) in 1991, thus dissolution of the "hidden" regime COCOM, which has been supporting the "official" regime NATO was only a matter of time.

However, it took more than 3 years since the WTO dissolved for COCOM to break up. Moreover, during this period, some of the Western states, particularly the military establishment in the US, strongly opposed the proposal to break up COCOM. This is because they still perceived the threat of the Soviet Union as a nuclear super power even after the Cold War had ended. As a result, they persistently resisted relaxing controls on technology transfer to the Soviet Union concerning "C^3I" (command, control, communications, and intelligence), which are the key technologies for the global military strategy of the US. Therefore, COCOM controls to Eastern European countries such as Hungary and Poland, that have rapidly shifted to the market economy system, were relaxed immediately. On the contrary, strict controls to the Soviet Union were laid down with respect to information and telecommunications equipment, and the so-called "two tiers" of regulations were promoted.

Undoubtedly, there are many other reasons why the "two tiers" of regulations, differentiating the Soviet Union from Eastern Europe, were generally adopted. Such factors as economic confusion before the demise of the Soviet Union, a delay in the shift to a market economy, and the vulnerability of President Gorbachev's leadership were also influential. Nonetheless, it was mainly because the Soviet Union still possessed nuclear forces exceeding those of the US, particularly in the strategy nuclear forces, that COCOM has treated differently the Soviet Union.

Nevertheless, export controls to Russia, were promptly relaxed after the demise of the Soviet Union and the shift to a market economy in January 1992. This followed the abortive coup d'etat in 1991 and in addition, the signing of the Strategic Arms Reduction Treaty (START

1) in 1991 and START II in 1992. These events were supported by the G-7's support for democratization and economic reforms executed by President Boris N. Yeltsin. Additionally, the COCOM Co-operation Forum (CCF) was organized, including Central and Eastern Europe and the CIS states, and held the first meeting in November 1993. This gives an impression that COCOM is losing its original character as the coordinating committee for the export control to the Communist Bloc. At this stage, COCOM secretly entered discussions when to exclude Russia from the list of states subject to export control.

Finally, deciding to dissolve COCOM means that Russia, after the demise of the Soviet Union, is no longer perceived to be a military threat to the West and that the Cold War has in a strict sense ended. In addition, the West now intends to include the CIS states, Central and Eastern Europe, and China in the New COCOM, which suggests that the term "strategic trade" is obsolete. Needless to say, Russian and Chinese participation in a New COCOM is necessary, if a renewed COCOM plans to change into a regime controlling conventional arms export and technology transfer to some concerned countries or regions.

2) Chinese participation in the New COCOM is needed

COCOM, which had started to function as an organization to control export to the Third World in the 1990's, has been promoting its cooperation with international export control regimes concerned with weapons of mass destruction, such as the Missile Technology Control Regime (MTCR), the Australian Group (AG), and the Nuclear Suppliers Group (NSG). That is to say, COCOM has been the core of this linkage structure. For example, through the CCF, Russia has received assistance and support to strengthen its own export control system, which also, bolsters its attempts to prevent technologies related to weapons of mass destruction from being transferred to countries in a conflict or potential conflict situation.

However, US-Japanese differences in views on Chinese participation in the CCF imply the possible re-occurrence of a dispute between the US and Japan on the process of including China in the New COCOM. The post Cold War relationship between the US and China seems tenuous, considering the US imposed economic sanctions on China in August 1993 over the export control issues surrounding the transfer of the M-11 missile and related technologies to Pakistan. As a result, it is difficult to predict whether China can participate in the

New COCOM without improving its relationship with the US. Nonetheless, as China is a permanent member of the UN Security Council, Chinese participation and cooperation is indispensable to make the New COCOM system, which controls conventional arms export and technology transfer to countries and regions in a potential conflict situation, effective. During the five years from 1987 till 1992, China exported major conventional arms to developing countries, which amounted to 7.5 billion dollars.[1] This means, China is now the third largest arms exporting country, following the Russia, and the US.

Surely, Chinese conventional weapons are by far inferior to American, Russian, and French weapons. However, considering the protracted and deepened Cambodian conflict owing to the supply of arms to the Pol Pot Faction, even the transfer of out-of-date arms can easily fuel regional conflicts. It is therefore necessary to promote Chinese involvements in the New COCOM so that the export control regime of conventional arms would be tenable.

3) Re-occurrence of disputes concerning regulated goods and new members

The next problem which the New COCOM might face is how to specify would-be concerned countries and regions, and how to expand (or narrow) the range of regulated goods and technologies. This is the problem that the present COCOM has been facing since its inception. Thus, it is uncertain whether the interests of the member states will always coincide, even though there will be a change applying control to any state as the need arise. It can be said that, the more unpredictable states and regions of concern are, the higher the possibility of conflict among the members over their security or trade interests.

Moreover, disputes among members, over specifying and interpreting the list of regulated goods and technologies, will occur as in the present COCOM. During the Cold War, disputes had repeatedly occurred with regard to making and revising the list of regulated goods, and in addition deciding an exceptional export. In short, it had been conflicts between the US policy of "Maximalist Approach" intended to expand the range of strategic goods and technologies as wide as possible, and European-Japanese "Minimalist Approach", narrowing the range. Though it cannot be predicted whether conflict will reoccur in the New COCOM, conflict of this kind will surely arise in the case of the US, which strongly feels responsible for building a new international order in the post Cold War era as the only superpower, continues to adopt the "Maximalist Approach".

What is more troublesome is deciding which states to allow as members. It is natural, on the one hand, that technologically-advanced neutral states, e.g. Sweden, Austria, and Switzerland should join the New COCOM. On the other hand, how to include developing countries which has an arms export record or export potential is a quite difficult problem. The same problem has been pointed out with respect to the transfer of weapons and technologies of mass destruction in such non-proliferation regimes as MTCR and so on. What is more, there are more than ten developing countries which possess the potential to export conventional arms ranging from rifles to aircraft or warships. By excluding such countries from the new regime, does the New COCOM bring economic aid to an end as a means of sanction in order to make export control to countries or regions under conflict situation, more effective? If this is the case, North-South friction may be more intense that previously experienced. Will not the policy guideline of the Japanese ODA be an ominous precedent?

4) A more difficult obstacle is US and Russian policies to expand arms exports

The topic mentioned in the previous section is not the only problem to hinder the effective operation of the New COCOM. Russia, which is moving to a market economy system at present, is suffering many difficulties in conversion from military to civilian production. From the days of the former Soviet Union, selling weapons overseas has been one of the main means to earn hard currency. Undoubtedly, the amount of arms export rapidly decreased owing to dramatic decrease in East European arms market following the dissolution of the Warsaw Treaty Organization, after the demise of the Soviet Union. However, as President Yeltsin himself has declared, Russia is making energetic efforts to regain its share in the international arms market.

At the same time, the shift from military to civilian production fully started by President Clinton, will promote arms sales at least in the short and near term, and may never cause a significant decrease in the amount of arms sold. The continuous reduction of the defense procurement budget has naturally reduced the opportunity to purchase weaponry. As a result, the US may inevitably have to sell arms in order to maintain production lines. In fact, in 1992 the US increased its share of the arms market in the Third World up to 60 percent, and became the principal arms supplier, surpassing Russia.

In addition, US weapons manufacturers requested support from the Senate for government loan guarantees. Thus, the Senate adopted an amendment to offer their loan guarantees for overseas arms sales, in response to the request.[2] This decision may facilitate arms races in the Middle East and Asia owing to the export subsidy policy, which will be adopted by such competing states as the UK and France. Although conditions surrounding the US and Russia are different, the US, facing difficulties in conversion as much as Russia, is going to accelerate overseas arms sales. The US diplomacy no doubt lacks logic, showing its leadership as a builder of the New COCOM to control arms and technology transfer on the one hand, and promoting arms sales from the viewpoint of economic security on the other.

This "double standard" diplomacy, more critically, "the forked-tongue diplomacy" is not new. The US-Japan conflict in 1981 over the export of Hitachi computers to China was a typical example. That is, the US protested the Hitachi computer export on account of possible. dangers of diversion to military use, while immediately after that rejection it showed its intention to permit IBM to export larger computers to China. Consequently the Japanese government was enraged. It is better to assume that the US will not always put its policy principles into practice after shifting to the New COCOM. The dilemma which the New COCOM will face can be easily imagined.

5) How to cope with the "dual use threats"

With regard to arms exporting and the transfer of dual use technologies, Chinese exports of M-11 missile parts to Pakistan were sanctioned by the US. The sanctions were applied by invoking the Helms Amendment of the Arms Export Control Act of 1990. Then immediately afterward, the US Government permitted supercomputer exports amounting to 8 million dollars to China in November. It was alleged that the US government allowed the sales to give relief to Cray Research, which was facing management crisis.[3]

This case recalls the another episode in August 1972 when the Nixon administration permitted Bryant Co. to export ball bearing grinding machines to the USSR, justifying it by claiming that it was a proof of detente. The true intention was to give relief to Bryant Co., which was in the midst of a financial management crisis, however, the Soviet Union consequently diverted them to military use and succeeded in converting the SS-19 missiles to multiple independently targetable re-entry vehicles (MIRV). Because supercomputers are the typical dual-use technologies, an emerging supercomputer export control regime has already been formed between the US and Japan.

What is more, the US promised Israel to sell her a new type of fighter aircraft, when Prime Minister Itzhak Rabin visited Washington in November 1993. Israel is still a country of proliferation concern in the Middle East. The US always justifies its overseas arms sales to conflicting regions on the grounds of maintaining or recovering the "regional military balance".

Japan is the rare state which has not exported arms since the end of the Second World War. Accordingly, Japan should show political initiative in opposing these contradictory tendencies as much as possible at any high level meeting in COCOM. Moreover, since it is reported today that Japan is trying to form an Asian export control regime, Japan has become the focus of attention on how it will deal with the "dual use threat" increasing in Asia.[4]

6) Chinese arms build-up and Western countries' dilemma

The most noticeable change among international military developments after the end of the Cold War is the Southeast Asian and Chinese intentions to expand their armaments. Besides, there are a lot of sources which will cause regional conflicts; for example, conflict over territory of the Spratley Islands in the South China Sea. Above all, in China a policy to increase the defense expenditure of 1994 by 22.4 percent compared with that of 1993 was announced at the National People's Congress held in March, which may raise other nations' fear of Chinese arms build-up. The Japanese Prime Minister Hosokawa's anxiety about Chinese arms built-up, expressed during the Chinese Deputy Prime Minister's visit to Japan in February 1994, is an illustration of these fears in the region.

In addition, there is still a possibility that a problem of sales of weapons of mass destruction and related technologies will recur, such as the previously mentioned problem of Chinese missile export to Pakistan. China already officially announced that it will observe the MTCR guidelines and increase its involvement in the non-proliferation export control regimes when the former US Secretary of State James

Baker visited China in 1991. However, China is not a formal member of the MTCR, the Australian Group, nor the NSG. Accordingly, Chinese participation in the New COCOM will not only make the conventional arms transfer control regime effective, but also its participation in the non-proliferation export control regime is necessary. It is quite clear that Japan should use its leadership role in multilateral negotiations to promote Chinese participation.

Chinese pragmatic diplomacy has been sharpening since the Cold War ended. With reference to the international export control regimes, China has announced that it will link its commitment to such non-proliferation export regimes as the MTCR with the US export of 150 F-16 fighters to Taiwan declared under the Bush administration in September 1992.[5] This occurred because from the Chinese perspective, the F-16 exports to Taiwan by the Bush administration were a violation of the US-Chinese Communique in 1982. Here, as well as in the case of F-15 fighter sales to Israel, the US's sophisticated avoidance of conventional arms transfer control principles is well observed. Therefore, it is quite natural that China announced that it would link MTCR commitment and F-16 sales to Taiwan, to cope with US pragmatic diplomacy.

However, the US can take this Chinese linkage policy as a China's intention to decrease its commitment to the MTCR. This will aggravate the US-China relationship, in addition to their on-going disputes over human rights issues. Undoubtedly, the Western states which make up the non-proliferation control regimes have discussed over and over again the possibility of Chinese formal participation in the MTCR. On the other hand, the Western states, particularly, the US have been afraid that sensitive technologies and data concerning the production of missiles might leak to the Chinese. It can be said that the US has completely changed its policy from the Reagan years, when the government rapidly relaxed military-related technology controls to China.

Chinese participation is indispensable for the non-proliferation export regimes to be workable. However, at the same time, leakage of sensitive technologies data to China should be avoided. The dilemma will surely arise under the New COCOM system. Therefore, if ways to solve this dilemma are to be considered, those are either: involving China in the non-proliferation export regimes and making it regulate arms itself through norms and rules of regimes, or keeping China outside the regime in order to avoid leakage of Western military related technologies to China. Needless to say, there are a wide range of alternatives between these two extremes.

Nevertheless, no consensus on which choice to make has been reached among states that are members of COCOM or already existing non-proliferation export control regimes. In short, a heated argument on Chinese participation exists. The argument is caused not only by different views on Chinese military power, but also by a contest over the huge Chinese market among states within the regimes. The original plan to reorganize COCOM at the end March 1994 seems to have been postponed because of disagreements over export control policy among COCOM member states. Above all, dispute between the US and European states, particularly France, the former being serious about non-restrictive technology transfer to China and the latter, seeking profit from trade with China, is keen. It is certain that the US, too, will look for profit to be gained from trade with China. Thus, although the US had banned the export of satellites to China as a result of Chinese violation of the MTCR guidelines in August 1993, the US was forced to remove the export ban out any plausible reason. This was because the US intended to avoid losing its major share of the satellite market in China. In brief, the US still suffers from the difficulty of balancing national security interests and commercial interests.

It is certain that, with the modification of the Export Administration Act near at hand, not only the government but also the Congress and business community of the US are willing to relax over-regulation in order to strengthen industrial competitiveness. Even the Department of Defense, which stood fast during the Cold War period, clearly shows its support, although subject to efforts to relax export controls. Permission for a third party to gain US developed technologies in return for US access to his markets, and a following plan to modify the Arms Export Control Law, announced by the Deputy Secretary of Defense John Deutsch is a good example.[6] On the contrary, some still strongly oppose the dissolution of COCOM as danger of nuclear proliferation may increase, as well as the relaxation of regulations, if the licensing mechanism based on multilateral consultations at COCOM disappears.[7] It is quite difficult to predict whether deregulation will be generally supported, or supports for stricter regulations will prevail. At present, it seems that the former is the general tendency. However, recent domestic trends in the US shows us that the future dynamics of US export control will fluctuate between these opposing trends, being largely dependent on the political situation in Russia.

7) Is it possible to establish an Asian regional export control regime?

Is it possible to establish a sub-regime in East Asia, to support global export control regimes? And if it is possible to do so with all difficulties concerning Chinese participation in the international export control regimes, then under what conditions?

The unstable situation in East Asia after the Cold War is not only made more uncertain by the Chinese arms build-up. It is well known that the Korean Peninsula, which is the last seat of the Cold War left in East Asia, the tension between both Koreas has been mounting since North Korean nuclear activities aroused international scrutiny. Moreover, the tension intensified through North Korean success in launching the ballistic missile 'Nodong-1'. Thus, the Korean Peninsula becomes the test site for forming a regional nonproliferation regime. In that case, not only South and North Korea, but also the U.S, Russia, China, and Japan, which are formally or informally participating in multilateral non-proliferation regimes, will play important roles. In addition, Taiwan, Hong Kong, and Singapore will be involved to some extent.

Needless to say, North Korea has been a target state for COCOM regulation not only as a remaining socialist state but also as a state in a potential conflict situation. Even after COCOM transforms itself to a conventional arms and related technology transfer control regime, the present control framework including nonproliferation regimes will not change much, as long as the Kim regime continues. Therefore, if China formally participates in the non-proliferation regimes or the post-COCOM regime, a regional regime targeting North Korea will, in practice, start to function.

However, the problem is how a regional regime, whose purpose would be controlling export to North Korea, should be organized. North Korea has rapidly become isolated from the rest of the world since the Cold War system was dissolved. Accordingly, it is the best way to avoid isolating North Korea further and forcing it to pursue a nuclear potential. Since the export control regimes targeting North Korea, such as the non-proliferation regimes or COCOM, are already working, it is unnecessary to create an additional regional export control regime.

Though there had been no regional export control regime, the newly industrialized economic states (NIES) became more careful in transferring military related high-technologies. This is because since the mid-1980s the US, led by Assistant Secretary of Defense Richard N. Perle under the Reagan administration, urged the Asian NIES that are not members of COCOM to organize and intensify their own export control systems. In addition, the US informal announcement of establishing an Asian COCOM had a great influence in that respect. As a result, sensitivity to militarily related high-tech export has dramatically risen. In fact, Taiwan, Hong Kong, South Korea, and Singapore, have started to establish their own export control system since the last half of the 1980s. It can be said, therefore, that these countries and areas are already involved in the non-proliferation export control regimes or a COCOM-like regime to a large extent.

With reference to militarily related high-tech led by electronics technologies, the NIES had made such remarkable progress that they have almost caught up with states that are COCOM members or other participants in the non-proliferation export control regimes. Therefore, role of the NIES in preventing proliferation of sensitive technologies related to weapons of mass destruction and conventional arms become logically important. It is quite natural that the Asian NIES should increase their involvement in the nonproliferation export control regimes or in the New COCOM. On the contrary, whether it is necessary to establish a new regional export control regime, including all these countries and areas, taken charge of by the U.S and Japan is a serious matter.

To sum up briefly, as previously noted, further isolating North Korea should be avoided. What is more, with the Taiwan issue, no policies that might arouse Chinese offensive posture are advisable from the viewpoint of stability in East Asia. Judging from the present strategic environment in Asia, it would be a better scenario to establish a soft system aiming at loose cooperation of concerned states than a hard system of export control.

Notes

1. World Armaments and Disarmament: SIPRI Yearbook 1993, (Stockholm: SIPRI, 1993) 444.

2. *International Herald Tribune*, November 4, 1993.

3. *Defense News*, November 1-7, 1993.

4. Lisa Burgess and Naoaki Wsui, "Japan Leads Quest For Asian Export Control," *Defense News*, (November 1-7, 1993).

5. Richard C. Barnard and Barbara Opall, "Chinese Ties MTCR to US-Taiwan F-16 Sale," *Defense News,* (March 7-13, 1994).

6. Stephen C. Lesueur, "US Likely Will Relax Third-Party Export Rules, " *Defense News,* (February 28-March 6, 1994).

7. For example see the statements of Stephen D. Bryen, the ex-Deputy Secretary of Defense. He was regarded as one of the most ardent Pentagon supporters of super-technology development during the Reagan administration. See Stephen D. Bryen, "After COCOM, A Danger of More Iraqs," *International Herald Tribune,* (March 5-6, 1994).

Chapter 3

Dual-Use Technology and Export Controls: An Economic Analysis

Yuzo Murayama

Introduction

Recent studies on nonproliferation export controls have started to pay more attention to the dual use nature of technologies.[1] One of the reasons behind this trend is that commercial repercussions of restricting technology flow are becoming more significant due to the increasing importance of dual-use technologies with military applications. This tendency is likely to become even stronger in the post-Cold War world, where economic factors are expected to play more significant roles.

Although there are numbers of studies available on the subject, all majority of these studies that deal with dual-use technology in an export control context have been policy oriented ones, because they lack an analytical perspective. The main purpose of this paper is to fill this gap, that is, by adopting simple economic analyses, I intend to provide a basic analytical framework for understanding the relationship between dual-use technology and export controls.

The first part is an economic analysis of transferring dual-use technology. This will be done by providing an analytical framework that covers cost-benefit relationships of commercial and military markets for private companies that produce dual-use technology products, I will point out that military technologies will depend more on commercial technologies in the dual-use technology area. Therefore, in the post-Cold War world, the military sector will be forced to use increasingly more technologies that are developed in the commercial sector. The second part is an economic analysis of export controls. Export control regimes are analyzed applying simple cartel theory and differences between COCOM and nonproliferation regimes are examined. I will point out some of the difficulties facing non-proliferation export control from economic perspectives.

In the last section, the above two analyses are combined and implications for non-proliferation export control of dual-use technology are examined. The main conclusion drawn from the examination is that the cost-benefit relationship of nonproliferation export control is worsening. In order to increase effectiveness of the control under these circumstances, three possible approach to the problems are suggested.

Although analyses here have limitations in incorporating such concept as power distribution among countries that are used frequently in international relations, they would provide different perspectives on the working of interactions between dual-use technology and export controls.

Economic Analysis of Dual-Use Technologies

A Framework for Analyzing Dual-Use Technologies

Analytical approaches to dual-use technology seem to be lagging behind considering the great amount of literature available on this subject.[2] One of the reasons that dual-use technology is a politically controversial issue related to both military and commercial industries, and thus, it induced more policy-oriented studies rather than the analytical ones.

In Japan, government policy also seemed to impede the development of studies on the transfer of dual-use technology. The Japanese government adopted a policy to separate national security issues from economic and trade issues. This policy indirectly influenced Japanese scholars to concentrate only on commercial aspects of technology studies. The national security aspects of technology transfer are neglected in academic research and issues concerning military aspect of dual-use technology have been only mentioned in the media rather sensationally. As a result, serious academic studies on dual-use technology totally divorced from the study of technologies in the Japanese academic world.[3]

In this chapter, I will employ analytical approaches to dual-use technology from two dimensions. They are, first, the degree of technology duality and second, the direction of dual-use technology development.[4]

Each technology has its own unique degree of duality. Here high technology duality refers to the situation where technology can be converted from commercial to military applications easily and *visa versa*. For instance, semiconductor memory is judged to have high technology duality because they can be incorporated both in military and commercial use without major changes. In the research and development (R&D) stages, the technology duality tends to be higher in basic research in comparison with applied research. This is because the development path to a final product, which is either commercial or military, has not been clarified in basic research stage. However, as the research goes into the application stage, a specific final product is in sight in, utilizing the research, therefore, technology duality tends to be lowered on this state.

At a product level, technology duality tends to be lowered as we advance from materials and parts to final products. It is obvious that as we advance to a final product, its use tends to be limited toward either military or commercial use. The reason why above-mentioned semiconductors have high technology duality is that they are electronics components, therefore, they can be used both in military electronics product such as missiles and in consumer electronics product such as VCRs. The similar distinction also can be made between product and process technologies, in which the latter technology's duality tends to be higher. Machine tools are a good example of the latter case.

Technologies with high duality tend to develop toward military applications in one time and toward commercial applications in another time. Because of these tendencies, it looks as if the nature of technology in terms of military and commercial applications changes over time. However, the dual-use capability of each technology does not change but direction of dual-use technology development is the one that changes over time.

In order to examine the direction of dual-use technology development, we have to look into cost-benefit environments in military and commercial markets for companies that produce dual-use technology products. In capitalist countries, dual-use technologies are usually developed by private companies. If we suppose that there is no coercion from government on private company's activities, companies that produce dual-use technology products have choices to develop their business in military or commercial markets. This choice depends on relative cost and benefit relationships in each market. For instance, if the military budget is plentiful and increasing at a rapid pace, and the government subsidizes those companies' R & D for developing military technologies, the companies have incentives to develop their business in the military market. On the other hand, if a commercial market is expanding more rapidly than military market and there are costly regulations imposed on military markets the companies would be pulled toward the commercial market.

Therefore, directions of dual-use technology development are influenced by such factors as military tensions (that is reflected in size and growth rate of the military budget), the government's R & D policy (that is reflected in research and development costs of companies depending on amount of subsidies available in military and commercial market), and the state of technology development (that influence whether the technology is developed enough to be cost effective in the commercial market).

Dual-use technology in the post-Cold War world

The time after World War Two (WWII) until the first half of 1960s in the US can be considered as a period when dual-use technology development was pulled toward military applications. As the Cold War developed after WWII, the US Government increased R & D funding for military and space development in order to maintain technological edge against the Soviet Union. This political decision provided dual-use technology companies (electronics and computer companies) enormous research funds.[5] In addition, the US government increased its military acquisitions budget at a rapid pace and acquired innovative but high priced products from dual-use technology companies. These provided ample incentives for dual-use technology companies to develop products for military and space markets. Furthermore, such important technologies as electronic components, jet engines, supersonic airframes, rockets, and computers were all in the early stages of their development and the US government played substantial roles in nurturing these technologies.[6]

On the other hand, prices of products that incorporated these new technologies were still too expensive for commercial markets. That is, these new technologies had not developed enough to provide cost effective products to commercial markets. Therefore, the profit oriented prerogatives of producers of dual-use technologies targeted military markets and as a result, development in this area was pulled toward military applications.

The circumstances surrounding dual-use technologies in the post-Cold War World are showing a clear contrast to the aforementioned situation. At first, world military expenditures are expected to decrease over time due to the ending of the Cold War. As a result, military markets will be shrinking markets for dual-use technology companies in general.[7] Secondly, it is widely perceived that, in the post-Cold War world, the role of economic factors are increasing their importance in comparison with military factors. This trend will encourage governments to support development of commercially valuable technologies. Furthermore, it is likely that government funding such as R & D will shift toward commercial sectors. Third, many important technologies that proliferated in mid-20th century such as semiconductors, computers, and telecommunications, are now in the application stage of the development cycle. Under these circumstances, companies can internalize their benefits of R & D by producing products that embody these new technologies. Therefore, these companies have strong incentives to develop technologies in commercial markets that are expected to expand steadily over the near term.

In sum, growth rate of the markets, government supports, and technological trends seem favorable for commercial development of dual-use technologies and companies that deal with these technologies would not have strong incentives to develop their technologies toward military applications. That is, military technologies will depend on commercial technologies in the area where technologies have high duality and notable dual-use technology will be mostly developed in commercial markets. This trend will force the military sector to be users of dual use technology that are developed in commercial markets. It is important to recognize that the need for nonproliferation control is increasing at the same time that the importance of dual-use technology in military technologies is increasing. We have to look at nonproliferation export controls in this historical context.

An Economic Analysis of Export Control Regimes

Export Control as an Extreme Case of a Cartel

Export control regimes can be considered as a kind of a cartel. In general, a cartel is formed to raise the price of a product or commodity by cutting the amount supplied to a market. Participating members of a cartel can get extra benefit due to the increase in the product price. In order to cut the supply, it is necessary for the members to collude and assign the amount of available to each of them. As such, an export control regime is an extreme case of cartel; that is, it tries to eliminate supplies to a certain number of countries, rather than limiting them. This kind of cartel does not make economic sense since members can not get any economic profits from this kind of cartel. Obviously, the purpose of forming an export control cartel is to get benefits in the national security area. By controlling the flow of technologies to undesirable countries, member countries can reduce the threat from these countries, and thus, obtain national security benefit by paying the economic cost of reduced supplies.

A simple economic theory implies that a cartel tends to break down under free competition. Since participating members are assigned a quota of supplies that are less than the amount without the cartel, they always have incentives to increase the amount supplied and obtain more profits. This incentive is especially strong because of the higher price set by the limited amount supplied to the market. If one member breaks the agreement of the cartel and increases the amount supplied to the market, other members, who perceive unfairness in the agreement, could follow the cartel breaker and the whole cartel would break down eventually.

This implies that in order to maintain a cartel under market pressure there must be an effective mechanism of monitoring each member's ill or deviant behavior and enforcing the agreements to prevent the members from increasing the amount supplied. Therefore, a maintainable cartel requires an effective system of monitoring and enforcement and it has to be provided at a low cost. The same line of the argument can be applied to export control regimes. That is, export control regimes are always in danger of breaking down from market pressure. However, only if the regime establishes effective means of monitoring member's less than prudent behavior and provides an effective method of enforcing agreements at a low cost, will the regime have the possibility of survival. It is important to start from the possibility of break down, rather than taking the persistence of a cartel for granted, as the basis for establishing an effective export control regime.

An Ideal Export Control Regime

Let us examine factors that are essential for maintaining effective export controls. In terms of the monitoring and enforcement aspect of maintaining effective cartels, the following six points can be considered as such factors (see the Table 1):

(1) Small number of member countries ----- It becomes less costly to monitor each other's behavior and enforce agreements as the number of member countries decreases;

(2) Small number of countries to which technology flow is controlled ---- It becomes less costly to control and monitor the flow of technology;

(3) Small number of items to be controlled ----- It becomes less costly to control and monitor flow of technology;

(4) High world market share of controlled technologies by member countries ----- If there are countries outside the regime that have the capacity to supply controlled technologies, these countries are happy to provide controlled technologies to undesirable countries. This incentive is especially strong because price of controlled technologies are set artificially higher due to the limited supply of technologies imposed by the export control;

(5) Strong common ideology among member countries ----- If the member countries share a common ideology, it becomes more difficult to break the agreement. This is because if one country breaks it, it would lose other member's confidence in that country and the country would worsen its position in international relations. Therefore, the ideological factor puts additional cost on breaking the agreement; and

(6) Severe punishment for breaking the agreement ---- If the punishment is severe, it makes it more costly to break the agreement.

If all of the above requirements are met at low cost, the export control regime can be maintained effectively.

A Comparison of COCOM and Nonproliferation Export Control Regimes

Next, let us examine COCOM and non-proliferation export control regimes with regard to the above criteria. In the COCOM regime, the number of member countries was seventeen and the number of countries to which technology flow was restricted was eleven. In non-proliferation regimes, both the number of member countries and countries to be controlled tend to be larger than the ones for COCOM. For instance, twenty-seven countries have participated in Nuclear Suppliers Group (NSG) guidelines for nuclear nonproliferation control and the US is proposing to include sixty countries in the control country list for a catch-all type export control system.[8] Although the numbers vary depending on the different export regimes, potentially large numbers in non-proliferation export control make monitoring and enforcement within the regimes more difficult compared with the COCOM regime.

The number of controlled items was about 300 under COCOM, and that appears to be a large number.[9] However, given the basic principle of COCOM, that is to control the flow of technologies that are not available in the Eastern bloc, the transfer of these items and capabilities is confined to high technology areas. This is because the technological level of the former Soviet Union was relatively high. This characteristic stands out clearly when we compare proliferation regimes. Nonproliferation regimes are mainly trying to control technology flow to Third World countries where the industrial capability is much lower than in the former Soviet Union. In addition, nonproliferation regimes sometimes try to control low technology items because production of biological and chemical weapons involve these items. These factors make the number of controlled items potentially large, therefore, the control lists of non-proliferation regimes tend to be longer. Of course, longer control lists cause difficult problems in monitoring technology flow.

As was mentioned, COCOM was trying to control relatively high technology items that were not available in the Eastern bloc. This, in principle, worked to raise the market share of technology controlled by the member countries of COCOM. Especially, after foreign availability concept was adopted, the market shares should have been maintained at a high level. This is a clear contrast to the nonproliferation regimes. Nonproliferation regimes sometimes try to control low technology items that are produced in the many countries. Therefore, in order to increase the market shares of these items by member countries, the number of member countries must be increased. This, in turn, makes monitoring and enforcement in the regimes more demanding. This trade-off between market share controlled by member countries and the difficulty of enforcement caused by the increased numbers is a very burdensome dilemma facing non-proliferation export control regimes.

One of the advantages that the COCOM regime possessed was its strong ideological ties. All the member countries had common perceptions about the danger of exporting important technologies to Eastern Bloc countries. The perceived threat from the Eastern Bloc was substantial enough to elicit a common ideology with the accompanying goal of containing communism. Because of this ideological factor, cooperation among the member countries was relatively easy and breaking the agreements was a costly behavior for the member countries. In addition, it also made it easy to identify the small number of countries to be controlled due to the ideological differences.

The ideological element is one of the difficult aspects of non-proliferation regimes. There is a general consensus that countries such as Iraq, Libya, and North Korea are the threatening factor in the international order and technology flow to these countries should be controlled. However, there are countries that perceive levels of threats differently depending on the country in question. Since there is no clear ideological difference between member countries and countries to be controlled, it becomes difficult to reach the agreement concerning which countries should be included in the control list. This is one of the difficulties in the post-Cold War world, where threats to a country are influenced more by such individual factor as the geopolitical position of a country. In addition to the difficulties of reaching agreement among member countries, it becomes easier to break the agreement due to the lack of common ideological ties among member countries.

Table 3.1:
Comparison of Export Control Regimes

	Ideal Type	COCOM	NPT
1) Number of members	small	17	7-27(?)
2) Number of controlled countries	small	11	possibly large
3) Number of controlled items	small	about 300	possibly large
4) Market shares by member countries	high	high	possibly low
5) Existence of common ideologies	strong	strong	weak
6) Level of punishment	severe	less uniform	less uniform

One weakness of the COCOM regime was the uneven application of rules by member countries. This is because COCOM was just a coordinating committee and violators were punished under each member country's domestic law. In addition, the mechanisms for enforcing COCOM rules were different in each country. This produced sense of unfairness in countries that had severe enforcement rules.

However, it cannot be denied that the US played a very important leadership role in alleviating this defect. The US government put pressure on other member countries to conform to the agreement by combining export control policy with economic assistance policy. This was especially important during the 1950s and 1960s. However, this role by the US government was reduced during the detente period of 1970s.[10] In nonproliferation control, issues are not clearly shaped yet regarding coordination of enforcement and punishment rules among member countries. Although the US government continues to play a leadership roles to forge a new regime, it is not clear that the US will be able to exert its influence as it was able to do during the 1950s when the COCOM regime was established.

Toward Increasing Effectiveness of Nonproliferation Export Controls

Worsening Cost/Benefit Relationships

The most important implication from the analyses in sections two and three is that the cost/benefit relationship of export control is worsening. On the cost side, as the roles of dual-use technology in military technology increase, it is becoming necessary to control more of the flow of dual-use technology in order to prevent proliferation. However, if we start to control larger flow of dual-use technology, it will have severe repercussions on commercial sectors. Since dual-use technology is also important in commercial business, dual-use technology companies have to sacrifice more of their commercial opportunities in participating the non-proliferation control. That is, opportunity costs facing dual-use technology companies are increasing. In addition, as was discussed in the previous section, costs to form effective regimes themselves are increasing. Therefore, it is becoming very costly both to forge regimes and control technology flows in the regimes.

The increasing importance of dual-use technology in export controls also affect the benefit side of control. If one controls the flow of military-oriented technology to prevent proliferation, its effect is direct; that is, it can directly control flow of military-relevant technologies. In comparison, the control of commercially-oriented dual-use technology has only indirect effects on proliferation. This is because, in most cases, weapons can not be developed by using only commercially-oriented dual-use technology, but it is necessary to combine these dual-use technologies with military-specific technologies or military know how. Therefore, unless the flow of military specific technologies and know how are controlled, benefits generated from dual-use technology export controls tend to be reduced.

In addition, the quality of national security benefits generated from export controls are different in the post-Cold War era. During the Cold War, if we allowed the free flow of technologies to the Soviet Union, it would have surely bolstered the Soviet Union's military strength, and increased their threat capabilities.

Compared with this Cold War period, the national security benefits generated from controlling technology flow to the Third World countries are sometimes different. In some cases, benefits from the export controls are economic ones, that is, we are trying to prevent regional conflicts that would cause economic threats to our countries. A typical case of this kind is the effort to prevent Gulf War type conflicts in the Middle East through export controls. In other cases, threats are ones to human rights, that is, we are trying to prevent infringement of human rights caused by regional conflicts, because we are concerned about the increasing trend of ethnic conflicts in the post-Cold War world. Although there remains the cases that the direct military threats to advances countries are the main reasons of export controls, it seems that the relative importance of the above-mentioned different kind of threats are increasing in the post-Cold War world.

Therefore, it is important to recognize that we are entering a very different period for nonproliferation export controls in terms of their costs and benefits. And in order to forge effective regimes for export controls, policies have to be built on the clear recognition of these different circumstances.

Possible approaches to effective export controls

The above examination of export control regimes suggests a few possible approaches to the problems facing nonproliferation export controls. Three of these approaches are presented below:

Shortening the control list - As was discussed in the previous section, the dilemma of non-proliferation export control is highlighted when attempts are made by member states to increase the market share of controlled items. One has to increase the number of the participating members to accomplish this objective, which in turn, makes monitoring and enforcement more difficult. This predicament becomes especially severe when the control list starts to include low technology items.

The only solution to this dilemma seems to be shorten to the control list by controlling only critically important items, that is materials and technologies specifically earmarked for weapons development and deployment. If the regime confines its control items at a minimum level, the following benefits in terms of monitoring and enforcement can be derived:

- the number of member countries can be kept small;
- the number of controlled items can be kept small;
- the market share of the products by member countries can be kept high;
- it becomes relatively easy to form the common ideology (shared goals, norms and values); and
- it becomes relatively easy to agree on the uniform enforcement and punishment rules.

Therefore, four out of five factors that make nonproliferation control difficult can be improved by shortening the control list. Although it is understood that shortening the list is important, a more difficult side of the story is how to make the control list shorter, that is, how we can determine the strategic importance of control items and sort out critical items to be controlled.

One way to approach this problem is to determine the technology's strategic value for national security. The standard approach is to judge product's strategic value by (1) the availability of its substitute, (2) the availability of different supply sources, and (3) the possibility of stockpiling.[11] That is, if the product has a limited number of close substitute product, a limited number of supply sources, and characteristics that make stockpiling difficult, the product's strategic value is high. For instance, supercomputers are a typical strategic product based upon the above three criteria.

A more meaningful approach in the case of export controls is the one presented in the Bucy report.[12] This report was published in 1976 and the main issue of the report is how to control technology flow effectively to the former Soviet Union. Although it looks as if there is no relevance to the nonproliferation export controls judging from the period and circumstances that this report was written, it still has great value in its analysis and in its way of thinking.

The most important point of this report, in terms of implications for nonproliferation export control, is its emphasis on controlling such technologies as design and manufacturing know how that are considered key technologies in weapon making. By controlling these technologies that provide bottlenecks to weapon making and releasing less important items from the control list, the report claims that export control can be maintained effectively at the lowest cost.

This approach is useful for nonproliferation export control because less critical technologies that are released from the control list have the potential to contribute to commercial development of the country. This becomes especially important if transferred technologies have only commercial relevance when they are transferred alone. This kind of thinking was irrelevant during the Cold War. If the former Soviet Union obtained the above kind of technologies and used them in commercial sectors, the situation would have been unacceptable for Western countries because it would have raised economic capacity of the Soviet Union and provided an indirect threat. The situation gets worse when these technologies are combined with military know how and contribute to the development of military technologies. This is not an unlikely situation given the high level of the former Soviet Union's military technologies.

This line of argument does not always apply for the Third World countries. It is possible for some countries to attain economic growth by obtaining commercially oriented technologies and their technological development pattern is pulled toward the commercial sector. This is a favorable development in terms of the non-proliferation of weapons. Therefore, if one tries to control technology flow extensively, it has the possibility of eliminating favorable development paths of economic growth in the Third World countries. Therefore, it seems important to distinguish between critical bottleneck technologies for developing weapons of mass destruction and other less important technologies in implementing an effective and meaningful system of non-proliferation export controls.[13]

Trying to forge a new common ideology - One of the primary strengths of the COCOM regime was the existence of a common ideology among member countries. However, as was discussed, this is not the case in non-proliferation export controls. This factor sometimes makes it difficult to identify countries to which technology flow should be controlled.

It is necessary to establish common criteria to judge these countries, that all the participating countries agree with, in order to form effective export control regimes. Given the different threat conditions that each country is facing, the common criteria would be difficult to be agreed upon, however, efforts to reach agreement should be continued. If the common factors that make countries undesirable for technology transfer are discovered through dialogues among member countries, it would become a firm basis for effective export control.

Standardized enforcement and punishment - Uniformity is also necessary for each member country's enforcement and punishment severity. This is an important factor because dual-use technology also plays a significant role in strengthening the international competitiveness of a country's industries. If one member country does not enforce the agreement severely and its punishment of violators is lenient, other member countries would feel the regime to be unfair. This is because the country can obtain commercial benefit by joining the regime but not by complying with the obligations of the agreement. In fact, if one country does not enforce the agreement while all other member countries conform to the prescribed requirements, that country can obtain great benefits by taking advantage of its monopoly position. If this kind of behavior prevails in the regime, others would be likely to follow by relaxing enforcement rules and it could eventually lead to the breakdown of the regime.

This kind of consideration is becoming more important in the post-Cold War world. There is an increasing recognition that economic factors, rather than military factors, are becoming more important in the international system. As was discussed; export control is a system to obtain national security benefit by sacrificing commercial benefit. If many countries start to perceive that national security benefits generated from export controls is not worth the sacrifice of economic benefits this kind of regime could not be maintained.

After all, it is important to recognize that creating a satisfactory export control regime is becoming a very difficult task in the post-Cold War world. Given this circumstance, a gradual approach to forming export control regimes seem to be more sensible. That is, by forming a solid regime among the small number of countries, the probability of reaching agreement on such elements as, a list of targeted countries, the list of controlled items, levels of enforcement and punishment, and the extension of that regime to other countries, increases appreciably. Even if the regime cannot control all the undesirable flow of technologies at the first stage, the regime can become a solid basis toward a better system.

Economic analyses of dual-use technology and export control regimes suggest that this kind of approach, that emphasizes prevention of regime break down, is optimal in the long run in constructing effective export control regimes.

Notes

1. For an example of studies of this kind see the following two studies by the National Academy of Sciences; *Balancing the National Interest: U.S. National Security Export Controls and Global Competition.* (Washington, D.C.: National Academy Press, 1987) and *Finding Common Ground: U.S. Export Controls in a Changed Global Environment.* (Washington, D.C.: National Academy Press, 1991).

2. For an important study that deals with the analytical aspects of dual-use technology see Part I in *The Relationships between Defense and Civil Technologies,* Philip Gummett and Judith Reppy eds., (Dordrecht, Netherlands: Kluwar Academic Publishers, 1988).

3. The important exception is Taizo Yakushiji, *Tekunohegemoni* [Techno-Hegemony](Tokyo: Chuokoron-Sha 1989) that deals with the importance of technological factors in establishing hegemony in international relations.

4. For details of the analytical framework of dual-use technologies, see Yuzo Murayama "Senryaku Ryoyo Gijutsu to Beikoku no Keizai Kyosoryoku Mondai" (Strategic Dual-Use Technologies and Economic Competitiveness Issues in the U.S.), *Gaiko Jiho*, No. 1292, October 1992.

5. For a study of U.S. Government involvement in the development of the computer industry, see Kenneth Flamm, *Targeting the Computer: Government Support and International Competition* (Washington, D.C.: The Brookings Institution, 1987).

6. Kenneth Flamm and Thomas McNaugher, "Rationalizing Technology Investments," in John D. Steinbrunner ed., *Restructuring American Foreign Policy* (Washington, D.C.: The Brookings Institution, 1989).

7. Military spending in Third world countries is expected to increase even in the post-Cold War environment. However, these increases will be more than offset by cutbacks in military spending by advanced countries.

8. *Asahi Shinbun*, November 17, 1992.

9.The number of controlled items under COCOM have changed over time. This number is the one that appeared in *Nihon Keizai Shinbun*, October 2, 1992.

10. See Michael Mastanduno, "The Management of Alliance Export Control Policy: American Leadership and the Politics of COCOM," in *Controlling East-West Trade and Technology Transfer* Gary K. Bertsch, *et al.*, ed., (Durham, N.C.:Duke University Press, 1988).

11. Brian McCartan, "Defense or Opulence? Trade and Security in the 1990's," *SAIS Review*, 1991.

12. The Defense Science Board, *An Analysis of Export Control of U.S. Technology - A DoD Perspective*, A Report of the Defense Science Board Task Force on Export of U.S. Technology (Washington, D.C.: Office of the director of Defense Research and Engineering, February 4, 1976).

13. The idea to make distinctions between technologies that have high relevance to militarization of a country and those technologies that tend to induce commercial development of a country was presented by Akihiko Tanaka, an associate professor at Tokyo University, during a study session of export controls at the International Institute of Global Peace on January 18, 1993.

Chapter 4

An Institutional History Of
U.S. Export Control Policy

William J. Long

> *-In the aftermath of World War II, in response to problems of the Cold War, security defined in military terms became the overriding purpose abroad-both in concept and organizational form. Today the concept has somewhat changed, but the organization mostly remains.*

> Graham T. Allison (1975)[1]

> *-The rationale for national security export controls has changed significantly, while the system-and the legislation that underpins it-has not.*

> Glennon J.Harrison (1994)[2]

Introduction

The fundamental problem of writing history is selection. Which are the crucial facts and circumstances from the vast volume of human experience that portray past events to a contemporary audience in an intelligible and compelling manner? The first step in meeting this challenge is the choice of an epistemic perspective that helps the author and reader makes sense of the past.

As the title of this paper and the quotations suggest, political institutions-state organizations and the institutions of law and bureaucracy-are factors that have had a particularly significant and enduring impact on the nature and evolution of US export control policy. Therefore, a history which is attentive to the importance of institutions on politics and policy is, I would argue, especially appropriate for understanding US export control policy and, perhaps, useful in anticipating its future direction.

An institutional perspective is just one of many useful in interpreting US export control policy. As part of international relations, US export control policy has been constrained by the basic structure of the international system. The dominant theory of international relations, structural realism, reminds us that the international system remains "anarchic" and that therefore states must be attentive to the distribution of power across units in the system and the importance of maintaining an overall balance of power within it. As applied to US export control policy in the post-World War 11 era, this framework tells us that policy was shaped by the bipolar competition of the Cold War. That the East Bloc and the "West" (including Japan) should compete for technological advantage and that technology controls would be used as an instrument of state power despite their welfare-reducing effects is not surprising.

Structural realism is a very sparse theory, however. It does not attempt to tell us what specific choices states will make but merely to identify the constraints under which they operate. As its proponents concede, structural realism is not a theory of foreign policy, it provides little guide to statecraft except to warn states to attend to questions of power and its distribution to survive.[3] Structural realism cannot explain the differences among the United States and its COCOM allies over export control policy or the ebb and flow of technology controls over the past two decades, for example.

Understanding the origins and evolution of policy requires the incorporation of other variables that influence policy decisions and outcomes. Among the relevant variables are societal factors, ideology, decision-maker cognition and belief systems, and many more. Each of these factors adds to our understanding of the history of US export control policy. Export control policy often was affected by societal forces and the concerns and interests of the American business community, for example.[4] US export control policy also reflected America's anti-communist ideology, the secular religion of American politics during the Cold War era which animated a wide array of policies. At times, export control policies were shaped by the motives and beliefs of individual actors.[5] Presidential attitudes, such as President Carter's visceral reaction to the Soviet invasion of Afghanistan or President Reagan's staunch anti-communism, had significant impact on the direction of US export control policy.

Without denying the importance of social context, ideology, and individual choice, this history of US export controls insists on a more autonomous and important role for the state and its political institutions. As James March and Johan Olsen have argued: "Institutions seem to be neither neutral reflections of exogenous environmental forces nor neutral arenas for the performance of individuals driven by exogenous preferences . . ."[6] Rather, state institutions define and defend interests and act with a degree of autonomy from external, societal, or individual decision-maker interests. Adopting this institutional perspective can provide unique insights into the history of US export control policy.

What can an institutional approach tell us? An institutional perspective can specify how historical processes and policy outcomes are affected by the specific characteristics of political institutions. This perspective can elucidate the "inefficiencies of history," i.e., changes that take longer than expected or that are not value-maximizing. It can explain why policy evolves in some directions but fails to evolve in other directions, and why history seems to repeat itself (something also suggested by quotations above).

The Statist/Institutionalist Approach

The statist/institutionalist approach holds that the strength and autonomy of the state matters most in determining national policy preferences and behavior.[7] The state-often defined as an elite group of executive branch institutions and officials-steers foreign policy in accord with the dictates of the competitive environment of international relations.[8]

This approach focuses on executive actors and institutions and their ability to shape foreign policy choices and behavior. The statist approach is not synonymous with the unitary, rational actor assumptions of some realists or game theorists. Rather, executive actors with goals and norms and certain enduring political institutions with established operating characteristics constitute the state.[9] These actors formulate policy in response to their internal goals and procedures and in response to the threats and opportunities provided by the international system.[10] The state's leaders and institutions possess a measure of autonomy from societal actors and the international system. National preferences flow from this interaction between the executive and its institutions as prompted by the international environment.

Statist approaches also remind us that policy preferences and choices are not simply traceable to the interests of one or more societal groups, they are affected by structures.[11] The approach is compatible, therefore, with institutionalism. As Stephen Krasner argues, "Statist orientations place greater emphasis on institutional constraints, both formal and informal, on individual behavior."[12] He summarizes two basic reasons why institutions are essential to understanding policy: "First, capabilities and preferences, that is, the very nature of the actors, cannot be understood except as part of some larger institutional framework. Second, the possible options available at any given point in time are constrained by available institutional capabilities and these capabilities are themselves a product of some choices made during some earlier period."[13] Responses to external stimuli or societal forces are neither automatic or without cost. In short, institutions matter because they shape preferences and define available options and act on that information.[14]

An Institutional Overview of US Export Control Policy

The United States has long controlled the export of dual-use goods and technologies, that is, civilian technologies with potential military applications such as computers or avionics, to further its national security interests. To further a broader set of "foreign policy" interests the United States has limited the export of dual-use items and purely civilian items as well. Since the early days of the Cold War, US policy was directed to implementing a strategic embargo against communist countries-adding an economic arm to containment.

Beginning with the Export Control Act of 1949, Congress gave peacetime statutory authority to the president to develop a list of controlled products and proscribed destinations to prevent the transfer of technology that could contribute to the capability of a real or potential adversary.[15] The president, through his designee, the Commerce Department's Office of Export Control, drew up a list of controlled dual-use products-the "Commodity Control List" (CCL)-and identified countries-the Soviet Union, China, and the Warsaw Pact nations of Eastern Europe-as proscribed destinations. The Commerce Department administered the system through reviewing and licensing individual exports with the advise of other agencies, primarily the Departments of Defense and State.

In addition to devising a system of unilateral restraints, the United States sought to promote multilateral participation in implementing national security export controls. To this end, the United States organized the Coordinating Committee for Multilateral Export Controls ("COCOM") in 1949. Although similar to the US system, COCOM's mandate was narrower in that it restricted only exports that had military or potential military utility and did not impose foreign policy controls.

During the early years of the Cold War, unilateral and multilateral export controls were extensive. Initial Western security strategy sought to prohibit the export of virtually all equipment and technology that would assist the military or economic capabilities of the East by licensing the export or reexport of technology within the West and between West and East. This comprehensive approach was not without its costs.

By the late 1960s growing allied and US business dissatisfaction with the economic consequences of an expansive embargo of the East led Congress to stipulate that export controls should govern only products and technologies that contribute *significantly* to a potential enemies military capabilities, and then only if a comparable product could not be obtained from foreign suppliers.[16] Preserving the West's superiority over the East in defense-related technologies, rather than economic warfare became the statutory goal of US and COCOM policy and the COCOM list was reduced somewhat.

Throughout the Cold War period, however, the strategy of containment remained the guiding principle of export control policy, albeit with a recognition of the importance of expanding non-strategic trade by the 1970s and 1980s. The operative premise of export control policy was that the quantitative superiority of the Warsaw Pact Organization's forces could be offset by maintaining NATO's qualitative, technological superiority.

Perhaps the most striking institutional feature of US export control policy-making is the diffusion of authority across executive bureaus. In time, more than a dozen agencies would administer US technology controls of one kind or another. A study of export control policy-making by the U.S. National Academy of Sciences was unable to find any analogous area of government with a comparable number of bureaucracies.[17] Moreover, these agencies hold distinctive and often diverse policy positions that reflect their historical mission and current constituencies. For example, the key administrative players-Commerce, Defense, and State-have vied for control over policy for over 40 years, each believing, perhaps correctly, that it brings a unique commercial, security, or diplomatic understanding to the problem. Equally true, however is that these multiple perspectives make it difficult and time-consuming to coordinate the economic, military, and broader foreign policy dimensions of US export control policy. The diffusion of policy-making authority within the executive branch ensured that the development of the domestic control lists.[18] and the export licensing process[19] were complex inter-agency dynamics that often made coordination among bureaus and with industry and allies problematic.

As a consequence of the multiple agencies and numerous statutory and regulatory regimes governing dual-use and military technologies, the exporting community, Congress, and independent auditors have often criticized US technology transfer policy as confusing, unnecessarily complex, inherently inefficient, slow to change, unable to resolve internal disputes, lacking clear lines of jurisdiction, and generally impenetrable to those societal groups most affected by controls.[20] Arguably, White House involvement or regular, effective congressional oversight could overcome some of these problems, but the administration of US export controls has not been the subject of sustained and systematic attention from either branch of government.

A second major institutional feature of US export control policy-making is the very broad delegation of authority from Congress to the Executive. Under the U.S. Constitution (Article 1, Section 8), Congress is given plenary power over foreign commerce and executive authority comes from legislative delegation. In practice, however, Congress reigns over export control policy while the executive rules. Despite meaningful differences among agencies and within Congress over the proper direction of policy, over the past two decade the executive branch has successfully retained substantial authority to use export controls to serve its conception of the nation's security needs and in promoting diverse foreign policy interests. Executive branch autonomy has been the norm despite Congress's repeated efforts to control executive discretion in the use of foreign policy controls and to ensure that national security controls be administered more efficiently, narrowly, and with greater bureaucratic accountability.[21]

There are many reasons for executive autonomy in US export control policy. The origins of broad executive authority can be traced to the emergency powers over exports it garnered during World War II that were retained and expanded significantly during two decades of unquestioned US hegemony, Cold War rivalry, and executive-congresssional-interest group congruence on the purposes to be served by US export controls. This extensive and generally unchallenged delegation of authority led the president to establish an elaborate and insulated export control apparatus that has preserved many of its prerogatives from congressionally-mandated reforms and societal pressures. In maintaining substantial authority over export control law and policy the executive has drawn on partisan influence, a historic role in protecting and promoting US security and foreign policy interests, and superior expertise and experience in export control administration. Throughout the 1970s and 1980s, executive prerogatives continued to dominate export control policy despite the resurgence of congressional authority in foreign policy in the 1970s, the erosion of Cold War norms, and the growing dissatisfaction of the US business community with the burdens of the export control system.[22]

Thus, by extension, as the President and executive branch institutions have dominated Congress in export control policy making, so too have they dominated societal groups whose primary channel of influence into the policy-making process are their elected representatives in Congress. During the first two decades of US export control policy-the height of the Cold War-the American exporting community remained generally quiescence over the widespread American-led embargo of the East. To do otherwise would have been perceived as "un-American." Moreover, American industries were focused on the domestic market and more familiar foreign markets in Western Europe and the Americas. This pattern of dominance over societal groups continued, in the 1970s and 1980s, despite the growing importance of international trade to American economic health and the importance of interest groups in shaping American trade policy generally.

In sum, a historical overview of US export control policymaking reveals three important features. First, numerous executive branch institutions with varying mandates and vested interests regulate the system. These structures tend to preclude certain reforms and generally limit the ability to undertake significant reform of any kind. Any institutional change needed to create policy reform will result in bureaucratic winners and losers and will create bitter opposition in one quarter or another. Second, although the bureaucracies are powerful determinants of US export control policy, the president can articulate and implement some measure of policy reform, when motivated to do so. The White House is not necessarily the hostage of the bureaucracy, although its involvement has been sporadic. Third, societal groups (the US exporting community) and Congress (the most representative branch of government) are important players in agitating and articulating demands for reform. If acting in opposition to executive interests, however, their effectiveness is limited.

The next section of this chapter contains a detailed account of how executive branch institutions dominated US export control policy in the 1970s and 1980s despite Congress's repeated efforts to reform the system. Specifically, it examines the last two major statutory reforms of US export control laws in 1969 and 1979. This discussion provides empirical support for my claims that executive branch institutions defined and pursued policies distinct from Congress and the American exporting community and for the value of an institutional approach to understanding US export control policy historically and presently. The readers is warned, however, that the path through the US export control system can be dense and slow going. Those readers more interested in the present day implications these institutional insights hold for post-Cold War policy should skip ahead to the concluding section of the paper.

The Export Administration Act of 1969 and US Export Control Policy in the 1970s

In 1969 Congress rejected the economic warfare objective of the Export Control Act of 1949 and placed a new emphasis on expanding American exports and opening up trade to the Eastern bloc. The new law provided that the bureaucracy could only deny export licenses for products contributing *significantly* to a potential enemy's military capability, and then only if a comparable product could not be obtained from a foreign supplier. In essence, the 1969 act represented a change in the congressional focus of American export control policy from a strategic embargo seeking to limit East-West trade toward a policy of qualified free trade seeking to promote exports that did not endanger national security. Despite Congress's and the exporting community's interests in loosening export control restraints, the Export Administration Act of 1969 did not quickly achieve many of its intended effects, and many were never realized.

The Executive initially opposed any relaxation in export control policies. Its attitude toward export controls did not change until three years later when, after securing certain concessions from the Soviet Union, and in the interests of detente, the Nixon administration expressed an interest in expanding East-West trade and loosening some export controls.

Congressional aims went unfulfilled, in part because of the Executive's opposition, but also because of the institutional implementation of the new Export Administration Act. Under the 1969 act, the method of implementing export control policy continued to be left largely to the Executive's discretion. The executive departments that would administer the 1969 act were the same offices that for two decades administered its predecessor. Embedded institutional practices, delays in license processing, and bureaucratic decisions regarding which commodities possessed "military significance," and when "foreign availability" of controlled commodities made continued licensing impractical all led to continued burdens on US exporters despite Congress's efforts.

Specifically, the new law attempted to: (1) limit the number of commodities subject to export controls for national security purposes; (2) instill a recognition within the Executive that the foreign availability of a controlled commodity should be an important factor weighed by the bureaucracy in granting licenses; (3) make export licensing processing more open and accountable to the business community; and, (4) harmonize the export practices of the United States with those of its allies through COCOM, that is, eliminate or reduce unilateral US controls.

The Executive-the president and his appointees in the relevant departments-emphasized the national security and foreign policy purposes served by the existing export control system and fought to maintain the Executive's administrative prerogatives. During the legislative debate, the relevant departments uniformly supported a simple extension of the 1949 act then in effect[23] and lobbied for language in the new act that made many of the congressional reforms into recommendations rather than requirements. The Executive's actions were consistent with the foreign policy of the Nixon administration, particularly National Security Council Director Henry Kissinger's policy toward the Soviet Union at the time.[24]

Although the executive branch recognized, at least in part, the changing conditions that prompted the congressional attempt to relax export controls, it believed that such action would have little positive impact on East-West trade and that any trade liberalization should be closely linked to political relations. This greater willingness of the Executive to link exports to other political or general "national security" interests represented an important distinction in the Executive's approach to policy from that of the majority in Congress and the business community.[25]

The Executive's overall approach to the new legislation was translated into specific opposition to the four major congressional reforms noted above. All three executive agencies (Commerce, Defense, and State) opposed any limitations on the president's authority to use trade controls for national security purposes.[26] The executive departments also made clear their opposition to the congressional recommendation that they give greater consideration to the foreign availability of controlled commodities as a factor in making licensing decisions [27] and claimed that existing agency policies and procedures were sufficiently responsive to business interests.[28] Furthermore, the State, Commerce, and Defense Departments unanimously justified the need to regulate more commodities than were controlled by America's COCOM allies, who regulated only goods and technology of direct military significance.[29]

During the legislative process the Executive won important compromises from Congress on several points. Under the final version of the 1969 act agency and presidential decisions were not be subject to judicial review and the president retained a good deal of flexibility in pursuing national security and foreign policy export controls.[30] The congressional approach to liberalization through procedures more responsive to business, assessment of foreign availability, and licensing practices more in line with America's COCOM allies were reduced to essentially non-binding recommendations.[31]

Although Congress had amended US export control laws to serve the dual purposes of national security and free trade, the Executive reserved the authority to maintain a system of trade controls that could be used for national security and foreign policy purposes as the Executive chose to define them. Equally important, embedded institutional practices and procedures ensured the continuation of a burdensome export control policy more restrictive than that anticipated by congressional reformers. Furthermore, to the extent reforms occurred, they came late and at the behest of the president or executive appointees.

Several factors contributed to the Executive's ability to prevail during passage of the 1969 act. Foremost, perhaps, were the divisions within Congress on the desirability of export control reform. Moreover, institutional procedures within Congress made it difficult to sustain momentum for reform. James Sundquist has noted generally that "in the process of overcoming the countless legislative hurdles, policies may be compromised to the point of ineffectiveness."[32] This tendency to compromise is particularly pronounced where, as in 1969, the Executive adopted a position in direct opposition to the congressional demands for change, marshaled the loyalty of the relevant bureaucratic agencies in opposing the legislation, and exercised partisan influence over House members during passage of the legislation.

Two additional factors contributed to the Executive's legislative effectiveness. First, the Executive possessed the technical expertise required to construct or obstruct meaningful reform of the export control system. Moreover, congressional involvement in export controls was episodic and lacked the depth and continuity of the administrative agencies. This informational problem was compounded by the highly technical and scientific information that is part of the export control policy-making process. On a daily basis, the ability to make the technological assessments crucial to export control policy resides within the Executive.

Finally, because export control policy is a topic directly related to national security, a congressional challenge to executive prerogative and executive judgment cannot be made without peril. Congress was constrained in some measure by the threat that the Executive will brand efforts to liberalize the export control laws as reckless and a threat to national security waged for particular commercial interests.

The president's opposition to expanded East-West trade underwent a reappraisal in the early 1970s-a time in which President Nixon reopened relations (including trade relations) with the People's Republic of China and negotiated, in 1972, an unratified trade agreement with the USSR-and the four major reforms sought by Congress in the 1969 act were slowly or incompletely realized. The reason congressional aims went unfulfilled lay initially in the Executive's ambivalence or re-definition of national security to include expanded, yet limited, East-West contacts. Additionally, the institutional implementation of the Export Administration Act profoundly influenced policy outcomes. Under the 1969 act the method of implementing export controls remained essentially unaltered.

The effects of institutions can be seen in the areas of attempted policy reform. First, institutional inertia contributed to the maintenance of national security controls on goods and technologies despite their widespread availability or increasing obsolescence throughout the 1970s. For example, despite the rapid technological advances and, hence, rapid technological obsolescence of computer technology, the relevant bureaucracies did not alter controls on computers from 1976 to 1985, and a similar situation existed with regard to circuit boards and other computer subassemblies.

Executive agencies also ignored Congress's second major reform effort, institutionalizing foreign availability assessment as a licensing criterion, even though Congress called repeatedly for its institutionalization in the 1970s and 1980s.[33] While entries were made to and withdrawn from the CCL periodically throughout the 1970s, the Commerce Department consistently maintained the right to add or retain commodities under full security controls regardless of foreign availability.

During the 1970s the Commerce Department made little or no progress in establishing a capacity to monitor foreign availability.[34] From 1980 to 1985 no licenses were granted for reasons of foreign availability, and until 1985 only two Commerce Department employees were assigned to the assessment of foreign availability. In fact, the Commerce Department did not develop formal regulatory guidelines governing foreign availability assessment until 1985.[35]

As to the third major initiative, simplifying the export licensing system, institutional rigidity and lack of accountability resulted in continuing licensing delays, unpredictability, and lack of responsiveness to American exporters,[36] notwithstanding Congress's expressed intent to the contrary. By the spring of 1972 Congress concluded that the Executive's consultation with business was limited because of insufficient agency procedures for consulting with domestic producers who knew the products, the foreign competition, and the "state of the art."[37]

In the Equal Export Opportunity Act of 1972 Congress sought to rectify this continuing lack of consultation by directing the Secretary of Commerce to appoint technical advisory committees (TACs) consisting of representatives of U. S. industry and government to review export control policy.[38] These committees were to be "consulted with respect to questions involving technical matters, worldwide availability and actual utilization of production and technology, and licensing procedures which may affect the level of (unilateral US and COCOM) export controls."[39]

In practice this reform did little to respond to American exporters' needs. American business believed that the executive departments essentially ignored or rejected TAC recommendations without further consultation or notification of the technical advisory committee involved.[40] Administrators within the Defense, Commerce, and State Departments during the period conceded that the effectiveness of the TACs in involving business in export control policy was, at best, limited. One former Defense Department official noted that his department was not averse to technical input from the business community before or after the creation of the TACS. He added, however, that business's advice on policy matters was never actively solicited by the Defense Department during the 1970s. Furthermore, the effectiveness of the TACs varied greatly. The semiconductor TAC was somewhat effective in funnelling business advice and expertise into the system. The computer TAC, in contrast, was largely ineffective and other TACs deteriorated as a result of decisions by business that their needs were not being served through continued participation.

The failure of the TACs to respond to business's needs stemmed directly from the manner in which the bureaucracy implemented the congressional directive. The majority of TAC deliberations were classified, limiting access to much information that business needed to participate actively and effectively in the process. Second, business and industry representatives on the TACs were originally limited to a two-year term, whereas government members served indefinitely. Business and industry believed that this arrangement "caused disruption and allowed very little time for an individual to become familiar with the other members of the committee before they are required to step down."[41] Finally, the legislation enabling the TACs specified that the TACs would report to the Secretary of Commerce. The receipt of reports, however, was delegated within the Commerce Department to the Office of Export Administration, an overworked and understaffed processing office with a long history of not wanting or accepting industry input.

Finally, in implementing the congressional aim of aligning US export licensing policy more closely with that of other COCOM members, the Executive's institutions continued to pursue a policy at odds with US allies and the wishes of American business. U.S. regulations governed many commodities not directly related to military application and subjected American exporters to lengthy license processing.

Because of the differing viewpoints between the United States and its COCOM allies on export controls, and because by 1970 the United States was no longer the sole or even principal source of high technology, the COCOM consensus weakened and a greater commercial rivalry among members arose. Although a general agreement about the need to maintain a military embargo against the Soviet bloc for reasons of Western security remained intact, the COCOM allies did not share America's interest in a strategy of broader economic or industrial warfare. Responding to this situation, Congress mandated in the 1969 act that U.S. licensing procedures become attuned with the changing economic and political balance between the United States and its COCOM allies. However, the Executive made clear its opposition to this recommendation in its testimony before the House and Senate.

Despite Congress's urging the United States continued to pursue a more restrictive policy toward exports than its allies after passage of the 1969 act. The United States continued to control a large number of product categories not controlled by its COCOM allies. In 1972 the United States maintained unilateral controls on 461 classifications of goods and technology not under multilateral (COCOM) control.[42] The U.S. Commodity Control List of September 1978 still contained, by one estimate, 207 entries, of which 123 were COCOM controlled and 84 were unilaterally controlled by the United States.[43] By another government estimate the United States unilaterally controlled 38 unique industrial item categories in 1979.[44]

Throughout the 1970s the United States continued to pursue a more restrictive export control policy than other COCOM nations. Gary Bertsch summarized the US position during this period: "Although supporting much East-West trade liberalization, the United States reacted negatively to most efforts to loosen the strategic COCOM embargo in the 1970s. The United States continued, for example, to utilize its veto to avoid decontrols involving deletions from and exceptions to the embargo list."[45]

The divergence between the United States and its COCOM allies with respect to commodity control practices was not solely the result of ideological or technological differences. Institutional processes also prevented US licensing practices from aligning with those of COCOM. The process by which the United States arrived at its position for COCOM's list reviews in the 1970s continued to involve complex and time-consuming inter-agency coordination within the US bureaucracy.

In addition to the Advisory Committee on Export Policy (ACEP), the interdepartmental committee which coordinated unilateral US export control policy, a second interdepartmental group, the Economic Defense Advisory Committee (EDAC), chaired by the State Department, coordinated US participation in multilateral export control policy through COCOM.[46] EDAC also decided whether COCOM exception requests to export controlled items should be approved. EDAC operated under a rule of unanimity as well. Its slowness in ruling on licensing and exception requests,[47] and business's lack of access to the administrative policy formulation process as it applies to COCOM contributed to lengthy licensing practices.[48]

In sum, institutional arrangements, abilities, history, and policy orientation interacted to influence policy outcomes resulting in policies different from congressional directives or the desires of the American exporting community. Institutions were slow to change during the 1970s and, lacking sustained pressure from within the Executive to liberalize policy, pursued a restrictive and cumbersome export control policy more in keeping with that of the 1950s and 1960s.

Before considering the "autonomous" role played by the president and high policy-makers within the Executive in shaping US export control policy, one final example of institutional influence on policy outcomes is noted. In response to chronic licensing delays in 1974, 1977, and 1979, Congress made significant amendments to the Export Administration Act in an effort to clarify, simplify, and thereby expedite the inter-agency export licensing process. Congress was responding to the business community's complaints of continuing delays and assertions that the commercial effect of delays is the same as a licensing denial- lost sales and sales opportunities and a damaged reputation for reliability. The heads of the executive institutions charged with processing licenses, however, lobbied against stricter licensing deadlines on the grounds that agency discretion and thoughtful review were required in licensing decisions to protect national security, that they were already sufficiently responsive and open to the export sector, and that they were making every effort to process license applications more efficiently.[49]

Although in 1974 Congress ultimately provided for ninety-day deadlines for most license applications unless delays were meaningfully explained to the applicant, inordinate licensing delays persisted. The number of license applications pending for more than ninety days in

1978 totaled almost 2,000 applications-nearly twice the 1977 figure.[50] In addition, private studies suggested that, with regard to many high-technology industries, delays actually worsened after the 1977 reforms.[51]

Rarely of direct concern to important executive actors, license-processing delays were in large measure attributable to the complex multi-agency license application review process. Occasionally licensing delays were purposeful. Executive institutions used delays to forestall either the approval or denial of a license application. Delays of this sort, however, were not the norm.

Institutional factors were more significant than purposeful actions in causing licensing delays. Especially in the area of high technology exports, export licensing was an increasingly segmented process subject to the scrutiny of several agencies. As noted earlier, the Department of Defense examined license applications from a broad gauge national security standpoint. The Department of State, responsible for reviewing export controls imposed for foreign policy purposes and for chairing COCOM multilateral reviews, viewed licensing from a diplomatic standpoint. The Commerce Department-as a result of the disparate views of the agencies it must consult and the ambivalent act that controls exports for national security, foreign policy, and short supply reasons while it simultaneously recognizes the need to stimulate American export performance-failed to adopt clear policy guidelines and frustrated many segments of the American business community because of its slow licensing procedures. Substantial evidence suggests that by the late 1970s differing agency viewpoints contributed to delay and hence a more restrictive export control policy.[52]

In addition to the number of varying orientations of agencies involved in export control licensing, the original decision-making process, based on precedent and the scrutiny of each item or technology to determine its military significance, remained fundamentally unchanged throughout the 1970s and contributed to the system's slowness and its resistance to reform. The ad hoc nature of the case-by-case method contributed to a lack of clear or uniform guidelines and to license-processing delays.

Export license processing was consistently at odds with congressional and interest group demands in the 1970s and 1980s. Executive institutions shaped policy to fit with institutionally defined goals and methods. Executive institutions with disparate but embedded mandates, insulated in some measure from societal pressures, and only periodically the focus of congressional inquiry, proved to be highly resistant to reform.

The Export Administration Act of 1979 and Executive Autonomy in the Exercise of Foreign Policy Export Controls

The Executive at times has articulated and pursued successfully a discernibly different export control policy than that of Congress or domestic interest groups. The autonomy of the president and highly placed officials within the executive branch is most clearly evident in the Executive's increasing use of export controls for foreign policy purposes beginning in the late 1970s.

The Executive's authority to undertake foreign policy export controls was virtually unbridled during the 1970s. Before 1979 the Executive's "foreign policy" authority was broader and less well-defined than its national security authority. In the 1969 act, Congress differentiated foreign policy controls from "national security controls," i.e., those controls intended to restrict exports that would make "a significant contribution to the military potential of any other nation or nations which would prove detrimental to the national security of the United States."[53] The president's national security control authority was limited by the 1969 act to regulating dual-use items, prohibiting in most instances their export directly or indirectly to communist countries. Unlike controls implemented for reasons of national security, the 1969 act did not attempt to limit the Executive's discretion to use export controls for foreign policy purposes. Export controls invoked for foreign policy purposes could be extended to all goods, strategic and non-strategic. Foreign policy controls, unlike national security controls, had no mechanism such as COCOM to coordinate their restrictions with the practices of US allies. Because allied nations were less likely to agree and cooperate with export restraints not directly linked to their security interests, foreign policy controls also became a source of policy divergence between the United States and its allies.

Furthermore, while the Export Administration Act of 1969, as amended, stated that the Executive should consider the foreign availability of comparable products before applying national security controls, it was mute with regard to the Executive's necessary considerations before imposing foreign policy controls. In a situation where comparable goods were available outside the United States a purchaser could simply shift to a supplier of comparable products in another country, thereby subverting the effectiveness of unilateral US foreign policy export controls. Finally, the 1969 act also required semi-annual reports on foreign policy export controls, but these reports, by most estimations, did not adequately inform Congress or the public.[54]

In rewriting the Export Administration Act in 1979, Congress sought to limit the president's authority in using export controls for foreign policy purposes. Foreign policy export controls came under increasing attacks from the business community, academia, and America's allies in the late 1970s. The business community opposed these policies, believing that they abrogated existing contracts and foreclosed future ones, and damaged the reputation of US exporters as reliable suppliers of goods and services without serving national security interests. Analysts criticized foreign policy export controls as an ineffective means of achieving foreign policy objectives and concluded that these policies were costly and served little more than symbolic, signaling, or displacement functions. Furthermore, because no means existed for coordinating unilateral US export controls promulgated for foreign policy purposes, foreign policy controls were a source of contention between the United States and its allies when they did not share foreign policy objectives or disagreed over the use of export controls as the best means to achieve shared goals.

As a result of these dissatisfactions, in the 1979 act Congress attempted to limit the situations where the president could use his foreign policy export control authority to those instances where the president had fully considered the likely effectiveness of the proposed controls, the compatibility of the proposed controls with overall US foreign policy, the effect of the proposed controls on US export performance, and the foreign availability of the goods or technology subject to the proposed controls.[55] Congress also attempted to instill greater accountability by the president to Congress and the business community through consultation and reporting requirements, including requiring the president to find that: (1) the controls will be likely to change behavior in the target state; (2) the controls will not cause undue hardship to the US economy or employment; and (3) successful negotiations with foreign governments eliminating the foreign availability of the controlled products are likely to occur.[56]

The Executive adopted a very different outlook on the foreign policy provisions of the proposed legislation. While espousing the need to expand exports, the Executive opposed any changes in the foreign policy provisions of the 1979 act that would effectively limit the Executive's flexibility to impose controls for foreign policy purposes, even in circumstances where the controls would not be effective in denying the country the goods or technology in question. In particular, the Executive opposed the imposition of strict criteria that must be considered before instituting controls for foreign policy purposes.[57] In addition, the Executive claimed that it already considered factors such as foreign availability in reaching its decisions,[58] but that it was executive practice to impose controls regardless of its findings should it desire to do so for moral or symbolic reasons.[59] The administration also opposed any provision that would permit Congress to veto the imposition of foreign policy controls and rejected a requirement that the Executive consult with affected industries or other governments *before* imposing foreign policy controls.[60] The Executive characterized these restrictions as either constitutional or practical encroachments on the president's ability to conduct foreign affairs.

During the lawmaking process the Executive won several important compromises from Congress. Congress wrote out of the new act the provision for a legislative veto of foreign policy export controls, instructing only that the president "shall consider" the criteria listed earlier before imposing foreign policy controls, provided that consultation with affected industries occur "as the Secretary [of Commerce] considers appropriate," and requiring that the president consult with and report findings to Congress prior to the imposition of controls "in every possible instance."[61]

In legislating these provisions Congress conceded their non-binding nature. The committee report accompanying the legislation noted: "that the [foreign policy] provision as amended would not preclude the President from reacting promptly to extreme situations, nor prevent him from imposing or maintaining export controls regardless of his conclusion with respect to the factors listed, nor require a public report if the President decided a public report was not in the national interest."[62] The committee further noted that the new foreign policy provisions did not establish criteria to be met but rather set forth factors to be considered, and recognized that the president, having considered them, might find one or more of the factors irrelevant to a decision to impose controls.[63] Similarly, with respect to foreign availability determinations, the committee pointed out that "the provisions will not preclude the use of export controls for foreign policy purposes despite foreign availability,"[64] and provided that the standard for assessing foreign availability in cases involving the imposition of foreign policy controls was not as strict as that required for national security controls.[65]

In sum, the foreign policy "restraints" on the Executive contained in the 1979 act were little more than procedural nuances. The Executive remained free to interpret if and when adherence to the requirements of the 1979 act was required. Sustained effort by the Executive to retain authority and flexibility over foreign policy controls, division within Congress over the degree to which it was willing to limit executive authority, and congressional deference to the Executive's foreign affairs powers and prerogatives conspired to produce a tenuous and ambiguous act.

In practice the foreign policy prerogatives of the president have predominated over congressional wishes that considerations of domestic economic costs and the effectiveness of the proposed controls be given greater weight. The new criteria written into the act and the consulting and reporting requirements did little to dissuade the president from extending existing controls and imposing new foreign policy controls is unprecedented numbers when that choice appeared expedient. New congressional guidelines did not curb executive efforts to limit exports to the Soviet Union following its invasion of Afghanistan.

In that instance President Carter's foreign policy export control initiatives, implemented under the Export Administration Act of 1979, received a mixed reception from Congress. Some controls, such as the Kama River truck plant controls and the Olympic boycott, were made with congressional support. The centerpiece of the Carter administration's sanctions imposed against the Soviet Union following its invasion of Afghanistan-the grain boycott-met with significant congressional opposition, however. Despite substantial domestic opposition to the boycott, the Carter administration held firm and did not lift the embargo, thus demonstrating the Executive's endurance as well as initiative in the use of foreign policy export controls.

The Reagan administration changed the direction of US export control policy in some respects but it did not differ from the Carter administration in either its willingness to use export controls for foreign policy purposes or its belief that, despite the 1979 act, the use and administration of export controls is the Executive's prerogative. President Reagan declined to impose controls on East-West grain sales but was willing to restrict both US and foreign companies from engaging in the sale of certain equipment and technology to the Soviet Union and its allies. Furthermore, while de-emphasizing the use of foreign policy export controls for human rights interests, the Reagan administration linked American export trade to its opposition to international terrorism and used export controls as a means of expressing its dissatisfaction with the policies of other nations. The presidential proclivity to use export controls for foreign policy purposes proved to be a decidedly bipartisan one; changes in administration and the substance of foreign policy did not reduced the Executive's willingness to use foreign policy export controls despite the 1979 act.

President Reagan issued foreign policy export controls over oil and gas equipment and related technical data to the Soviet Union. These controls were imposed in two parts. The first part, imposed December 30, 1981, expanded the existing requirement for validated export licenses for exploration-and-production-related goods to include those related to transmission and refinement. In addition, processing of all export licenses on goods destined for the Soviet Union was temporarily suspended. The second part of these controls, initiated in June 1982, expanded coverage of the oil and gas controls extraterritorially, i.e., beyond the territorial jurisdiction of the United States, to include exports of foreign-oriented goods and technical data by U. S.-owned or controlled companies abroad and foreign-produced products of US technical data not previously subject to controls. The pipeline controls were made at the urging of the National Security Council over significant domestic and international opposition. President Reagan also expanded existing foreign policy controls against Libya and in 1984 made two additions to the foreign policy export control programs governing trade with Iran, Iraq, and Syria.

In continuing its use of foreign policy controls, the Executive largely ignored the guidelines set forth in the 1979 act. The Carter administration's reports to the Congress regarding foreign availability assessment reveal that the Executive was not dissuaded from imposing foreign policy export controls, despite the foreign availability of the controlled product, and did not feel compelled to explain to Congress its decision to impose the controls.[66] Similarly, the Reagan administration was chastised by its staunchest supporters in Congress for its "disappointing" assessment of foreign availability in extending foreign policy controls and its failure to consider adequately the statutory criteria before imposing such controls.[67] The Reagan administration continued foreign policy export controls regardless of the foreign availability of the controlled commodities and technology and without demonstrating to Congress the efficacy of such controls.[68]

The Executive also repeatedly ignored the requirement of the 1979 act that Congress be notified before imposing export controls for foreign policy purposes. For example, although President Reagan imposed additional foreign policy controls on exports to Libya on March 12, 1982, the Commerce Department did not notify and report to Congress until more than two months later.[69] The Executive's disregard of the statutory requirements was even more apparent in the case of the expanded pipeline controls. On June 19, 1982, President Reagan directed that additional foreign policy controls be placed on exports of oil and gas exploration, production, transmission, and refining equipment, and technical data to the Soviet Union. Although these controls were *terminated* on November 13, 1982, following a severe rift between the United States and its allies over the extraterritorial application of these controls, Congress was not notified of their imposition until November 28, 1982-two weeks after their termination.[70]

In summing up the executive-congressional struggles over foreign policy export controls, one longtime insider to the process estimated that the Executive possesses greater latitude and power vis-a-vis Congress and interest groups in export control policy than in any other area of foreign economic policy. This estimation is presented-along with the considerable evidence of Executive autonomy offered in this chapter-to highlight the difference between the conventional wisdom suggesting that congressional dominance or equivalence best characterizes US trade policy, or that Congress has become increasingly re-assertive in foreign policy since the mid-1970s, and the real situation. Furthermore, those who would dismiss executive preeminence as simply an aberration because they believe that national security aspects of export control policy permit the Executive greater latitude in this policy arena, must also explain away the Executive's dominance in the use of foreign policy export controls discussed above.

The Present Debate: Rewriting the Export Administration Act for a Post-Cold War World

Needless to say, the world has changed a great deal recently, but Congress has not undertaken a major revision of US export control laws since 1979.[71] The end of the Cold War represents a watershed in the history of US export control policy. By the late 1980s, four changes in the international system challenged the traditional directions in US export control policy. The foremost change was the end of the geopolitical and ideological hostility between East and West and the military threat posed by the Soviet Union and the Warsaw Pact. Instead, the residual concern from the East became economic decline and political instability that could create regional conflicts and encourage the outflow of military technologies from this region to other areas of instability. One of the unanticipated consequences of the post-Cold War "peace dividend" was the substantial overcapacity of military industries in the former Soviet Union. Until the final conversion of these industries to civilian projects, Soviet successor states face near-term economic pressures to export weapons and dangerous technologies to earn foreign exchange. Second, revolutions in Central and Eastern Europe and the dissolution of the Soviet Union required US and Western economic and technological assistance-an affirmative technology transfer to former adversaries. Third, US economic and technological competitiveness increasingly depend on open international flows of technology. US technological supremacy is no longer a given, and policy makers can no longer slight the competitive costs of export controls. Finally, nuclear, chemical and biological weapons, and missile technology have proliferated throughout the developing world. Countries acquiring these dangerous technologies include several in unstable regions or known terrorist states. Although the nature of this threat is less acute than that presented by a Soviet superpower, the problem of regional instability and proliferation are the fundamental security and arms control issues facing the United States in the post-Cold War era. In this changed environment, the effectiveness of US export control policy will be measured by how well it serves several divergent goals: promoting modernization and democracy in former rival states of the East; enhancing American competitiveness; and, slowing the proliferation of dangerous technologies to nations and regions that threaten regional or international stability.

To meet these new challenges the Executive has re-oriented its technology transfer policies in several ways. To confront the threat of proliferation, the United States has strengthened its technology controls to regions of proliferation concern under President Bush's Enhanced Proliferation Control Initiative (EPCI) and fostered the development of new multilateral institutions such as the Nuclear Suppliers Group (for nuclear-related technology), the Australia Group (for chemical and biological weapons technology), and the Missile Technology Control Region (for missile systems technology) to coordinate multilateral technology controls. Member states in each of these regimes include most advanced industrial states (including some former Cold War rivals), and the member countries have achieved general consensus over the technologies to control and the potential countries or regions of concern. To strengthen US competitiveness, licensing agencies have, under the COCOM "core list" exercise, reduced some requirements on technology transfer for US exporters for formerly-controlled destinations and raised permissible thresholds of exportable technologies. To strengthen nascent efforts to establish market economies and democratic governments in Central and Eastern Europe and the former Soviet Union, the United States has encouraged technology transfer provided the recipient guarantee its peaceful use and that the technology would not be re-transferred to a third party in a region of instability. US assistance in helping countries establish their own technology transfer systems and US encouragement of the new governments to join the emerging multilateral nonproliferation regimes have become mainstays of US technology transfer policy. More recently, the United States, bowing to the wishes of its allies, has agreed to disband COCOM to be replaced by a new multilateral organization that would focus on arms-related exports to certain destinations. COCOM's successor is likely to include several new states, including Russia. Unlike COCOM, the new regime's licensing policies are likely to be based on national discretion rather than unanimity.

After several false starts, the writing the first post-Cold War export control bill is underway in Washington. The process began in earnest in the Fall of 1993. Encouraged by Clinton administration rhetoric about the need for an overhaul of America's export control system, Representatives Toby Roth (R-WI) and James L. Oberstar (D-MN) introduced legislation (H.R. 3412) that would limit the ability of the US government to impose unilateral controls (increasingly important with the end of COCOM near), focus US controls more narrowly, and consolidate licensing in the Commerce Department as a means of strengthening the process. The legislation has the strong backing of the US exporting community and Senator Patty Murray (D-WA) introduced companion legislation (S. 1846) in February 1994.

Congress expected the Administration's position at hearings in January, but inter-agency disputes over unilateral controls and licensing authority delayed the proposal. On February 24 the Administration presented its proposals to the Senate Banking Subcommittee on International Finance and Monetary Policy. As feared by the business community, the bill did not contain the fundamental reforms earlier expected. Under the Administration's plan, the Executive would retain authority to impose unilateral national security export controls over goods presently controlled in COCOM. Commerce officials claimed that the use of unilateral controls will be constrained by a set of statutory considerations[72] but the Defense Department spokesman made clear that unilateral controls were clearly necessary in many cases, including telecommunications, computers and machine tools.[73] The Administration also promised to assess the affects of unilateral controls on the export performance and competitiveness of American businesses as a means of assuring that such controls would not be imposed for symbolic purposes. In contrast the Roth-Oberstar legislation would require the Executive to take one of three actions regarding unilateral controls after six months: (1) eliminate the control; (2) secure multilateral adherence to the controls; or (3) upgrade the controls to a full embargo against the target country.[74]

As to licensing procedures, presidential intervention was needed to break a deadlock between the Commerce Department and the State and Defense Departments over the freedom to impose unilateral controls and the role of the agencies in licensing review. In the end, the interagency review process was not substantially altered although the Commerce Department spokesman assured Congress that all interagency reviews and disputes would be resolved within 90 days under the timetable of the Administration's bill.[75] Noticeably absent from the Administration's proposal was any liberalization control thresholds.

American industry was disappointed by the Administration's initial presentation. The Coalition for Export Control Reform (a collection of more than 100 leading US companies) expressed profound disappointment adding that the administration's proposal would rely excessively on unilateral controls, prolong lengthy licensing 'turf wars' among the bureaucracies, and provide exporters with few assurances that goods widely available on world markets would ultimately be decontrolled.[76] Perhaps in response to business dissatisfaction, the Clinton administration later moved to eliminate most export controls on shipments of telecommunications equipment and computers to Russia, China, and most former communist countries. The Executive's actions were consistent with legislation moving through the House Foreign Affairs Subcommittee on Economic Policy, Trade, and Environment and was received enthusiastically by American exporters.[77]

The institutional history of U. S. export control policy presented here allows us to appreciate this familiar pattern in the law-making process. First, we see again some divergence between congressional reformers' and the business community's demands for reform and the Executive's insistence on greater autonomy and ability to intervene in market activity. Contrary to the congressional/interest group emphasis on making the export control system more efficient, more accountable, and less burdensome to exporters, and its use as a tool of foreign policy exceptional, the Executive stresses the need to use export controls as a means of furthering its national security and foreign policy goals. The institutional perspective also anticipates independent executive initiatives such as President Bush's EPCI or President Clinton's most recent actions.

The institutional structure and patterns of state autonomy also allow it to dominate export control policy-making process. American business has rejected some of the Administration's recent proposal, in part, because it anticipates that the implementation of policy will, if left to bureaucratic discretion, follow the interests of executive institutions, not industry and Congress. Commenting on the latest set of criteria for the Executive to consider before implementing unilateral export controls, one anonymous industry source said, "The Clinton proposal is so wishy-washy that subsequent administrations will laugh at the criteria; if they want to impose or continue the controls they will-easily."[78] That statement, I would offer, reflects industry's keen understanding of the importance of institutional strength and state autonomy in export control policy-making. Time and some future study will tell us whether the partial reforms of the new legislation adhere more toward the traditional interests of the bureaucracy or whether fundamental policy change occurs.

To date, however, institutional factors have been critical determinants of export control law-making and policy-making. Early indications suggest that institutional factors will slow the pace of change despite revolutionary alterations in the ideological and geopolitical bases of the system.

Notes

1. Overview of Findings and Recommendations from Defense and Arms Control Cases," *Commission on the Organization of Government*, Appendix IV, June 1975, p. 21.

2. Export Controls: Background and Issues," *Congressional Research Service (CRS) Report for Congress*, January 12, 1994, p. 1.

3. Kenneth Waltz, *Theory of International Politics*, (Reading, Mass: Addison-Wesley, 1979), pp. 121-22.

4. Pluralism, a variant of liberal theory, views the political process within states (particularly the United States) as dominated by interest group activities. It suggests that state behavior is the result of bargaining and compromise among many, voluntarily, randomly-arranged interest groups. Understanding the dispersion and fragmentation of authority among domestic groups and the process of forming a consensus is essential to understanding policy. Executive branch actors and institutions, which are the focus of statist theory, are seen by pluralists as merely aggregating and averaging the preferences and power of societal actors. For an application of this perspective to U.S. export control policy see Gary K. Bertsch, "American Politics and Trade with the USSR," in Bruce Parrott, ed. *Trade, Technology, and Soviet-American Relations* (Bloomington: Indiana University Press, 1985).

5. Policy preferences and actions can be identified with individual cognition and choice. See for example, Robert Jervis, "Hypotheses on Misperception," *World Politics*, vol. 20, no. 3, April 1968, pp. 454-79; *Perception and Misperception in International Politics* (Princeton: Princeton University Press, 1976); Irving L. Janus and Leon Mann, *Decision-making: A Psychological Analysis of Conflict, Choice, and Commitment* (New York: Free Press, 1977).

6. James G. March and Johan P. Olsen, "The New Institutionalism: Organizational Factors in Political Life," *American Political Science Review*, vol. 38, no. 3, September 1984, pp. 734-49.

7. See, for example, Robert Gilpin, *U.S. Power and the Multinational Corporation* (New York: Basic Books, 1975); Stephen Krasner, "State Power and the Structure of International Trade," *World Politics*, vol. 28, no. 3 (April 1976), pp. 317-47; Peter Katzenstein, "Introduction" and "Conclusion" to "Between Power and Plenty: Foreign Economic Policies of Advanced Industrial States," *International Organization*, vol. 31, no. 4, Autumn 1977, pp. 587-606, 879-920.

8. Peter F. Cowhey, "'States' and 'Politics' in American Foreign Policy," in *International Trade Policies,* John S. Odell and Thomas D. Willet eds. (Ann Arbor: University of Michigan Press, 1993), p. 225.

9. One of the conceptual shortcomings of statist theory has been a lack of clarity and consistency in defining "the state." See Stephen D. Krasner, "Approaches to the State: Alternative Conceptualizations and Historical Dynamics," *Comparative Politics,* vol. 16, no. 2, January 1984, pp. 223-46.

10. See John Ikenberry, "Conclusion: An Institutional Approach to American Foreign Policy," *International Organization,* vol. 42, no. 1, Winter 1988, pp. 219-43; David A. Lake, "The State in American Trade Strategy in the Pre-Hegemonic Era," *International Organization,* vol. 42, no. 1, Winter 1988, pp. 33-58; William J. Long, *U.S. Export Control Policy: Executive Autonomy Versus Congressional Reform* (New York: Columbia University Press, 1989).

11. Peter Gourevitch, "The Second Image Reversed: The International Sources of Domestic Policies," *International Organization,* vol. 32, no. 4, Autumn 1978, p. 903.

12. Stephen D. Krasner, "Approaches to the State," p. 225.

13. Stephen D. Krasner, "Sovereignty: An Institutional Perspective," *Comparative Political Studies,* vol. 21, no. 1, April 1988, pp. 71-72.

14. Robert O. Keohane, "International Institutions: Two Approaches," *International Studies Quarterly,* vol. 32, no. 4, December 1988, p. 386.

15. At their origin, immediately after World War II, peacetime export control laws authorized the president to prohibit or curtail all commercial exports of any article, materials, or supplies (including technical data) except under such rules and regulations as he might prescribe for reasons of national security, foreign policy, or domestic short supply. Operating under this broad delegation of authority, the Executive established a relatively autonomous institution within the Department of Commerce-the Office of Export Control (OEC)-to issue export control regulations, grant or deny applications for export licenses, and investigate violations of the regulations of the Export Control Act itself.

16. Export Administration Act of 1969, Pub. L. No. 91-184 (emphasis supplied).

17. Committee on Science, Engineering, and Public Policy , U.S. National Academy of Sciences, National Academy of Engineering, and Institute of

Medicine, *Finding Common Ground - U.S. Export Controls in a Changed Global Environment,* Washington, D.C.: National Academy Press, 1991), p. 71.

18. For example, by the 1970s, the preparation of national security controls on the CCL began with the Defense Department's generation of a "Militarily Critical Technologies List" that was adapted through interactions with Commerce, State, and Energy Departments and the intelligence community along with advice from industry. Inevitable disputes arising from list-making exercises were aired in an ascending series of inter-agency review groups beginning at the senior civil service level, through the assistant secretary level, and ending at the National Security Council in the White House if the dispute could not be resolved at a lower level.

19. Three principle agencies currently administer most export licenses (as they have under various names for decades): the Bureau of Export Administration at the Department of Commerce is charged with licensing items on the CCL; the State Department's Center for Defense Trade, Office of Defense Trade Controls issues licenses for munitions, coordinates U.S. multilateral controls, and plays a key role in reviewing foreign policy control licensing, and the Defense Department's Defense Technology Security Administration serves in an advisory capacity to both agencies. The lines of jurisdiction among these agencies is often unclear and overlapping. Disputes over whether an item is properly classified as a munitions item subject to State Department licensing or a dual-use items under the jurisdiction of the Commerce Department, for example, have erupted periodically.

20. See for example, U.S. Congress, House Committee on Government Operations, *Strengthening the Export Licensing System,* 102d Cong., 1st sess., July 2, 1991.

21. See generally, William J. Long, *U.S. Export Control Policy: Executive Autonomy Versus Congressional Reform* (New York: Columbia University Press, 1989).

22. *Ibid.*

23. The Nixon administration proposed a simple extension of the date of expiration of the Export Control Act until June 1973. S. 813, H.R. 4293, 91st Cong., 1st sess., 1969. During hearings on proposed amendments Acting Assistant Secretary of State Joseph A. Greenwald told the Senate committee, "[T]his isn't either the time or the circumstances to make what would be a major change." U.S. Congress, Senate Committee on Banking and Currency, Subcommittee on International Finance, *Export Expansion and Regulation,* 91st

Cong., Ist sess., 1969, p. 273 [hereafter Senate Hearings].

24. See Raymond L. Garthoff, *Detente and Confrontation: American-Soviet Relations from Nixon to Reagan* (Washington, D.C.: Brookings Institution, 1985), pp. 90-91.

25. See Senate Hearings, p. 270 (statement of Joseph A. Greenwald, acting assistant secretary for economic affairs, Department of State); U.S. Congress, House Committee on Banking and Currency, *Hearings before the Subcommittee on International Trade to Extend and Amend the Export Control Act of 1949,* 91st Cong., 1st sess., 1969, p. 1 18 [hereafter House Hearings], (statement of G. Warren Nutter, assistant secretary, international security affairs, Department of Defense); and *Ibid.,* p. 123 (statement of Kenneth N. Davis, assistant secretary for domestic and international business, Department of Commerce).

26. See Senate Hearings, pp. 274-75.

27. See House Hearings, pp. 119, 122.

28. *Ibid.,* p. 128.

29. *Ibid.,* pp. 116, 119, 121.

30. Under the 1969 act the president remained free to elect the purposes for which export controls were to apply and could avoid export restraints entirely by declaring that a control was implemented for foreign policy purposes, as opposed to national security reasons.

31. For example, the 1969 act required the president, before implementing national security controls, to determine that the commodities or data regulated were not readily available to such controlled nation or nations from other sources, *unless* the president determined that an export control restriction was "necessary in the interest of national security" and reported his reasons to Congress. Export Administration Act of 1969, sec. 4(a)(2)(6).

32. James L. Sundquist, "Congress and the President: Enemies of Partners?," in Henry Owens and Charles L. Schultze, eds., *Setting National Priorities: The Next Ten Years* (Washington, D.C.: Brookings Institution, 1976), pp. 583-618.

33. Congress explicitly strengthened its call for improved foreign availability assessment in the 1972 and 1977 amendments to the 1969 act. See *Export Administration Act of 1969 as Amended by Equal Export Opportunity Act of* 1972, Pub. L. 92-412, 86 Stat. 644, sec. 4(b) (2) (B), 1972; *Export*

Administration Amendments of 1977, 95th Cong., 1st sess., 1977, p. 9.

34. An exhaustive analysis of export control administration by the U.S. General Accounting Office concluded: "[S]imply put, no single person was in charge of managing the foreign availability analysis. The task groups [made up of various executive agencies] dealt with the intelligence agencies on differing bases and there was some apparent breakdown in the use of information that was available." Comptroller General, *Export Controls: Need to Clarify and Simplify Administration, Report to the Congress of the Comptroller General of the United States,* March 1, 1979, p. 29.

35. See 50 *Federal Register* 10503, March 15, 1985.

36. See Comptroller General, *Administration of U.S. Export Licensing Should be Consolidated to be more Responsive to Industry, Report to the Congress by the Comptroller General of the United States,* October 3 1, 1978.

37. U.S. Congress, House of Representatives, *International Economic Policy Act of 1972,* H. Rept. 1260, 92nd Cong., 2d sess., 1972, p. 4.

38. *Equal Export Opportunity Act,* Pub. L. 92-412, 86 Stat. 644, sec. 103, 1972.

39. *Ibid.,* sec. 105. As a result of the legislation, the Secretary of Commerce established seven TACS.

40. See U.S. Congress, House Committee on International Relations, *Extension of the Export Administration Act of 1969,* 95th Cong., Ist sess., 1977, P. 601.

41. See Comptroller General, *Administration of U.S. Export Licensing Should be Consolidated to be more Responsive to Industry, Report to the Congress by the Comptroller General of the United States,* October 31, 1978.

42. U.S. Congress, Senate, S. Rept. 890, 92nd Cong., 2d sess., 1972, p. 3.

43. John R. McIntyre and Richard T. Cupitt, "East-West Strategic Trade Controls: Crumbling Consensus?," *Survey: A Journal of East and West Studies,* vol. 25, no. 2, Spring 1980, pp. 81-108.

44. Comptroller General, *Export Controls: Need to Clarify Policy and Simplify Administration, Report to the Congress by the Comptroller General,* P. iii.

45. Gary K. Bertsch, "Western Strategic Trade Controls: Goals, Policies,

Politics, and the Future," paper presented to the Conference on East-West Economic Relations in a Changing World Economy, Toronto, Canada, June 13-15, 1984.

46. EDAC was chaired by the assistant secretary of state for economic and business affairs. This inter-agency committee consists of representatives from the State, Defense, and the Commerce Departments and from the Nuclear Regulatory Commission and the Central Intelligence Agency.

47. See U.S. Congress, House Committee on International Relations, *Extension of the Export Administration Act of 1969*, p.310.

48. See *Report of the President's Task Force to Improve Export Administration Licensing Procedures* (draft), September 22, 1976, P. II 2.

49. See U.S. Congress, House Committee on International Relations, *Extension and Revision of the Export Administration Act of 1969*, 95th Cong., 1st sess., 1977, pp. 518-20 [hereafter House Hearings 19771.

50. Office of Technology Assessment, *Technology and East-West Trade* (Washington, D.C.: Government Printing Office, 1979), p. 139.

51. See House Hearings 1977, pp. 505-18.

52. See Comptroller General, *The Government's Role in East-West Trade Problems and Issues, Summary Statement of Report to Congress by the Comptroller General of the United States*, February 4, 1976, pp. 42, 43.

53. *Export Administration Act of 1969*, Pub. L. 91-184, 83 Stat. 841, sec. 3(l), 1969.

54. U.S. Congress, House Committee on Foreign Affairs, *Extension and Revision of the Export Administration Act of 1969*, 96th Cong., 1st sess., 1979, p. 259 [hereafter House Hearings 1979], (statement of Mr. J. Kenneth Fasick, International Division, General Accounting Office).

55. U.S. Congress, House of Representatives, H.R. 2539, 96th Cong., Ist sess., 1979, sec. 6 (b).

56. Ibid.

57. House Hearings 1979, p. 632.

58.See U.S. Congress, Senate, S. Rept. 169, 96th Cong., Ist sess., 1979, P. 8; House Hearings 1979, p. 132 (testimony of William A. Root, director, Office of East-West Trade, Department of State).

59. House Hearing 1979, P. 685.

60. Ibid., p. 687.

61. *The Export Administration Act of 1979,* Pub. L. 96-72, 93 Stat. 503, sec. 6(e), 1979.

62. U.S. Congress, Senate, S. Rept. 169, 96th Cong., Ist sess., 1979, p. 8.

63. *Ibid.*

64. *Ibid.,* p. 9.

65. *Ibid.*

66. See U.S. Department of Commerce, Office of Export Administration, *Foreign Policy Report to Congress,* December 31, 1980.

67. "Banking Committee Members Hit Foreign Policy Controls Report," *International Trade Reporter's U.S. Export Weekly,* March 30, 1982, pp. 763, 765.

68. See, for example, the conclusory report sent by the Reagan administration to Congress in 1985-a report virtually identical to the one submitted by the Carter administration in 1980. U.S. Department of Commerce, Office of Export Administration, *Foreign Policy Report to Congress,* January 18, 1985.

69. Malcolm Baldridge, secretary of commerce, to the Honorable George Bush, president of the Senate, June 23, 1982, reprinted in *Export Administration Annual Report for the Fiscal Year 1982,* p. 162.

70. *Ibid.,* p. 169.

71. For a discussion of reform effort of the mid-1980s, see William J. Long, *U.S. Export Control Policy,* Chapter Six.

72. The criteria include: an evaluation of controls compatibility with other U.S. foreign policy objectives; the likely reaction of other countries; foreign policy gains to be realized; the economic costs incurred; the likelihood of changing the

behavior of the target country; the ability to deny the target country access to the controlled commodity; and the likelihood of establishing multilateral cooperation. "Administration Proposes Major Revamp of Export Controls; Industry Critical," *International Trade Report,* March 2, 1994, p. 328.

73. *Ibid.,* p. 329.

74. "Industry Rejects Administration's EAA Proposals," *Export Control News,* February 28, 1994, p. 2.

75. Administration Proposes Major Revamp of Export Controls," p. 328.

76. *Ibid.*

77.   Thomas L. Friedman, "U.S. Ending Curbs on High-Tech Gear to Cold War Foes," *The New York Times,* March 31, 1994, pp. Al, C4.

78. "Administration Proposes Major Revamp of Export Controls," p. 328.

Chapter 5

Japanese Export Controls, COCOM and the United States: A Historical Perspective

Yoko Yasuhara

The purpose of this chapter is to offer a historical perspective on Japanese export controls after World War II. This chapter will, first of all, discuss briefly the origins a postwar Japanese export controls, and second, examine their unique feature, i.e., the "economic interpretation of military issues" which the Japanese government, bound by the Japanese Constitution, has taken since the early days of the postwar export controls. Finally it will examine how such a situation changed under the impact of the 1987 Toshiba-Kongsberg case and why.

In tracing the origins of the postwar East-West export controls (including the origins of postwar Japanese controls), scholars have usually focused only on COCOM in their analysis. But the export controls initiated by the United States, had in fact a dual structure, i.e., COCOM on one hand, and on the other the export control network linked to the Mutual Defense Assistance Agreements (MDAAs), which the United States formed with recipients of US military assistance under the Mutual Defense Act of 1949. Developed through these MDAAs, a global export control network indeed encompassed more countries than COCOM members.COCOM, consisting of the most advanced industrialized countries at that time, was in this sense only the tip of the iceberg. On the basis of "self help" and "mutual aid", the United States requested aid recipients to observe certain "obligations"--one of which was export controls--in return military assistance.

The first MDAAs, with Western European countries in 1950 made no mention of export controls. Only declassified primary sources reveal that Article 7 of the draft MDAAs referred to "effective controls over the export of war-potential material, equipment and, in so far as practical, technical data" to accomplish mutual security. However, the Western Europeans opposed the article on the grounds of parliamentary difficulties, so that the United States finally agreed to its deletion obtaining written assurances of cooperation on export controls in either "some form of secret minutes or letter."[1]

The first MDAAs with the Western Europeans, thus hid the role of export controls in secrecy. Yet the MDAA with Korea, signed on January 26, 1950, one day before the European accords, has exactly the same sentence in Article 7, that was deleted from the European version. Many of the other MDAAs also requested export controls, such as Article 8 of most of the Latin American agreements, Article 6 with Spain, Article 7 with Ethiopia, and Annex (D) with Japan.[2]

Postwar export controls originated in September 1945 when Japanese trade was placed under control of the Supreme Commander for the Allied Powers (SCAP). Initially the United States exercised its controls not against Communist countries but against Japan itself. These Second World War type of export controls restricted exports of heavy industrial goods and raw materials to Japan to prevent a resurgence of Japanese war industries (i.e., heavy and chemical industries) and of Japanese militarism. To be a 'peaceful country,' its industrial capacity had to be limited to light industry such as textile production.

These Second World War type of export controls, however, did not last long due to changing US global strategies. In 1947 and 1948 the initiative for a change of the early occupation policy came from the Department of the Army which for financial reasons wanted to avoid a protracted occupation, and from the Policy Planning Staff (PPS) and its chief, George Kennan, whose main concern was the intensifying US-USSR conflict. General Douglas MacArthur's initiative for a Japanese peace settlement in 1947 was, thus, eventually replaced with a "virtual peace" embodied in the report by the National Security Council (NSC). "Recommendations with Respect to United States Policy toward Japan" (NSC13), whose revised version, NSC13/2, was approved by President Harry Truman in October 1948.[3] Given a very different Cold War perception of the future of Asia in these NSC 13 series, Japan would now become a "workshop" in Asia to counter Communist influence, resuscitating its heavy industries, while modifying reparations. Under this "virtual peace," basic premises of early demilitarization policy no longer worked as effective guidelines.

Export controls in Japan began to shift into the Cold War type especially when impending Communist victory in China became clearer in the fall of 1948. The State Department was busy preparing its new export control policies, and the resulting paper "United States Policy Regarding Trade with China" (NSC41) of February 1949, urged the Truman Administration to enlist cooperation on export controls from other countries concerned and to establish a close liaison between the US government in Washington and SCAP.[4] Following the directive sent by the Joint Chiefs Staff (JCS) in March, the Office of the Under Secretary of the Army and SCAP began to coordinate closely their export control policies.

Further tightening of Japanese export controls occurred in 1950 when war broke out in Korea. The subsequent Chinese entry into the war shattered Japan's sanguine expectations for the China trade, which reached a nadir in December 1950 when SCAP directed the Japanese government to suspend all export license applications to Mainland China, Manchuria, North Korea, Hong Kong and Macao. Despite the gradual relaxation of export controls under a "virtual peace" settlement, SCAP throughout the war retained its control over exports of strategic items until the very end of the occupation. It was only in March 1952, one month before the end of the occupation, that SCAP transferred its control authority fully to the Japanese government.

The conflict in Korea certainly made it easier for the US government to induce the Japanese to maintain export controls. Japan gave the United States its commitment to hold the level of export controls until the end of the war. But with a strong pent-up desire for Sino-Japanese trade among Japanese and with an approaching peace settlement, the United States needed to circumscribe Japanese trade within non-Communist countries by some other means, i.e., by placing Japanese export controls within a multilateral framework.

The United States raised the issue of Japanese export controls in the COCOM meeting of September 1951, where the members agreed to give the Japanese government access to information of the Paris group, including the Consultative Group (CG), the upper decision-making body, and the Coordinating Committee (COCOM), the standing lower-rank committee.[5]

Yet, the Europeans were not fully in concert with the United States, especially when the US tried to merge COCOM with NATO, and as recently declassified Japanese primary sources reveal, to establish a Far Eastern Group which would consist of a Far Eastern Consultative Group and a Far Eastern Coordinating Committee, as a subordinate body of a future collective security system in East Asia.[6] A new Far Eastern organization on export controls within a collective security system in East Asia, together with an integrated COCOM with NATO, could have further tightened world-wide export controls, which the Europeans of course wanted to eschew.

From July 28 to August 2, 1952, the United States, the United Kingdom, France, Canada, and Japan met in Washington. There the Europeans, supporting a Japanese entry into COCOM, opposed the US initiative for establishing a separate Far Eastern organization. A compromise was eventually reached, however: the establishment of the China Committee (CHINCOM), a new working group   focused on Communist states in Asia, under the CG was accepted. The United States also approved Japanese entry into COCOM, but only after gaining a Japanese bilateral commitment to the United States to maintain controls more stringent than COCOM's.[7]

Not until an armistice in Korea could the Japanese government relax its export controls to COCOM levels. During the Korean War Japan greatly benefitted from US special procurement, which could easily compensate for the loss of the China trade and led to a remarkable economic recovery in Japan. Thus, decline of procurement after a cease-fire might have resulted in a severe recession like the one in 1949, a nightmarish experience for the Japanese business community. Increasing desire for Sino-Japanese trade and for decontrol of restricted items finally led the Japanese government to place the export control issue on the agenda of the US-Japan negotiations on a MDAA from 1953 to 1954.

As the Japanese government had been committed to strict export controls during the Korean War the armistice was a timely occasion for a relaxation of Japanese export controls. During the US-Japan MDAA negotiations, the United States, still continuing a virtual embargo on its China trade, solicited Japan for stricter export controls than Japan was ready to do, while the Japanese tried to gain decontrols as much as possible.

As were the cases of other MDAA negotiations, the US government initially tried to include Article 7 on export controls in the draft of the US-Japan MDAA.[8] Yet the Japanese government strongly resisted this article due to difficulties in convincing the Diet, amidst the increasing Japanese opposition against trade restrictions. One of the Japanese negotiators even asked to handle the matter as the Europeans did, i.e., in a secret side letter.[9] In the end, to obtain the deletion of Article 2(3) of the US draft which aimed at restricting Japanese acceptance from any third party any assistance of the MDAA type, the Japanese government agreed to include export controls in Annex (D),[10] while the United States acquiesced to the relaxation of Japanese controls to the COCOM levels in a gradual three-month process in 1954.

The conclusion of the US-Japan MDAA was not just a matter between the two countries, but had a global implication: By entering into a MDAA network initiated by the United States, Japan promised to support US global strategies against Communist countries and the global export control network also, in return for US military assistance, as other countries did in their MDAAs.

Despite such a significant role of Japanese export controls in the overall US strategy against Communist countries, however, the Japanese government had downplayed this strategic approach in explaining COCOM and Japanese export controls. In contrast. with US polices, where COCOM and East-West trade controls were a part of its grand anti-communist strategies, export controls in Japan were a matter of Japanese cooperation with Western countries or with the United Nations, or, a matter of economic importance, not a matter of containment strategies against Communist countries.

A key to understanding this peculiar standpoint of the Japanese government lies in the Japanese Constitution of 1946. This Constitution, hastily prepared under pressure by SCAP, has divided the Japanese into *kaikenha* (proponents of its revision), and *gokenha* (it supporters). *Kaikenha* often called it *Oshitsuke Kempo* (the constitution forced by SCAP and the United States), insisting on its rewriting. But, today few people realize the circumstances at that time which necessitated its quick drafting by SCAP.

The making of the Japanese Constitution was closely related to the Far Eastern Commission (FEC) and to the Emperor system. In December 1945 the United States, the United Kingdom, and the USSR agreed in Moscow to establish the FEC as the top decision-making body of the allied occupation. The United States was then given no discretionary power in "the fundamental changes in the Japanese constitutional structure," General Douglas MacArthur, who sought a unilateral hand in occupation and in preserving the emperor system, accelerated the drafting process of the Constitution to avoid interference by the FEC.

The first meeting of the FEC was scheduled on February 26, 1946. But before a FEC decision was made on the matter of the Japanese Constitution, SCAP interpreted that it could operate as if it had sole authority. Thus, with the Japanese drafts prepared since the end of the war deemed unacceptable, SCAP started its own drafting on February 4, 1946, and on February 13 the draft was handed over to the Japanese government. The Japanese government, although at first stunned by many unacceptable parts, under pressure by SCAP quickly revised it, and made its summary public on March 6. Despite the opposition by the FEC, the first general elections carried out on April 10. After a subsequent four-month debate the Diet passed the Constitution on October 7; the Constitution was promulgated on November 3.

The important matter here in relation to export controls, however, is not the hastiness of the drafting process but the overall Second World War framework of the present Constitution. The lessons of World War II are strongly evident, for example, in its preamble and in Article 9. The preamble expresses the ideal of the Constitution, "the Japanese desire for peace for all time." The Japanese, it states, trust in "the justice and faith of the peace-loving peoples of the world" to preserve the security and the existence of Japan. And "the Japanese recognize the right of all peoples of the world to live in peace." Pacifism is also clear in the famous Article 9 where the Japanese "forever renounce war as a sovereign right of the nation and the threat or use of force as means of settling international disputes." "The right of belligerency of the state," it also writes, "will not be recognized." This quest for peace and renunciation of war, which apparently grew out of World War II experiences and the spirit of the Potsdam declaration, was desirable to make the Constitution palatable to war-ravaged countries and thus counter-balancing the preservation of the Emperor system, still a target of persecution by many countries.

It was after the intensification of the US-USSR conflict, especially after the Truman Doctrine of March 1947, that a gap appeared between the Japanese Constitution based on the Second World War framework and the Japanese role in the Cold War. Since then, the Japanese government has been struggling to adjust its military policies to the principles of the Constitution.

Japanese export control policy well illustrates this gap. As a peace-loving country the Japanese government has denied that Japan has potential adversaries, which of course contradicted the Japanese role in the US Cold War strategies. Therefore, in explaining COCOM and export controls, the Japanese government minimized the military aspect as much as possible. By the time when the Foreign Exchange and Trade Control Law was formed in December 1949, Japanese export controls had already been targeted against Communist countries. Yet the law only listed "balance of international payments" and "healthy growth of foreign trade and domestic economy" as reasons for license requirement, without reference to any military factors.

The first case which gives some insight into Japanese export control policies is the debate in the Diet on the Japanese entry into COCOM in 1952. At that time the Korean war was still going on and the UN resolution on embargo on China had been made in May 1951, so the Japanese government could defend Japanese export controls either as a measure to bring about peace in Korea, or as a matter of Japanese cooperation with the United Nations. In May 1952, an official of the Ministry of International Trade and Industry (MITI) told the Diet that on the basis of Japanese cooperation' with the United Nations, the Japanese government would decide which export control policies were beneficial to Japan.[11] For Ryutaro Takahashi, the Minister of International Trade and Industry, Japanese support for the Battle Act came as a result of Japanese cooperation with the United Nations, and in his view US assistance rather than the China trade was more advantageous to Japan.[12] On the other hand, Minister of Foreign Affairs Katsuo Okazaki emphasized Japanese export controls as a war-time emergency measure during the Korean War.[13]

Despite the subtle differences of rationale, there was a significant lack of analysis of the Japanese role in global US strategies against Communist countries. The Japanese membership in COCOM had to be a matter of peace and of the United Nations, or the one of economic advantage or disadvantage.

Another example of the gap between rhetoric and reality is the case of the Japan Industrial Fair of 1969. Organizers of the fair initially planned to exhibit around 7,000 items in Peking and Shanghai from March to June. MITI, however, rejected export license applications for 19 items, including electronic equipment, measuring instruments and synthetic fiber, by invoking the Export Trade Control Order and the Foreign Exchange and Trade Control Law, which allowed MITI to disapprove items detrimental to "a healthy growth of foreign trade and domestic economy." Due to poor turnout of the items in the Peking fair. China assailed the "reactionary government policy of Prime Minister Eisaku Sato" and cancelled the Shanghai fair. While the Japanese organizers filed suit for the loss of prestige and transactions, the real issue questioned was the legality of applying informal COCOM restrictions in Japan.

As there was no UN resolution on the China trade in 1969, "the economic interpretation of military issues" is clearer in this Japan Industrial Fair case than in 1952. In the Tokyo District Court, the Japanese government had to defend COCOM controls with economic reasons specified in the Foreign Exchange and Trade Control Law (i.e., "healthy growth of foreign trade and domestic economy"). Under then-current international relations, the government reasoned,' Japan could develop its economy only in close cooperation with liberal countries. If Japan violated COCOM the United States and other liberal countries would retaliate against Japan, which would be detrimental to the Japanese economy. In this light, Japanese observance of COCOM agreements was legitimate.[14]

The paper by MITI submitted to the Tokyo District Court in February 1969 developed this economic interpretation in more detail, pointing out "detrimental" elements in the case of the export of the 19 COCOM-restricted items.[15] Japanese violation of COCOM agreements, it stated, would undermine Japanese international credibility, weaken Japanese influence in the world, and bring isolation of Japan by destroying close economic ties with liberal countries. Due to various restraints imposed by other countries, Japan would suffer in many fields such as (1) the import of technologies from abroad, (2) Japanese export and import in general, and (3) the introduction of foreign capital.

In July 1969 chief judge of the Tokyo District Court Ryokichi Sugimoto handed down the decision on the case. Although he rejected the suit, he questioned the legality of the MITI disapproval of the 19 items. The application of the Export Trade Control Order should be, he said, limited to "pure and direct" economic purposes, so that domestic legislation would be needed to apply an informal COCOM agreements.[16] It was not until 1980 that the Foreign Exchange and Foreign Trade Control Law included a security provision in its Article 25 (controls on the export of technology), and only after the Toshiba case were "international peace and security" added to Article 48 (controls on the export of goods).

The Toshiba-Kongsberg case, became indeed a turning point in the peculiar post-war history of Japanese export controls. In April 1987, the Japanese police raided Toshiba Machine Corporation on the grounds of COCOM violation. Its export of four sophisticated propeller milling machines to the USSR was soon found to be one of the most "egregious diversions" in the history of COCOM. Although the case became public in 1987, the investigation had originated in a letter of December 1985 by Kazuo Kumagai of Wako Koeki, a small Japanese trading firm, who informed COCOM of the sale. The Japanese government, received the letter from COCOM, thereafter held hearings ten times and inter-ministry meetings five times. By April 1986 MITI concluded that the alleged sale could not be substantiated. Yet, US government officials, unconvinced by MITI's conclusion, raised the issue to the Japanese government in June 1986, in December of the same year, and in March 1987. MITI still denied the allegations. However, "some evidence" which the Japanese government received from the United States in March 1987 led to a renewed investigation by MITI.[17] And the letter from Defense Secretary Casper Weinberger to Defense Agency Minister Yuko Kurihara in April expedited the pace of the investigation, resulting in a public revelation of the sale in April 1987.

In this Toshiba-Kongsberg case, Toshiba Machine, as well as Japanese trading firms Ito Chu and Wako Koeki, made a contract with the USSR in April 1981 to sell four propeller milling machines capable of nine-axis simultaneous control, which would enable Russians to produce propellers for ship use with a diameter of up to 11 meters and increase production capability. The size of the machine was about 10 meters high, 22 meters wide, and it weighed 250 tons.

As COCOM prohibited the export of a metal-processing machine capable of more than two-axis simultaneous control to the USSR, Toshiba Machine imported NC-2000 controllers for two-axis use from Kongsberg Vaapenfabrikk of Norway, a state-owned munitions maker, and incorporated it into the machines. Subsequently, MITI granted an export license for the transfer of two-axis simultaneous-controlling milling machines.[18] At the same time a computer program for nine-axis simultaneous control was exported from Japan via Kongsberg as a part of the documentation for other machines. As the NC equipment for two-axis use could easily be changed into the one for nine-axis use, the machines in the end could work as nine-axis controlling machines in the USSR.

The Toshiba-Kongsberg case led to an intense investigation both in Norway and in Japan. A report by the Norwegian government revealed that the Kongsberg violations involved not only companies in Japan, but in France, West Germany, and Italy as well.[19] Exports of five-axis machines by Toshiba Machine and Kongsberg from 1974 to 1980 were also disclosed, which exacerbated the outrage against Japan.

As the US Congress had been reviewing the Export Administration Act (EAA) of 1979 since the beginning of 1987, the Toshiba-Kongsberg case was immediately taken into the review process. The resulting EAA of 1988, incorporated in the Omnibus Trade and Competitiveness Act of 1988, included a section on "Multilateral Export Control Enhancement." Its section 2443 levelled against Toshiba, Toshiba Machine and Kongsberg mandatory sanctions, including a three-year prohibition on the imports of all products made by Toshiba Machine and Kongsberg.

Significant in this Toshiba-Kongsberg case was a wide gap in perception between the Americans and the Japanese. The Reagan administration and congress, assailed the diversion from a military perspective. The sale, they argued, caused enormous damage to the US anti-submarine warfare capability. Toshiba and Kongsberg, Congressmen criticized, "sold out the West and the free world to make a few bucks," causing "irreparable harm" to US security. This "most damaging diversion in history," was nothing but "treachery" and a serious "breach" which would cost the United States billions to counter.[20] Resentment in Congress was even more intense, because of US frustrations over a sudden change of the United States into a debtor nation, to a rise of the Japanese economic power in the 1980s. Japanese low levels of military spending together with lenient export controls, Congressmen criticized, increased Japanese economic competitiveness, while the US economic performance was suffering from enormous military spending. The Toshiba-Kongsberg case, thus, developed into an issue of "burden sharing" of the defense cost.

In contrast to the US reaction, the Japanese took the Toshiba affair in a very different context, i.e., as an economic issue. They were skeptical about the US charge. And their initial skepticism grew into resentment when smashing of a Toshiba radio was televised throughout Japan. Many Japanese regarded Toshiba Corporation and Toshiba Machine as scapegoats of distressed US domestic industries, including the US machine tool industry. The US allegation of COCOM violations, they argued, was not supported by strong evidence. So why did Japan have to apologize? Deliberately singled out by the United States, Toshiba Machine was only "a poor victim" with "a deep scar" being "beaten" by the United States. The real aim of the United States in this "tragedy" was to control and undermine the Japanese economy and technology under the rationale of military defense.[21]

This wide divergence of views on both sides of the Pacific Ocean is striking, especially if we consider it derived from the same Toshiba-Kongsberg case. Why did such a perception gap occur? The main reason lies in the Japanese postwar history of export controls. Many Japanese failed to see a military aspect of the Toshiba Kongsberg case, simply because in Japan there had been little discussion on export controls from a strategic point of view. Due to the legacy of World War II and the Japanese Constitution, export controls had been treated mostly as economic matters with Western countries. Even in the Toshiba case the Japanese government was reluctant to give enough details on its military implications. Moreover, the firm presence of US power in the Pacific Ocean enabled Japan to take the "economic interpretation" of export controls and to handle them technically without having to provide its own strategic analysis.

The most significant effect of the Toshiba-Kongsberg case, therefore, ties in the demise of the "economic interpretation" rationale. As Japanese economy became highly developed, producing the most-advanced dual use technologies, normal economic activities were no longer immune from application to military purposes. This new awareness, derived from the Toshiba case especially changed MITI which had long taken the economic interpretation of export controls. MITI took the initiative in establishing the Center for Information on Strategic Technology (CISTEC) in April 1989 and in introducing US-style compliance programs into Japanese companies.[22] The number of export license inspectors in MITI also increased. The Japanese government is now trying to take military factors into consideration in its economic policy making, although it still does not have a clear. projection -- for the future role of Japan in the world.

With the collapse of the USSR and Communist countries in Eastern Europe, a completely new, but more unstable era is upon us. Today, global strategies of the United States are no longer targeted against the USSR but focused on regional conflicts. The role of the MDAA network is also changing, and world-wide export controls have moved from COCOM to nonproliferation controls. This shift of US strategies, together with the changing relations within the Western world, have affected Japanese policies considerably. As Japan is no longer "the super-domino" in US strategies against Communist countries in Asia, more and more Japanese are searching for a new Japanese role in international relations.

One of the most important issues today is whether the Japanese Constitution, especially Article 9, should be revised or not. The Japanese also questioned the role of the so-called "55 *nen taisei*" (the 55 year system), where the Liberal Democratic Party (LDP), the ruling party, and the Socialist Party, the opposition party, had been dominant since 1955. This "55 *nen taisei*" worked well in the days of the US-USSR conflict. Yet Japanese political parties also need to adapt to the new situation.

In the July 1993 election, the "55 *nen taisei*" was brought to a close due to the loss of the LDP as the ruling party for the first time since 1955. Thereafter the Japanese government has changed twice, and in the spring of 1995 Japanese political parties are still in the process of being reshuffled. Indeed, the demise of the USSR, together with the changing relations within the western world, has brought among Japanese a new awareness of military aspects of export controls and of the role of article 9, as well as a search for a new political alignments and for its future role in international relations.

Notes

1. *Foreign Relations of the United States (FRUS)*, 1950, 3:9-11, 4:72; Lawrence S. Kaplan, *A Community of Interest: NATO and the Military Assistance Program,* 1949-1950 (Washington, D.C.: GPO, 1980) 62-64. The Mutual Defense Assistance Act of 1949 was formed in close relation to the North Atlantic Treaty of the same year. The act authorized the President to furnish military assistance to North Atlantic Treaty countries under Title I; to Greece and Turkey under Title II; to Iran, Korea, the Philippines, and the general area of China under Title III. Section 408(e) allowed the President to transfer equipment, materials or services not only to nations under Titles I, II and III, but also to those countries which had collective defense and regional arrangements with the United States. Section 408(e), thus could cover Latin American countries as well. For recent works on COCOM see, Michael Mastanduno, *Economic Containment and the Politics of East-West Trade* (Ithaca: Cornell University Press, 1992); Tor Egil Førland " 'Selling Firearms to the Indians': Eisenhower's Export Control Policy, 1953-54," *Diplomatic History* 15:2 (1991), Robert M. Spaulding, Jr., "Eisenhower and Export Control Policy, 1953-1955," *Diplomatic History* 17:2 (1993).

2. The following is a list of articles on export controls in MDAAs:
Korea - Article 7, January 1952; Ecuador - Article 8, February 1952; Peru-Article 8, February 1952; Cuba - Article 8, March 1952; Brazil - Article 9, March 1952; Colombia - Article 8, April 1952; Uruguay - Article 8, June 1952; Chile - Article 8, July 1952; Dominican Republic - Article 8, March 1953; Ethiopia - Article 7, May 1953, Spain - Article 6, September 1953; Japan - Annex (D), March 1954; Nicaragua - Article 8, April 1954; Honduras - Article 8, May 1954; Pakistan - Article 6, May 1954; Guatemala - Article 7, January 1955; and Haiti - Article 8, January 1955.

3. NSC13/2, October 7, 1948, *FRUS,* 1948, 6:858-862.

4. NSC41, February 28, 1949, *FRUS,* 1949, 9:820-834.

5. As the ninth *Battle Act Report* states: It is widely believed that COCOM was formed in November 1949 by the United States, the United Kingdom, France, Italy, the Netherlands, Belgium and Luxembourg. See International Cooperation Administration, *The Ninth Report to Congress under the Mutual Defense Assistance Control Act of 1951* (Washington: GPO, 1957): 17.
Yet, primary sources reveal that the Netherlands and Belgium, especially the former, vigorously opposed its formation in the November 1949 meeting. See also "From E.L. Hall-Patch to Clement R. Attlee," November 29, 1949, UR11993/45/98, F0371/77816; United Kingdom Delegation to O.E.E.C., No.

5. January 26, 1950, UR348/6, F0371/87186.

6. The twelfth declassification of Japanese primary sources in November 1994 by the Ministry of Foreign Affairs, Reel E'00 15 (hereafter cited as MFA): 270.

7. On September 5, through the exchange of notes and memoranda of understanding, Japan formally promised to restrict more items than COCOM was controlling. The declassified Japanese primary sources shed new light on Japan's entry into COCOM. First, the European opposition against US policy continued even after the Washington meeting of 1952. The United States tried to make the China Committee independent from COCOM, while Europeans tried to place CHINCOM at a lower level than that of the CG/COCOM. The name of the new committee, the China Committee, was also questioned by Canada (MFA, 414). Second, from the end of 1951,to 1952, a mysterious person called "*rei-no-jimbutsu*" (that person in question), whom we cannot identify due to excision, approached the Japanese and often tried to induce them to the European side. It is likely that person was D'orlandi, the COCOM chairman at that time, See Yoko Kato, "Declassification of Primary Sources on COCOM and Export Controls Today" presented at the US-Japan Nonproliferation Export Controls workshop, University of Georgia, March 27, 1995; See also "Gaimusho bunsho ga kataru nihon no kokomu kanyu keii: Shin kokomu eno tembo wa?" *Jetro Sensor*, (April 1995), 64-67.

8. "Draft Mutual Defense Assistance Agreement With Japan," July 1, 1953, RG59, *General Records of the Department of State, Bureau of Far Eastern Affairs, Office of Northeast Asian Affairs*, Alpha-Numeric File on Japan, Box 4, (Washington: National Archives).

9. From Tokyo to Secretary of State, No. 633, September 9, 1953, 794.5 MSP/9-953, Decimal File, RG59, *General Records of the Department of State.*

10. Article 7 of the US draft of the US-Japan MDAA states that "In the interest of their mutual security, the Government of Japan will cooperate with the Government of the United States in taking measures to control trade with nations which threaten the maintenance of world peace," while Annex (D) states that "In the interest of common security, the Government of Japan will cooperate with the Government of the United States of America and other peace-loving countries in taking measures to control trade with nations which threaten the maintenance of world peace.
The wording "mutual security" in the original US draft was changed to "common security" in Annex (D). Also "and other peace-loving countries," was added to soften the impression that the annex was an anti-Communist measure and to show the MDAA was within the framework of the Peace Constitution.

11. *Records of the Committee of Trade and Industry, Lower House*, No. 42, 13th Diet, Tokyo, Japan, May 28, 1952, 2-3.

12. *Ibid.*, No. 44, May 30, 1952, 3.

13. *Ibid.*, No. 49, June 6, 1952, 11.

14. "Sugimoto saibancho no hanketsu riyu, " *Asahi shinbun*, July 9, 1969.

15. "Nikkoten mondai de ikensho," *Asahi shinbun*, February 15, 1969.

16. "Sugimoto saibancho no hanketsu riyu."

17. *Records of the Committee of Commerce and Industry, Lower House*, No. 3, 109th Diet, August 21, 1987, 14. For works on the Toshiba case, see for example Beverly Crawford, "Changing Export Controls in an Interdependent World: Lessons from the Toshiba case for the 1990s," in *Export Controls in Transition: Perspectives, Problems and Prospects*, Gary K. Bertsch and Steven Elliot-Gower (Durham: Duke University Press, 1992); Gordon B. Smith, "Controlling East-West Trade in Japan," in *Controlling East-West Trade abd Technology Transfer*, Gary S. Bertsch (Durham: Duke University Press, 1988); William C. Triplett II, "Crimes Against the Alliance: The Toshiba-Kongsberg Export Violations," *Policy Review* 44 (Spring 1988).

18. Hitori Kumagai, *Mosukawa yo saraba: kokomu ihanjikenno haikei*, Bungei Shunjyusha, 1988.

19. *Congressional Record* (hereafter cited as *CR*) S15035-SI5043, October 23, 1987.

20. *CR*, H5035, June 16, 1987; S8397, June 19, 1987; H7303, August 7, 1987; S16305, November 13, 1987.

21. "Tatakarete fukai kizu', *Asahi shinbun*, March 22, 1988; "Toshiba kikai: beikoku ni honro saretsuzukeru higeki", *Sentaku*, May 1988.

22. In 1994, the Center for Information on Strategic Technology (CISTEC) was renamed the Center for Information on Security Trade Control (CISTEC).

Chapter 6

Export Control Policies in Japan: The Current System and Stream of Change

Jun-ichi Ozawa and Takeshi Ito

Introduction

The rosy expectations for international relations that emerged with the end of the Cold War are steadily fading. This worrisome process is being hastened by the fact that developed countries are focusing their attention on domestic concerns, instead of seizing the opportunity to contribute to the construction of a "new world order." Compounding the problem, certain aggressive countries are still seeking to expand their interests abroad.

In these uncertain times, the United Nations has become an increasingly important organization in the resolution of regional conflicts through both Security Council resolutions and peacekeeping (PKO) activities, although the problems and conflicts the UN is attempting to mediate are not easily settled. Today's world has become a very difficult creature; the number of independent countries has drastically increased. Actions of the former Soviet Union (FSU) alone has created 15 new states; regional organizations such as the EU, NAFTA, and APEC have created new, freer markets more favorable to the member countries; in Japan, Italy, and South Korea, political uncertainties are creating confusion and a lack of clear policy measures; while in western countries looming economic recession draws people's concentration to domestic matters.

On the other hand, in accordance with the collapse of East-West tension, disarmament has emerged as a major international issue - one that is having a profound influence on the global military industry. East Asian states, for example, with their still-accelerating economic advantage, are reported to be upgrading and improving their existing weapons arsenals. Clearly, as the Middle East weapons market shrinks in the aftermath of the Gulf War, the "emerging" East-Asian market is becoming the most prosperous for the military sector.

This is not a favorable trend for either the US nor Japan. North Korea, China, India, Pakistan - any or all of these countries could become a significant new threat to world order. What should we do next? Given the circumstances that world order is becoming determined not by supremacy but by coordination, will collective security be any more attainable than in the past? Are the existing measures against proliferation of weapons of mass destruction valid? In other words, after the abolition of COCOM, what kind of order should - or should not be - established to meet global expectations? Moreover, is it possible to develop coordination among existing regimes (i.e., Australian Group, MTCR, NSG, etc.)? One principle that may elicit universal agreement in export control circles is that a new world order could be constructed more on the basis of non-proliferation rather than COCOM-type regulations.

The more desirable scenario would be to have related regimes completely unified, but in 1992 Dr. Paul Freedenberg (former US Commerce Undersecretary for Export Administration) left no doubt as to the American assessment of such a possibility when he called it an "unrealistic" expectation. On the Japanese side, the government is deeply concerned about the destabilization of world (and especially Asian) order through the indiscriminate proliferation of weapons and technology; therefore Japan's specific and expected role in international regimes is to work to reduce proliferation of weapons related to Japanese-based technologies.

In recent years, export control regimes in Western countries have come to a historic turning-point. The end of the Cold War, the collapse of the Soviet Empire, the War in the Persian Gulf--a series of global incidents has altered the structure of international political and economic interaction and has forced dramatic changes in the traditional export control regime which was formulated during the East-West confrontation.

Although Japanese export control also faces the same wave of change, the historical turning-point of Japan's export control policy could be considered to be 1987, the year when the COCOM violation of Toshiba Machine Co., an independent subsidiary of Toshiba Co., was revealed. From that year on, Japanese export control policy has put a much higher priority on "security" criteria. Japan's National Security Export Control Committee issued a report last year, "On the Future of Security Export Control," which outlined the changing world situation and possible measures the Japanese government can take to combat the proliferation of weapons of mass destruction and related items.

This chapter briefly looks back at the history of Japanese export control policy after World War II, describes the current control system, briefly reviews government activities following publication of the committee's report in 1993, and presents the future scope of change. It also presents a short review of Japanese government activities, following publication of the committee's report last year, as well as a brief outline of perspectives for the near future.

A Historical View of Japanese Export Control

The legal basis of the Japanese export control system was formulated in 1949, and its basic structure has not changed since. Although the structure has been the same, the environment in which it exists has changed according to four distinct periods.

The first period was during Japanese occupation by the Allied Powers. At that time, Japanese trade was under the control of the Supreme Commander of the Allied Powers (SCAP), which essentially meant Japan was under U.S. control. The initial aim of occupation policy was to restrict Japanese heavy industry so as to suppress the revival of militarism. But the growing Soviet threat, as well as the increasing costs of occupation, made the United States shift its stance, allowing Japan to restore its industry and be brought into the western free trade regime. From 1947, Japanese trade was gradually decontrolled, and in 1949 the Foreign Exchange and Foreign Trade Control Law, which is the legal basis for Japan's export control system, was enacted. Under this law, the Japanese government has controlled foreign exchange, trade which affects the domestic economy, and the trade of strategic goods.

The second period was the 1950s, when Japan joined and became involved in the COCOM regime. In the early 1950s, there was a dispute between the United States (for) and its European allies (against) on establishing another COCOM-type regime targeting Asian countries, especially China, which would have entailed stricter regulations than COCOM had it been established. Also, the Japanese government itself preferred to participate in the original COCOM from the standpoint of staying in close cooperation with Western countries, and, at the same time, of securing the minimum level of restrictions on trade to communist China, which the government regarded as highly important. Thus, Japan joined COCOM in September, 1952.

The third period, from the 1960s to the early 1980s, at which time Japan participated in COCOM activities without incident. In the 1960s and the 1970s, the period of *detente* between the two superpowers, there was an increased interest in trade with the Eastern bloc in Japan as well as in major Western countries'.[1] But in the early 1980s, when decline in US industrial competitiveness and the illegal flow of sensitive technologies to the USSR became obvious, the United States began to take the initiative in reinforcing COCOM. In response to this US initiative, the Japanese government reviewed its organization in 1985 to establish the "Security Export Control Office" in the Export Division of MITI to specialize in COCOM and related regimes.

The final period began after the Toshiba Machine case in 1987. This incident was, as mentioned before, the turning-point for Japan. Since then, Japan has taken a more active stance on export control.

A Change in Motives

The Japanese export control policy in the first three periods was based on the motive of cooperation with Western countries in the field of trade and in other economic activities. This was absolutely necessary for the healthy development of the Japanese economy; therefore, the observance of such international arrangements as COCOM was inevitable if Japan was to preserve this cooperation.

Based on this motive, in principle export was free insofar as it was consistent with the objectives of the healthy development of the Japanese economy."[2] Therefore, export control as a means of security (or diplomacy) was not considered the main priority in Japan; the security standpoint was not directly incorporated into Japanese export control legislation. As a result, violators of the regulations could be subject to penalties under the same provisions regardless of the nature of the violation. However, it did not necessarily mean that Japan had a "decidedly pro-trade oriented policy."[3] In other words, Japan pursued both national security and prosperity through cooperation with the Western allies, but domestically, only economic benefit could bestow legitimacy on export control for a country fettered in the "taboo of security." The situation changed in 1987 when the Toshiba Machine case revealed to observers that Japanese technology had the potential to significantly affect international security. Since then, the standpoint of international security has been greatly taken into account in Japanese export control policy.

In addition to control on East-West trade, Japan has taken a rather strict position on the proliferation of nuclear weapons and arms trade. This is based on its own strong belief in peace, as the sole country with the actual painful experiences of nuclear attack and with a constitution which renounces the right to wage war. Japan has been a strong advocate of the Treaty on the Non-Proliferation of Nuclear Weapons (NPT) from its early stages and has enforced control over trade in nuclear-related goods and technologies. In the arena of arms trade, in 1967 the Japanese government announced the "Three Principles of Arms Export,"[4] which were originally intended as a restriction, but later generally came to be recognized as a ban on arms trade. In 1976, a new policy, the "Unified View of the Government on Arms Exports,"[5] which further strengthens the "Three Principles," was announced. According to these policies, most arms, arms parts, and equipment and technology for arms production can not be exported.[6]

Japan, as one of the leading countries in the economic and technological arenas as well as a country which possesses special feelings about peace, promotes the field of non-proliferation export control on weapons of mass destruction, now an important agenda item for international security. Japan has actively participated in related regimes, such as the Nuclear Supplier Group (NSG), MTCR, and the Australia Group, from the beginning.

In recent years, Japan has come to seek a more positive and constructive role in the political arena of international relations. In 1991, the government established the ODA Assistance Charter, which states that in extending ODA, full attention should be paid to trends in the recipient country's military expenditures, its development and production of weapons of mass destruction, and its import and export of arms. The Charter is an indicator of the Japanese government's intention to take more strategic initiatives in its diplomacy. In 1991, the

Japanese government, along with other European countries, also proposed a resolution to the U.N. General Assembly advocating transparency in arms transfer.

The Export Control System in Japan Legislation and Organization

The export control system in Japan is based on the Foreign Exchange and Foreign Trade Control Law and two related cabinet orders, the Export Trade Control Order (ETCO) and the Foreign Exchange Control Order (FECO). The export of goods is controlled under the former order and the export of technologies (including software) under the latter. Concerning the export of goods and technologies, the Ministry of International Trade and Industry (MITI) is the sole authority with the right to administer these laws and orders. MITI also holds the right to direct customs, which institutionally belongs to the Ministry of Finance." The Foreign Exchange and Foreign Trade Control Law and ETCO were both established in 1949 and FECO was enacted in 1980.

Articles 25 and 4-8 of the Law require exporters to obtain an export license from MITI in exporting certain goods (Article 4-8) and technologies (Article 25) that may have security implications to specified destinations. Before the Toshiba Machine case, Article 4-8 did not directly refer to security considerations. A provision for security considerations was first incorporated into Article 25 in 1980, when the Law was amended to adapt to the liberation of service transactions in order to specify which types of transactions (regarding the export of technology) would require government approval. Then in 1987, the same provision was incorporated into Article 4-8 to make distinctions regarding the causes which would inflict heavier penalties on violators of security export control.

Controlled goods and technologies and their destinations are listed and described in the Attached Tables of the Orders. These Tables are often amended in response to revisions of the Law and of international arrangements. Because of the introduction in 1987 of the security provision into Article 4-8 of the Law, ETCO's Attached Table was separated into two tables, Table No. 1 and No. 2, and the former was designated for the goods controlled for security reasons. In 1991, when COCOM introduced its Core List, Table No. 1 of ETCO and FECO's Table were completely reorganized and made more plain: For example, Table No. 1, which formerly listed nearly two hundred items at random, now consists of 15 categories which correspond to the types of control objectives, such as "arms," "nuclear," "COCOM," etc. Subsequently, each category list is composed of individual items and destinations. Further specifications for the items are detailed in the Ministerial Ordinances and other announcements and notices issued by MITI. Thus, though perhaps complicated, the control lists, which substantially correspond to those of various multilateral regimes, are made public.

The sections responsible for implementing export control from a security point of view are the Security Export Control Office and related offices in MITI. The number of staff engaged in security export control was drastically increased from 40 in 1987 to 103 in 1988, and has reached 115 in 1992. Although MITI is the sole authority in export control, MITI closely cooperates with other government bodies, especially the Ministry of Foreign Affairs.

Concerning the relationship between the government and business, MITI has advocated the concept of Compliance Programs, which about 850 companies have already committed themselves to. About 80 percent of the total of Japanese exports is covered by these companies. For those companies which have committed to and followed the program closely, MITI may issue comprehensive licenses with specific conditions. In 1989 exporting companies, in cooperation with MITI, established the Center for Information on Strategic Technology (CISTEC) as the advisory organization on technical matters related to security export control.

Japan's recent export control activities

1993 saw important international breakthroughs on regimes critical for non-proliferation. Most notably, the Chemical Weapons Convention (CWC) was made available for signature at the UN, and other export control regimes (AG, MTCR) reached new agreements.

The Japanese government regards its security export control policy as one of the most important issues to have emerged since the end of the 1980s. In this context, it is an active contributor to international regimes such as the NSG and the UN Register. Specifically, since the Toshiba Machine Co. export-violation case in 1987, MITI has been imposing ever-stricter controls on the export of high-tech commodities and technologies.

Japan's export control policy is closely coordinated by the responsible ministries (Ministry of Foreign Affairs [MOFA], Ministry of Finance [MOF], and the Ministry of International Trade and Industry [MITI].   Combined with Japan's strict ban on weapons export (established by Cabinet decisions in 1976 and thereafter), Japan can more easily establish a national consensus on such controls than can the United States, where there are several strongly independent agencies (DOC, DOS, and DOD), and where the military industry is an essential element of the economy.   Japanese government measures taken in line with international agreements in fiscal year 1993 were as follows:

1) Amendment of the Cabinet Order on Export Trade Controls, and of the Ministerial Order Determining Goods and Technologies, Promulgated in June 1993.   According to the Australian Group agreement of December 1992, biological weapons-related items (microorganisms, toxins and genes used for the production of warfare agents, physical containment facilities, fermenters, centrifugal separators, cross-flow filtration equipment, freeze-drying equipment, protection equipment used in P3 or P4 containment housing, and aerosol inhalation chambers) have been newly included in the Export Control List.   In addition, based on the March, 1993 MTCR agreement, the technical standards of items such as individual rocket stages, solid propellant rocket engines, and reentry vehicles have been revised.

2) Amendment of the Cabinet Order on Export Trade Controls, and of the Ministerial Order Determining Goods and Technologies, Promulgated in December 1993.   According to international agreement achieved at COCOM meetings prior to October 1993, specially designed components of optical fiber communication cable etc. have been removed from the List and waveform digitizers and non-contact measurement equipment for optical surfaces (lens or reflection mirrors) have been added to the List.   Moreover, in line with international agreements, the technical parameters for ICs, digital computers, and telecommunication transmission equipment have been revised.

3) The Czech Republic and Slovakia were removed from the List in early 1994.

4) 1993 saw additional changes in governmental organizations. For example, the Ministry of Foreign Affairs created the Non-

proliferation Division in the new Foreign Policy Bureau, and MITI upgraded the Security Export Control Office to the status of division.

New non-proliferation schemes

With the ending of the Cold War, COCOM approached the end of its useful role. The end of the Cold War and the strong request of President Boris Yeltsin at the April 1993 Russia-US summit led COCOM members to began talks on new arrangements that would reflect the changed international situation. At a high-level informal meeting on November 16, 1993, the following agreements were reached:

(1) COCOM would be abolished by March 31, 1994, at the latest;

(2) The present members will start talks on a new arrangement that covers the non-proliferation of weapons and related items;

(3) The participation of Russia is indispensable, so negotiations to this effect will be initiated;

(4) Working groups will be set up in order to properly advance the procedures necessary for the above three measures;

(5) The next high-level meeting was to be held in the middle of January 1994, based on the results of the working groups (this was postponed until March 29 and 30th of the same year).

Moreover, the high-level meeting in the Hague that ended on March 30, 1994, reached the following ad hoc conclusions:

(1) The key aim of the organization that replaces COCOM will be to prevent regional conflicts;

(2) The next meeting was be held in October 1994, with extended participation from the present 17 member countries and 6 cooperative countries, as well as Russia and possibly China.

Additional ad hoc measures include:

(1) The controlled items in the COCOM list will remain controlled;

(2) Major strategic items such as acoustic sonars will remain under strict control. Negotiations will continue on issues of membership and what the controlled items (including weapons) and countries should be included.

New measures from MITI

Inspired in part by these international changes, Japan's own export control policy is entering a new era. The National Security Export Control Committee (chaired by Ambassador Ryukichi Imai of the Industrial Structure Council), an official MITI advisory body, submitted a report with important proposals for the future of security export control in Japan.

Having received the proposals, MITI is preparing to introduce the following measures:

(1) Introduction of a new comprehensive system of permission.

(a) With regard to countries already participating in international export control regimes, the new system is designed to consolidate controls and streamline the permission process - while refining full oversight authority. After permission is acquired under this new system, individual applications for the export of goods or services to the above countries for a limited period become unnecessary.

(b) As for countries other than the above: even if exports are made to non-participating countries, it will be extremely difficult, if not impossible, for proliferation to occur. One line of reasoning is that almost all Japanese exporters operate under a strict export control system that requires a Compliance Program [CP], and some also have a close capital relation with their end-users. The new system will, for exporters satisfying both conditions, introduce more comprehensive permission regulations for the export of items and services related to weapons of mass destruction. Ultimately, the new permission system will deregulate the present export control system - principally by reducing the number of applications by an estimated 60 percent.

(2) Simplification of application procedures (abolishment of prior reporting system). According to present application procedures, "prior reporting" before formal applications are made is required for strict enforcement of the export control law when items and services relating to weapons of mass destruction are to be exported to countries not participating in the international export control regimes. In order to reduce applicant burdens, the present system will be abolished this April and a new system with simplified application procedures and a reduced examination period will be reduced.

(3) Delegation of power to local MITI bureaus (9 divisions). At present application forms for the export of items and services relating to weapons of mass destruction must be delivered to the Tokyo headquarters of MITI; but as of this August 1994, local bureaus will accept and examine applications.

(4) Introduction of simultaneous application of the permission system when an item and its related (technological) service are exported at the same time, under the same contract.

Currently, as the exports of items and services are regulated under different cabinet orders, separate application for each is required, even if both originate from the same contract. In order to streamline the approval procedures, simultaneous applications for items and services will be accepted from April 1994. The new system will apply to about 60 percent of the present applications for the export of services.

Other schemes planned in MITI

The Export Control Committee's report deliberately refers to the importance of the nonproliferation export control known in the West as the "know" (catch-all) regulation. This everything-on-a-string type of regulation seems to be a rational and useful tool for a regulator searching for a true criminal. However, many questions must be resolved before this new type of regulation is introduced in Japan. Most important, what kind of information should be submitted? Is it reasonable to expect a particular exporter to gather and provide complete information on end-use and end-users? And a legally exported item might, of course, be altered for undesirable ends, e.g. weapons use, after a long trip through the complex world trade network. New regulations will thus require clarification of application criteria for exporters, along with international coordination so that legal exports will not inadvertently draw blame from other allied countries if they wind up used for illegal or otherwise unexpected purposes.

MITI's chemical weapon and drug-control policy office is now preparing to introduce new legislation restricting the trade of chemical weapons and related products (in accordance with the 1993 Chemical Weapons Convention) for the purpose of non-proliferation. The CWC - related committee - chaired by Professor Toyohiko Hayakawa of the Tokyo Institute of Technology - of the chemical products council will submit its recommendations for legislation this month.

MITI will in July 1994 nominate a new senior officer to the newly-established post of deputy director general. This official will be principally responsible for security export control issues, in order to enforce the controls more effectively. The termination of COCOM is expected to accelerate the relaxation of the export control regulations of participating countries, including Japan and the US. For example, a complete review of the countries formerly on the list as suspicious is to be carried out. In line with this, the Japanese government is expected to introduce new deregulation measures sometime in April in cooperation with 16 other members.

Outlook on the Japanese Export Control System:
The Security Export Control Committee

Recently, non-proliferation export control, particularly in regard to the suspicious third world countries, has attracted the government's attention as it considers how to prevent regional conflicts. Since this type of control would require more strict investigation of the end-use and end-user of the goods and technologies to be exported in addition to inquiries into the performance of those goods and technologies which are required under the current control system, the United States, Germany, and Britain have already introduced new regulation systems under what is called the "catch-all" system.

In response, the Japanese government decided to examine its future export control policy which corresponds to the non-proliferation export control. For the first time in 1992, MITI set up the Security Export

Control Committee as a subcommittee of the Industrial Structure Council, which is an official advisory council to the Minister of International Trade and Industry.   The Committee, comprised of members from various sectors -- from academia to business -- has met six times since last September, and completed its recommendation report for the Minister on the 25th of March 1993.

The Report of the Committee

This report, entitled "The Future of Security Export Controls: For the Nonproliferation of Weapons of Mass Destruction" consists of the following three sections: (1) International Trends Surrounding Security Export Controls, (2) Japanese Security Export Controls: Current Situation and Issues, and (3) Future Security Control Export Policy.

The first section of the report is given over to an analysis of the current situation concerning international security and export control, and suggests the need for a shift in emphasis from a COCOM-type control system to a non-proliferation type.

The second section, briefly looking back over the evolution of the Japanese export control system, points out the following three issues as the topics of future Japanese export control:

(1) The need for intricate and sophisticated control systems: Since the aim of nonproliferation export control is essentially to prevent the spread of weapons of mass destruction as well as the excessive accumulation of conventional weapons, regulations must be restrictive so as not to hinder the economic development of a target country.   Therefore, a more intricate and sophisticated control system is required for close investigation of the end-use and end-user to prevent diversion of exported goods and technologies.

(2) The renewed need for international cooperation: Because the details of regulations such as identification of suspicious countries has yet to be fully agreed upon on an international basis, the implementation of export control largely depends on each country's individual decision. Therefore, international cooperation is needed, such as the sharing of security-related information or establishment of common control guidelines.

(3) The need to expand the scope of controlled items: The threat of goods of less strategic use and wider-application which are not on the control lists of existing multilateral regimes being diverted to the development and manufacture of weapons of mass destruction is increasing. There is a growing awareness that Japan, as a major world supplier of industrial products, must take swift measures in addition to enforcing existing controls.

Having described the future subjects of Japanese export control in Section II, the first part of Section III addresses the significance of export control policy:

(1) The role of security export controls in overall security policy. In establishing a security framework, a combination of policy measures is required. Diplomatic efforts, such as strengthening the role of the UN or establishing regional security dialogue; economic cooperation which contributes to regional stabilization; and arms control and disarmament. Although security-related export control is important as a means of arms control, it must be regarded as one of a number of policy measures which would mutually complement each other to establish a peaceful order, not as a self-concluded policy measure which could completely prevent, by itself, the proliferation of weapons of mass destruction and the excessive accumulation of conventional arms. Besides, the purpose of security export control is not to broadly restrict the economic activities of a certain country as economic sanctions do, but to prevent proliferation and excessive arms accumulation in a country. Therefore, it may be possible, through economic development, to prevent a country's isolation or to remove destabilizing factors in a region. It may be adequate, in some cases, to have economic and technological cooperation with the proscribed country. In this sense, careful consideration should be given to implementing security export controls so as not to hinder the economic development of a proscribed country.

(2) The significance of security export controls to Japan: Considering that Japan is producing and exporting various high-technology products, it is increasingly important that Japan establish an effective export control system in order to prohibit diversion of such products for development and manufacture of weapons of

mass destruction. This is the inevitable responsibility of Japan itself, as its economic prosperity greatly depends upon a free and stable international society.

Thus emphasizing the significance of the policy, the last two parts of the Section make policy recommendations. Relating to the international arena, the recommendations are as follows:

(1) The coordination of multilateral security export control regimes: The report requests Japan to take the initiative in harmonizing various multilateral regimes of export control in such areas as items to be controlled and sharing of views and information on security-related matters including the assessment of threat of a country of concern. Further, the report also proposes the establishment of a new framework which unifies the various existing regimes in order to make a firm and swift determination in implementing export control.

(2) Promotion of international controls on transfer of conventional weapons: The report also requests that Japan take the initiative in reinforcing export control on conventional arms to countries of concern through international cooperation.

(3) Assistance to other countries to establish their export control systems: It is increasingly important to encourage countries in the former Soviet Union (FSU), in eastern Europe, and in Asia to participate in the existing multilateral export control regimes. Many of these those countries possess significant industrial capability, and especially regarding the countries of the FSU, there is great concern that the munitions they possess may find their way to other countries. Japan is called on to cooperate in organizing export control systems in these countries, while at the same time encouraging them to join the existing multilateral regimes.

Regarding domestic issues, the report makes the following recommendations:

(1) Future export controls:
A. Introduction of new export controls for the prevention of the proliferation of weapons of mass destruction: Introducing so-called

"catch-all" regulations concurrent with distinct criteria to judge whether the end-use and end-user of exports is suspicious or not. The identification of dangerous countries and the creation of a set of exempt items are also required in order to keep regulations at the necessary minimum. It is also necessary to harmonize regulations among countries for the purpose of securing international fairness in regulations.

B. The implementation of focused export controls by streamlining procedures: To implement more efficient and rational export control, it is necessary to streamline controls where possible, set priorities, and allocate the limited administrative resources accordingly. To this end, the rationalization and simplification of licensing procedures is necessary.

(2) Further improvement of private and public systems: The strengthening and improvement of the administrative organization is necessary for effective implementation. The establishment of a self-management system in the private sector, e.g. Compliance Programs, will also foster this.

(3) Collecting, analyzing, and providing information: the creation of system for collecting, analyzing and disseminating security-related information, for example on the development plans of weapons of mass destruction, is increasingly important.

Upon receiving these recommendations, MITI will examine whether an amendment of the Foreign Exchange and Foreign Trade Control Law itself is needed. A possible option would be to revise the two Orders, ETCO and FECO, so as to put the suggested new export control system into practice.

Toward a world export policy

Given current circumstances, where the most appropriate measures to maintain world security seem to consist of deterring low intensity conflicts, proper stratagems to reduce the real sources of the conflict are needed more than ever. In this sense, the abolishment of COCOM and the creation of a new non-proliferation regime presents a pivotal occasion where COCOM's present members and would-be countries can participate in the construction of a new world order.

Two major issues were raised at the COCOM March 29-30, 1994 meeting where the formation of the new regime was discussed: what will the controlled items be, and which countries are to be identified as dangerous? Agreement is not easily obtained on these questions - there are serious differences of opinion as to what constitutes risky technology and which countries can be viewed as friendly. Furthermore, the coming (1995 and thereafter) non-proliferation regimes (both COCOM-type and others) still lack clarity in many key theoretical areas, including:

a) What is the real goal of the new arrangement? The stabilization of world order through a reduction of conflicts in the Third World? The introduction of human rights principles? Or is the developed world pursuing its own private interests? In reality, a mixture of the above factors is the most acceptable, and likely scenario.

b) How should items be controlled for the purpose of non-proliferation? To date, items identified as dangerous under export control regimes such as COCOM are all subject to standard control measures in participating countries. But this doesn't apply to the new "know" regulation, on which consensus has not yet been reached in Japan.

c) Is it weapons of mass destruction or their related items and technologies that should be controlled? The dominant phenomenon of the post-Cold War world is expanding regional conflict. In order to reduce the incidence and intensity of such conflict, the most effective measure is strict control of conventional weapons. This necessitates firm coordination with member countries that still support proxy wars for their own political and economic interests. Conventional weapons control will also help to reinforce traditional control measures for high-tech items and services -- measures that are losing effectiveness under the indirect influence of conventional weapon proliferation with the end of the Cold War.

d) What will the most feasible non-proliferation measures be? A stick-and-stick policy (export control laws and economic sanctions), as opposed to a carrot-and-stick policy, may seem the only effective measure available. But there is an alternative: a purely economic approach, which would leave all exports free of restrictions. Exporters would only have to concern themselves with ensuring that their products or technologies are not copied by the recipient country.

From a Japanese viewpoint a new world order might be better constructed by reducing regional conflicts (such as those in eastern Europe and South Asia) through non-proliferation measures high-tech items and related weapon technology. But, the most useful measure would be to control conventional weapons. Although the UN Charter prescribes the right of nations to acquire arms to defend themselves, this right, which is exploited through the worldwide weapons trade, may accelerate regional conflicts. The global military industry creates a complicated and agonizing problem: while our goal is non-proliferation, recession in the arms industry coupled with disarmament--especially after the end of the Cold War--has had a negative effect on the economy and employment rates of arms-producing countries. Governments may find themselves forced to support the arms trade simply because it is a key national industry. Another serious problem is the "brain drain" of scientists and engineers who can no longer find employment in military or high-tech sectors in their native countries. Governments should take measures to find employment for these people before they are recruited by a hostile country. Asia is seemingly stable, and economically vibrant; but countries in the region are accelerating the modernization of their arms and armed forces in tandem with economic growth. This trend shows no signs of abating, Furthermore, tensions over North Korea's nuclear ambitions are becoming increasingly acute. The lack of Japanese reaction to North Korea's launch of a missile into the Japan Sea last year was a great surprise to international security circles. Japan's attitude is now changing little by little. Most importantly, as the largest economic power in Asia, Japan is now required to take political measures for regional security and disarmament, in addition to its positive leadership role in the NSG and the UN. These measures could include disarmament through the reduction of Japan's defense budget (the largest in the region) and UN activities (peace-keeping operations or even economic sanctions) in cooperation with its allies. As a peace-loving nation, Japan has much to do to advance the cause of international cooperation and development in a confused world.

Appendix 6.1: Outline of Japanese Export Control System

I. Legislation

A. Export Control from Security Viewpoint

(1) Goods

When exporting specific kinds of goods to a specified destination which has been designated as one considered to be obstructive to the maintenance of international peace and security, an exporter must obtain a license from MITI. (Article 4-8, Paragraph 1 and 2 of the Foreign Exchange and Foreign Trade Control Law)

Controlled goods and destinations are described in the Attached Table No. 1 of the Export Trade Control Order. Table No. 1 consists of the following 15 sections, which correspond to the control lists of the international arrangements:

> Section 1: Arms
>
> Section 2: Nuclear
>
> Section 3: Chemical Weapons
>
> Section 4: Missile
>
> Section 5-14: COCOM goods
>
> Section 15: Computers and 4--WD vehicles to South Africa

(2) Technology

When making a transfer to a specified destination with a non-resident of which the objective is to offer technology concerned with design, production, or use of specific kinds of goods designated as those considered to be obstructive to the maintenance of international peace and security, a person must obtain a license from MITI. (Article 25 of the Law) Controlled technologies and destinations are described in the Attached Table of the Foreign Exchange Control Order.

(3) Export Control from an Economic Viewpoint

When exporting specific kinds of goods to a specified destination, MITI may obligate an exporter to obtain an approval, within the limits of necessity, for the maintenance of the balance of payments and for the sound development of foreign trade and national economy. (Article 48, Paragraph 3)

Controlled goods and destinations are described in the Attached Table No. 2 and No. 2.2 of the Export Trade Control Order.

Appendix 6.2: Japanese Export Control Organization and Staffing:

Ministry of International Trade and Industry (MITI)

Trade Administration Bureau

Export Division (Number of staff - 2): General coordination of export control

Security Export Control Office (51): General coordination concerning security export control

Strategic Commodities Export Inspection Office (27): General coordination of inspection concerning security export control

Basic Industries Bureau

International Trade Office (4): Processing of export licenses for those goods which the Bureau is in charge of.

Machinery and Information Industries Bureau

International Trade Office (16): Processing of export licenses for those goods which the Bureau is in charge of.

Regional Bureaus, Including Okinawa General Bureau (15): Regional processing

Total staff. 115

Notes

1. In 1972, the view that further decontrol or the abolishment of COCOM would be considered in order to promote trade with Communist countries appeared in a report of the working group of MITI's advisory council.

2. In answer to a lawsuit concerning the legitimacy of export control based upon the Foreign Exchange and Foreign Trade Law, the judgement of a lower court was that the prohibition of exports by reason of COCOM regulations deviates from the objective of the Law and that special legislation for COCOM would be required to control exports. However, as the suit itself was won by the Government, there was no chance to appeal to a higher court, and the precedent remains undisputed. In an amendment to the Law in 1987, the phrase, "obstructive to the maintenance of international peace and security" was added to Article 4-8; but Article 1, which describes the objective of the Law, was left untouched.

3. Gordon B. Smith, "Controlling East-West Trade in Japan," in *Controlling East-West Trade and Technology Transfer, Power, Politics and Policies* Gary K. Bertsch, ed. (Durham: Duke University Press, 1988), 138-158.

4. The Three Principles of Arms Export--The export of arms is restricted by the Export Trade Control Order of Cabinet and is subject to the approval of the Minister of International Trade and Industry. The approval shall not be granted, in principle, if the destination of the export is as follows: (a) a communist country; (b) countries to which the export of arms is prohibited by a resolution of the United Nations; and (c) countries which are now involved in or may be involved in international conflicts.

5. The United View of the Government on Arms Export -- In order to avoid escalation of international conflicts, the Japanese government has been carefully dealing with arms exports from the standpoint of a peace-loving nation. The government will not promote arms export and will hereafter pursue the following policy: (a) the export of arms to destinations covered in the Three Principles shall not be permitted; (b) based on the spirit of the Constitution and the Foreign Exchange and Foreign Trade Control Law, the export of arms to destinations other than those covered in the Three Principles shall be refrained from; and (c) the export of equipment and facilities which are used in the manufacture of arms shall be treated with the same regard as arms exports.

6. The United States was dissatisfied with the unilateral flow of arms technology to Japan, and required the transfer of Japanese military technology according to the Mutual Defense Assistance Agreement (MDAA) between the

two countries. In 1983, Japan agreed to the transfer of arms technology to the United States exclusively under the framework of the MDAA.

Chapter 7

Export Controls: Related Issues and Measures in Japanese Industries

Michio Yoneta

Introduction

Reflecting on the present international situation, the context and substance of export controls practiced by Japanese industries is shifting from COCOM controls to specific nonproliferation control. In other words, export controls focusing on items in the lists pursuant to the existing strategic commodities controls against the Communist bloc are giving way to those centering on sensitive items which may contribute to the development and manufacture of weapons of mass destruction and missiles. In addition to list-based controls of commodities related to nonproliferation, controls of so-called end use/end user are becoming increasingly important.

Under such circumstances, Japanese industries, to deal with the new nonproliferation export controls in place of COCOM controls which they have practiced for years, are engaging in the preparation of an internal management system, education for the change in perception, etc. The Center for Information on Security Trade Control (CISTEC), for its part, is conducting surveys, research papers, and publication of various institutions and consulting services which may be useful to industries in implementing and administering export controls properly.

Nonproliferation export controls, however, are often broad, diverse and complicated, bringing industries face to face with new issues and challenges.

The following describes, in part, the perceptions of Japanese industries on security trade controls, the present state of export controls and related issues, and measures to be taken in the future.

Perceptions of Japanese industries on security trade controls and international cooperation

Export promotion and international harmonization in export controls

With the prolonged domestic economic recession, Japanese industries are coping with restructuring in order to strengthen their corporate nature. At the same time, they are coping with the earliest stages of economic recovery.

This recovery necessitated activation of the domestic market, orderly expansion and promotion of exports, and the exploration of new markets. As for their promotion of exports, the industries perceive that it would be imperative for them to carefully conduct export controls according to each destination, so that the commodities exported from Japan could not be used for the development or manufacture of weapons of mass destruction and missiles, or misused for the manufacture of weapons by countries involved in conflict.

On top of complying with Japanese laws and regulations, many industries have implemented their own compliance program (CP), employing necessary voluntary controls, based upon their appropriate administrative judgement in order to maintain their international reputation.

Under these industry perceptions, it is strongly suggested that there should be an international harmonization of controls so that countries may compete in export trade on an equal footing, while Japanese companies should continue to conduct adequate export controls.

Cooperation of Japan with other Asian countries

For Japanese industries, Asian countries, particularly NIES and ASEAN countries, are important not only as the markets for their export products but also as their overseas production bases. This indicates the existence of a strong relationship between Japanese industries and those areas. Thus, controls of end user/end use are becoming increasingly important in assuring that no commodities exported to these Asian markets from Japan would be transferred to countries involved conflicts or those engaged in the development or manufacturing of weapons of mass destruction and missiles via diversion. In the meantime, preparation and support with respect to the export control system of these Asian countries are now being done by the Center for International Cooperation on Export Controls which was newly established in the CISTEC in cooperation with the Japanese government. One example of such cases is that the first seminar of international security export controls of Asia which was held from 26th to 28th in October, 1993 under the auspices of the Japanese government with six ASEAN countries. One positive result of that seminar was that the significance of preparing security export control systems was recognized by these countries.

Present state of Japanese industries and measures to be taken

As regards export controls, Japanese industries comply with laws and regulations with regard to COCOM-listed items and items related to nonproliferation such as nuclear weapons, missiles, etc. At the same time, industries have implemented voluntary controls.

However, it still remains to induce and educate export related industries, including small and medium size enterprises, to conduct proper nonproliferation export controls. In 1992, when the nonproliferation export controls became an important issue for industries, CISTEC sent out questionnaires to its supporting members. (The results of that questionnaire survey are shown in the Appendix 7.1).

With regard to the drastic reform of COCOM and its impact on the export controls involving companies in the post-COCOM era, contents of new COCOM regime have yet to be clarified. Thus, companies wait and see with interest how things will be developing.

As for Catch-all/Know controls which have been implemented in the US, U.K. and Germany, methods of introducing them, controlling techniques, etc. are being considered by the administrative authorities concerned in Japan. Meanwhile, Japanese industries are asking for the following in the case of catch-all/know controls introduced in Japan:

(a) Objectivity and clarification of standards of judgement;

(b) Designation of controlled countries;

(c) Restriction of controlled items by preparing excluded items, special treatment for goods of small value, etc.

CISTEC's committees discussed these matters and compiled in the proposal of March, 1994. (See Appendix 7.2)

Future directions and measures to be taken with regard to export controls

As the momentum for the review of controls progresses, the Japanese industries are watching with concern what will happen to the Export Administration Act in the US in 1995, how the Clinton Administration's export promotion policy and the potentially modified Act will be balanced, how the EU's unified export regulations will be finalized, and how and when new export controls (know controls) will be shaped and introduced in Japan.

In the meantime, it is thought that now is the time to promote the exchange of opinions for harmonization in export control areas among industries of the US, Europe and Japan. Whether export controls will be more tightened or relaxed as a whole from 1995 onwards is a matter of concern for industries in each country. Attention is being paid to how the international situation, which will have a great impact upon export controls, is going to develop from this point forward. While recognizing anew the significance of security trade controls, Japanese industries are making proposals for the streamlining and simplification of the existing controls and systems. They desire that the contents of their proposals will be implemented soon.

It is a positive development that the above proposals have been reflected to some extent in the recently revised regulations by MITI for relaxations of export control procedures.

The Role and Business Activities of CISTEC

(a) Establishment of CISTEC - CISTEC is a nonprofit, non-governmental organization in Japan founded in April 1989 to deal with export control matters. CISTEC aims at maintaining and securing international peace and security. In this direction, CISTEC promotes its objectives to implement reasonable export controls in harmony with

Japan's economic activities, and thereby ensures the harmonious enforcement of laws and regulations based on international treaties.

(b) Roles of CISTEC - CISTEC supports Government activities in various types of international export control regimes in terms of technology and information and CISTEC aims at the implementation of Japan's reasonable and effective export control system. To meet such an objective, CISTEC collects opinions and requests from related business circles concerning the amendment of the export control system and improvement in practical procedures, and makes recommendations to the Government.

(c) Examples of its activities -

(i) Gathering and providing information on security trade CISTEC systematically gathers and analyzes the relevant information essential to customer management and the examination for confirming the end use of the items in nonproliferation export controls, etc., and information publicized on situations relating to weapons of countries of concern. CISTEC is planning to store such information in computers, etc. and create a database, thereby providing the necessary information when necessary.

(ii) International cooperation - There is a growing recognition of the importance of nonproliferation oriented export controls and an increasing necessity for international cooperation among nations including those in Asia. Given these changes in the international climate for export controls, CISTEC has cooperated in holding seminars and study meetings sponsored by the Government to support the preparation of export control systems directed toward these countries. In addition, CISTEC regularly carries out its own support activities for other countries in terms of export control legal compliance systems, inspection systems, and voluntary control within companies.

(iii) International harmonization activities on export controls CISTEC is going to make efforts to promote international harmonization in export controls via the exchange of information and opinions on security trade issues, with industries and research institutions in the US and Europe.

Appendix 7.1: The Results of questionnaire survey on Actual Status of Internal Management in the Companies for Nonproliferation Export Controls

Introduction

CISTEC has carried out a questionnaire survey on the management system of non-proliferation export controls implemented by the supporting member companies. The results of this survey are as shown below:

Number of companies contacted: 197

Number of companies responded: 175 Response rate: 88.8 percent

Surveyed: in October, 1992

Note: This survey was made in October, 1992. Since then, many efforts have been made by companies to cope with nonproliferation export control issues, therefore, the figures in the survey result don't reflect the present situation in Japanese companies.

1. General Remarks

(1) Nearly 100 percent of the companies responding to the survey showed an understanding of the trend of export controls after the Gulf War and the necessity of establishing an internal export management system in their companies.

(2) As for the understandability of export laws and regulations as well as nonproliferation export controls, most of the personnel responsible for the export management can explain them. But the greater part of the staff of a company cannot explain them satisfactorily

(3) With the exception of a few companies, most of the companies are taking, in their judgment, some kind of operational or practical measures to address nonproliferation export controls. Only 14.8

percent of the companies have revised their compliance programs.

(4) 86.7 percent of the respondents think their current export management systems can fully cope with COCOM export controls. But only about half of the respondents feel their current systems can fully cope with nonproliferation export controls.

2. Export Management Systems

(1) 87.9 percent of the respondents have established a permanent export management division and are trying to improve their export management system. However, only 36.4 percent of the respondents have appointed a full-time executive (director) responsible for export controls.

(2) 70.2 percent of the respondents are centralizing the entire in-house information on export controls, and the figure increases to 93.6 percent if we include companies that have replied that the "information is partially centralized." On the other hand, 19.8 percent have replied that they cannot sufficiently centralize the control over customs requirements. This shortcoming suggests that the centralized management of in-house information becomes perfunctory.

3. Screening System

(1) 74.1 percent of companies have established a screening system based on non-proliferation export controls.

(2) 64.7 percent of companies are implementing, with a view to greater security, in-house management of the items that are not subject to the controls of Foreign Exchange and Foreign Trade Control Law.

(3) 65.1 percent of them are implementing a shading control (priority control) according to destinations. (Judgment of commodity classification)

(4) In the case of manufacturers, most of them are judging by themselves, but 46.6 percent of them feel that they have not enough

information to judge the commodity classification. They expect CISTEC to make up for their insufficient information.

(5) On the other hand, in the case of non-manufacturers, some of the companies (27.9 percent) judge the commodity classification by themselves but 69.2 percent think their information is insufficient. (Screening of transaction)

(6) Only 29.5 percent have correct information about the end-users and end-use of their transactions.

(7) When they have to ask outsiders to check the end-users or end-use of their transactions, the greater part of them usually ask trading companies with which they have business connections.

(8) 90.2 percent have authorized their export management division to suspend or approve their export transactions. 89.6 percent are implementing a multi-step screening system by their export management division on transactions that may fall under the controls of Foreign Exchange and Foreign Trade Control Law.
But, 10.4 percent of the respondents say that their export management division participates in screening their transactions only when they have "doubts about them. " From this we can see that multi-step screening is not fully functional.

4. Education

(1) 94.2 percent of companies are holding an annual education and training course.

(2) 69.2 percent of companies think that it may be better to have an outside educational institution specializing in export controls, and 72.5 percent are actually utilizing some outside educational institution. As for an outside institution, CISTEC plays an important role (67.7 percent).

5. Audit

(1) 81.4 percent are implementing an audit on export controls at least once a year and 85.2 percent are undertaking the task of

improving and guiding the in-house practices based on the audit.

(2) Only 8.0 percent have dealt with accidents based on CP when customs accidents had occurred.

6. Others

(1) 27.0 percent of the companies have increased their personnel responsible for export management. Also, 39.1 percent have increased their budget for export management.

Appendix 7.2:

A. Proposals For Export Controls

(1) International harmonization - Harmonization in relation to Catch-all/Know controls

(a) Export controls are in the process of changing. It is becoming extremely important to internationally harmonize export controls and equalize the opportunities for companies of each country to export in light of the anticipated COCOM's dissolution and establishment of a post-COCOM mechanism and unification/reorganization of nonproliferation regimes.

With regard to nonproliferation controls of weapons of mass destruction, it seems most effective and less burdensome for exporters to impose a list control focusing on "choke-point technologies", namely, bottleneck technologies essential to the development and manufacturing of weapons of mass destruction, with the export to countries of concern targeted, rather than to try to control a broad range of commodities but list controlled items by catch-all/know controls. In the meantime, it is understood that, if most of the Western countries are to adopt catch-all/know controls following the changes in the international situation, Japan might be obliged to assume its international responsibility by introducing catch-all/know controls.

In implementing new export controls, it is naturally anticipated that loose controls may invite international criticism and excessively strict ones might make it more difficult for exporting companies to compete internationally.

Thus, it would be better for Japan to act in concert with the majority of advanced countries in the West in the areas of standards and operation of controls.

Particularly, with regard to catch-all/know controls, it is more difficult to internationally unify the method of operation of such controls than is the case for list-controls for the following reasons.

- without lists of controlled items, the range of application is unclear and subjective,

- there is inconsistency as to the controlled countries,

- the standard of operation is subjective.

Thus, it is important to harmonize in introducing catch-all/know controls.

(b) As for catch-all/know controls, only the US, UK and Germany are incorporating these controls into their domestic systems. Most countries are not practicing such controls. With catch all/know controls being imposed by US, U.K. and Germany, there exist problems described below.

US: catch-all/know controls are too broadly defined with almost everything covered. In introducing such controls, highly sophisticated intelligence is needed.

U.K.: Range of responsibilities exporters should take is quite wide as "Reason to know" is included.

Germany: Penalties and applications are severe even with conventional weapons controlled.

Thus, it is necessary to watch how this control system will be judged or reviewed.

(c) At present, introduction of catch-all/know controls based on the unified export control regulations is being studied by EU members. Once the study is completed, the EU's fifteen countries, including the U.K. and Germany, will have unified controls (some say that it will be completed at the end of 1994). Meanwhile, in the US a comprehensive review of export controls including catch-all/know controls is in progress, in line with the revision of the Export Administration Act (EAA) (scheduled in 1995 or 1996). As for Japan, it is better to harmonize with advanced nations of the West, while watching and confirming the trends and contents of the EU's unified regulations and the US's Export Administration Act potential revision. In case Japan is to implement export controls in its own way, it would be advisable to have well-balanced ones, taking into full account the trends of such regulations in the EU and US

(d) When implementation or review of catch-all/know controls by major advanced countries (including EU members) is completed, it will be recommendable to internationally unify controlled countries and commodities/technologies, controlling methods and guidelines as soon as possible.

(2) Requests on export controls in general

(a) It would be advisable to harmonize and simplify controls, by integrating each international review of nonproliferation controls and standardize the contents/level of control lists.

(b) Even if export controls are implemented by members of an international regime, the effectiveness of controls may be reduced, in terms of the items of low technological levels that could be available through non-members. Thus, coupled with the preparation of COCOM's core list, the preparation and review of lists should be carried out on the basis of preparation standards of control lists depicted below.

- Strategic use for weapons of mass destruction

- Availability of procurement from non-members

- Controllability of regime members

(c) With respect to nonproliferation controls, it might the most effective to impose controls focusing on choke-point technologies against countries of concern. It may be efficient to control entirely against a country, restricting the controlled items to choke-point technologies as a general rule (export would be permissible only when it is guaranteed that the item is for civil use).

(d) Regarding nonproliferation controls, controls would be less effective and a gap enlarged in economic activities among companies of each country, unless controlled countries are clarified and controls practiced by each country concerned.

(e) Japan, as the only "country controlling export of weaponry", should support more strongly the efforts to stop the proliferation of conventional weapons.

It would be advisable for Japan to conduct effective controls, having Russia and China participate.

(f) It would be advisable to establish an information center in each regime, through which information on refusal cases is accumulated. It is also recommendable to share the information among the administrative authorities concerned and to promote the; unification of operational standards. With respect to the international regimes, there should he no differences in the interpretation and operation of nonproliferation export controls among members.

(3) Requests concerning post-COCOM matters

(a) It would be necessary to list sensitive commodities/technologies with a high probability of being used for the development or manufacturing of weapons.

(b) As to the commodities to be included in more sensitive lists than the existing COCOM lists, Japan should request that listed items should be restricted to specific-purpose ones, taking into consideration foreign availability.

(4) Japan's export controls

Statutory controls such as catch-all/know controls are to be considered separately from voluntary control standards of companies for their internal use.

The request concerning statutory controls are as follows:

A. Controlled commodities

(a) Controlled commodities should be limited to dual use items for nuclear, chemical and biological weapons and their missiles as delivery systems, with conventional weapons excluded.

(b) Controlled commodities should be limited to those capable of directly being used for the development or manufacturing of weapons of mass destruction (excluding, however, items listed in the attached table of Export Trade Control Order), preparing positive lists, if possible.

As for the items contributing less to the development or manufacturing of weapons of mass destruction and uncontrollable items in terms of end user/end use in transactions (such as general-purpose, intermediate materials or ultimate products sold widely in the market), streamlining and efficiency of controls and tightening of the burden home by industries should be executed, by expanding the range of excluded items or taking measures of excluding such items under the actual control procedures.

(c) In order to clarify commodities to be controlled, commodities should be classified on the basis of US code of customs duty.

(d) Even if it is impossible to have positive lists as referred to in the lists of excluded items (commodities/technologies to be excluded without doubt) should be known.

(e) Exclusive rules as to commodities of small value shall be set up.

B. Controlled countries/areas

Controlled countries/areas should be restricted to those engaged in the development or manufacturing of weapons of mass destruction. Countries of no specific concern in terms of diversion should be excluded. Controlled countries of concern should be limited and lists of such countries should be shown. Taking into account the effectiveness of controls, the number of controlled countries should be limited to a minimum. In selecting controlled countries, reference should be made to those being uniformly controlled by the US, UK and Germany. It would be recommendable to unify the controlled countries (or areas) among nations practicing catch-all/know control in the future.

C. Requirements (Conditions)

In exporting a controlled commodity to a controlled destination (or ultimate destination), individual export license should be applied for, with reference to the following requirements.

(a) In cases where the item(s) are related to the development of weapons of mass destruction is the recipient country will be informed by the government.

(b) In case there is a "positive knowledge" that the item will be for the use relating to weapons of mass destruction.

The case of "have reason to know/suspect" should be excluded. There should be no obligation of "negative" proof that the item will not be for a use related to the development of weapons of mass destruction.

D. Introduction of bulk license system

Due to a wide variety of controlled items, catch-all/know controls seem to require a lot of work relating to export controls. Thus, this much burden should be averted by introducing bulk license system. Moreover, in introducing the bulk license system, application procedures, conditions for authorization, etc. should be simplified and conducted speedily so that exporters of small and medium size can utilize the system.

E. Clarification of definition, interpretation, etc.

As catch-all/know controls are subjective and have many ambiguous factors, it would be advisable, in effecting such controls, to wipe away exporters' anxieties about the way violation of Foreign Exchange and Foreign Trade Control Law is judged, by clarifying requirements and the scope of responsibilities (conditions for exemption).

In addition, it is recommended that the method of implementing the administrative controls should be less strict than initially planned.

F. Objective standard

In catch-all/know controls being implemented by several countries, there seem to be no examples of requiring "the contents of business done by ultimate user", in place of "know" requirement. Usually, if "the contents of business done by the ultimate user" are required, exporters are obliged to conduct a specific investigation, which is a great burden on them in exporting non-controlled items (except where such a requirement is really necessary). Thus, the objective standards should be limited to the following.

(a) As for end-users, what can be known in usual transactions should be acceptable. Considering the fact that in the US, "examination is to be conducted within the context of the usual transactions and no specific written oath or investigation required", exporters should not be too heavily burdened.

(b) Objective standards should be narrowly limited to the cases where there is a clear link between the contents of the business and weapons or mass destruction (definition of items related to weapons of mass destruction should be clarified).

Chapter 8

Export Controls and the U.S. Congress: New Issues, New Policies?

Glennon J. Harrison

Introduction

US dual-use export control policy has undergone a fundamental transformation in the years since the Berlin Wall came down in 1989.[1] The policy of containment, which provided the essential rationale for national security export controls,[2] has been superseded by a policy aimed at preventing the proliferation of weapons of mass destruction.[3] The Clinton Administration and many Members of Congress have called for the overhaul of US dual-use export control laws to take account of the changing international environment. Much of the postwar export control system is now in the process of being renegotiated: the Administration is negotiating with allies over the organization of a successor regime to replace the Coordinating Committee on Multilateral Export Controls (COCOM) and the Congress is considering legislation to re-authorize export controls.

Revision of dual-use export control legislation raises a number of problems for policy-makers. These problems cannot be readily grouped into distinct categories, nor can they be solved easily. With the end of the Cold War, nearly every aspect of export control policy has grown more complex. Instead of a policy based on denial of strategic technology exports to the Soviet Union, its allies, and other Communist countries (e.g., China, North Korea, Cuba), the United States and its allies now confront the threat of proliferation and a related series of lesser threats. Where general agreement on policy existed during the Cold War, people now differ on the best approach to non-proliferation and also differ somewhat on the priority non-proliferation should be given.

The fundamental issue that has arisen in the debate over EAA re-authorization, and one which the Clinton Administration has recognized, is how to liberalize export controls to expand exports and boost the economy, while effectively countering efforts by certain countries or groups to acquire weapons of mass destruction. Can export controls be effective in efforts against proliferation? What will be the economic impact in the United States of such a system? Will the economic impact fall disproportionately on US business? Will a COCOM successor regime rely on broad multilateral controls, or will each member exercise discretion in deciding which controlled goods may be exported?

The National Security/Economic Security Quandary

Businesses have frequently cited studies that show that export controls have a very significant negative impact on high-technology businesses, jobs, research and development and, ultimately, the wider economy. Recent studies have estimated the value of foregone exports at around $10 billion per year.[4] Businesses have long held that this constraint on exports reduces the ability of the United States to raise the level of exports (and thus the level of imports), and prevents US exporters from receiving the highest and best price for their goods in international markets. The loss of sales by high-technology firms, they argue, may have serious long-term consequences for some of the most dynamic firms in the United States. Furthermore, the extensive use of unilateral export controls (i.e., those that are unmatched by similar controls in other countries) would tend to increase the burden on US exporters without necessarily enhancing US security.

The removal of export controls would, in all likelihood, raise the level of trade (both exports and imports), although net exports would not necessarily change. The composition of trade would change to favor high technology exports. But if this change produces a net increase in the output of this sector, output in some other sector (possibly an export-competing sector) would decline as resources (capital or labor) are drawn away from it. A 1987 study of export controls by the National Academy of Sciences estimated the cost of export controls in terms of lost exports and lost jobs:

> A reasonable estimate of the direct, short-run economic costs to the U.S. economy associated with U.S. export controls was on the order of $9.3 billion in 1985. This is a very conservative estimate.... Associated just with lost U.S. exports was a reduction in U.S. employment of 188,000 jobs. If we were to calculate the overall impact on the aggregate U.S. economy of the value of lost export sales and the reduced R&D effort, the associated loss for the U.S. 1985 GNP would be $17.1 billion.[5]

Export controls lead to a lower level of exports (and a lower level of imports) than would otherwise obtain, and cause the composition of exports to shift away from the controlled goods to other goods. The terms of trade should be worse as a result of export controls (the same quantity of exports would buy fewer imports). While employment may be reduced by 188,000 jobs in the sector or sectors affected by export controls (this particular point is unclear in the NAS study), the shifting composition of exports would not change the level of real employment in the economy. In other words, absent a change in macroeconomic policy, it is unlikely that export controls could cause overall US employment to fall, although welfare might be reduced as a result of the overall costs imposed by export controls.

Some arms control analysts tend to minimize the impact of export controls by suggesting that only a tiny fraction of US GDP (4/10ths of 1 percent, or $23.7 billion of a $6 trillion economy) is subject to Department of Commerce licensing requirements. Furthermore, they argue that "only $790 million in applications were denied --which is *one hundredth of one 1 percent of the US economy* and less than half the cost of one B-2 bomber" (Emphasis in original).[6] It is likely that the $790 million in license denials represent only a small part of the total value of goods that were not sold because of export controls. But even additional high-technology exports contribute more to economic security than they cost in terms of national security. In the quotation above, Richardson somewhat mystically argued that "exports and export sectors often have special economic value beyond what the market registers." Investing exports and export sectors with "special economic value" is neither precise nor quantifiable. But it may be the crux of this particular problem.

Both "national security" and "economic security" have properties that cannot be reduced to numbers or values. In assessing them, each policy-maker brings a certain set of views, values, and definitions to each concept: some would always favor national security over economic security, while others might believe there is a balance that can be struck between them; a third group might believe that they are essentially identical; while a fourth would believe that declining economic security could only mean declining national security. The economic costs of export controls (plus the "special economic value" of exports) may not be insignificant, but such imprecise measures do little to advance the debate.

Rethinking Export Controls

In the post-Cold War world, it is not necessarily clear that the choice is *either* national security or economic security. There is no longer a single threat emanating from one country. A more reasonable approach to export controls might be to refocus the debate away from the numbers (which, in any case, do not allow a balanced assessment of the risks and rewards of export controls) and start thinking about what it is we want to achieve with export controls. This is fundamentally not an economic question. The objectives of an export control regime are primarily to promote the national security and foreign policy interests of the United States and its allies.

Peace-time controls on exports of dual-use items date back to 1940, when exports of steel scrap to Japan were prohibited. After World War II, export controls were continued on a year-to-year basis as an important component of US policy towards the Soviet Union and its 'satellites.' The Export Control Act of 1949 confirmed the policy of containment, providing the President with the authority to prohibit all commercial exports to the Soviet Union and the other Communist countries. The Congress authorized the President to control goods of both direct and indirect military utility.

The 1949 act authorized export controls for three purposes. First, to prevent domestic economic shortages, a serious concern after World War II. Second, to promote national security. And third, to promote US foreign policy.[8] Despite the evolution of export control policy during the Cold War, these three goals have been maintained in statute by the Congress and pursued by the various executive branch agencies charged with implementing the legislation.

During most of the Cold War period, national security controls have been the backbone of the export control system. The national security rationale for such controls was articulated by former Secretary of State Lawrence Eagleburger in a Foreign Affairs subcommittee hearing in September 1993:

> the rationale has been to reduce the military capabilities of the Soviet Union, its allies, and other Communist countries; to promote the intelligence gathering capabilities of the United States and its allies; and as part of the Western effort of waging economic warfare against the Soviet Union.[9]

To promote Western adherence to the system of national security export controls, the United States formed the Cooperating Committee on Multilateral Export Controls (COCOM) in 1949. The United States encouraged Western European country membership with a carrot-and-stick approach. Countries that joined would be eligible for Marshall Plan assistance to redevelop their war-shattered economies. The United States had such a wide technological lead over most other countries in the aftermath of World War II that refusal to join COCOM would almost certainly have made acquisition of many new technologies very difficult, if not impossible. The Western European countries' participation in the multilateral export control system may also have been promoted by the fact that the United States was mainly attempting to control goods that it alone produced. By 1950, the basic domestic and international institutional relationships were established, and the export control system that governs today was in place.

The export control system was reformed in 1969, 1979, and 1988 to reflect changes in US relations with the communist countries, and also to reflect the fact that the United States was no longer the sole source of technology or innovation. The 1988 legislation also reflected the emergence of developing countries as suppliers of high technology goods. These reforms liberalized export control policy, but they also demonstrated the limits of reform for the US and multilateral export control system. While detente was a factor in export control liberalization, the emergence of strong foreign competitors was a much stronger impetus. Export controls became much more contentious as Japan, the Western Europeans, and non-COCOM countries began producing dual-use goods that were only nominally under COCOM control.

The revolution in Eastern Europe and the collapse of the Soviet Union provided the backdrop for the three most recent attempts (during the 101st, 102d and 103d Congresses) to reform the export control system. These events raised serious questions about the export control system, which, with respect to the former Soviet Union, was -- and to some extent remains -- strategic in its purposes. While some observers believe that Russia or some of the other former Soviet republics continue to pose a threat to the United States and its allies, very few would agree that the residual threat is even remotely similar to the one posed by the USSR and its Warsaw Pact allies.

Refocusing Export Controls I: New and Old Threats

The end of the Cold War provides an opportunity to review export control policy and to consider whether the goals of that policy may have changed. Of the original justifications for US export control policy, national security and foreign policy continue to be sources of concern for policy-makers. The national security rationale appears to have changed significantly as a result of the breakup of the Soviet Union and the virtual end to the strategic threat that country once posed, but other threats (proliferation, terrorism, and regional conflicts) have the potential to affect US national and international security interests.[10]

Under the Export Administration Act of 1979, as amended, these other threats generally have been treated as foreign policy concerns. However, in the wake of the 1991 war with Iraq, many believe that the proliferation threat has come to pose one of the most serious threats to US national security. Indicators of the extent to which proliferation has become an overriding concern in the export control arena include the passage of numerous laws that have required successive Administrations to focus on the problem of proliferation, the gradual buildup of proliferation-oriented export control regimes,[11] the Bush Administration's Enhanced Proliferation Control Initiative (EPCI),[12] and the Clinton Administration's stated aim of countering proliferation through the use of export controls.[13]

The proliferation of weapons of mass destruction (and their delivery systems) is regularly identified as the main international security threat of the post-Cold War era. Concerns with proliferation suggest that the future dual-use export control system may be heavily weighted toward countering that threat. Such a reorientation of priorities would suggest significant revision of the statute authorizing dual-use export controls. For policy-makers, export control reform raises several questions about proliferation, including:

- What is the most effective way to stop proliferation?
- What is the role of export controls in preventing proliferation?
- Who will bear the costs of such a system?
- Are the costs of such a system warranted?
- Do the United States and its allies agree on nonproliferation goals?
- Are the US and its allies willing to create multilateral and complementary proliferation control systems?

Refocusing Export Controls II: Targets

Threats are one focus of a dual-use export control system. The ability of a system to deal effectively with threats is dependent on identifying and targeting the specific countries or groups that are the sources of the threats. The countries that are usually identified as high priority targets among US policy-makers for proliferation export controls include Iran, Iraq, Libya, and North Korea. But there are also other countries that are developing chemical and biological weapons, missiles, and/or nuclear weapons.

Countries that are identified in the Export Administration Regulations (15 CFR 778) special country list for nuclear non-proliferation include not only so-called rogue countries,[14] but also India, Pakistan, and Israel, among others. Countries identified as being of concern for chemical weapons proliferation include China, Bulgaria, the entire Middle East region, Russia and the other republics of the former Soviet Union, Taiwan, South Africa, and others. Missile technology projects are also identified for a number of countries: Brazil, China, India, Middle East, Pakistan, and South Africa, among others.

The question is: should the list of target countries include only the rogue nations, should there be some universal standards, or should all countries with proliferation objectives be identified as target countries? Should all countries so identified be subject to stringent end-use controls, or should exports be controlled on a more selective basis? Will a target strategy be effective, or will "friendly countries" with proliferation goals merely be antagonized?

The United States and its allies have occasionally disagreed about whether a particular country should be the target of proliferation export controls (e.g., the recent dispute between the United States and Germany over export control policy toward Iran). For countries like Pakistan or India, should controls focus narrowly on limiting sales of dual-use goods that may find their way into a project of concern?

The cases of Russia and China also raise questions. Some Members of Congress have warned that democratic reforms in Russia and some of the other nuclear-armed states may be reversible (although none have suggested the reemergence of a Soviet-type threat); others have suggested that the Russian military continues to demonstrate an interest in acquiring new or enhanced capabilities in nuclear and conventional areas. Of course, there are others who argue that to deny exports to civilian end users and uses can, at this point in Russia's transition to democracy, be economically destructive without enhancing US security. There is also the question of persuading Russia and the nuclear successor states of the former USSR to implement fully arms control treaties, as well as convincing other governments to adhere to non-proliferation regimes. The potential for diversion of weapons and technologies from Russia and the other former Soviet states presents a special challenge to non-proliferation policy. China is another country subject to national security and proliferation export controls. As with Russia, overly restrictive treatment could be counterproductive-- especially if China reacts by refusing to cooperate with multilateral export control regimes.

Such disagreements over export control targets have been a stumbling block to forging a common approach to export controls and have threatened to undermine nonproliferation objectives. The United States has frequently used unilateral controls while seeking multilateral agreement on the use of export controls against third countries. This strategy has been criticized by business and foreign governments alike as inflexible and counterproductive. Proponents of unilateral controls argue that abolishing their use would reduce the prospects of halting the flow of dual-use goods to proliferators and eliminate whatever leverage the US Government could hope to bring to bear in favor of strengthening multilateral export controls. Issues for US policy include:

• Should US and multilateral policies differentiate between so-called "rogue countries" and other countries that are pursuing programs aimed at developing weapons of mass destruction?

• What level of agreement is necessary among export control regime partners? Should the US and its allies be in substantial accord as to the export control measures to be taken toward countries with proliferation objectives?

• How much flexibility should participating members of non-proliferation regimes have with respect to the use of export controls against countries that have projects of concern?

• The United States and one or more of its allies cannot agree over whether a third country should be treated as a target (i.e., a known or suspected proliferator) for export controls, should the United States use unilateral controls? Should the use of such controls be restricted?

• What are the advantages and disadvantages of a "target" country approach to export controls?

Refocusing Export Controls III: Technologies

Technology is a third major focus of an export control system. The control of certain dual-use technologies to countries or end-users that pose a threat (whether of proliferation, terrorism, or regional stability) is a critical link in constructing an effective national or multilateral export control system. The focus of the US and multilateral export control systems has shifted from the strategic threat posed by the USSR to proliferation and other threats.[15]

The question for policy-makers is whether this shift requires a new approach to technology. If the intent of policy-makers is to deny access to technologies that could contribute materially to the proliferation of weapons of mass destruction, how broadly or narrowly focused should such controls be? If the intent is to prevent the acquisition weapons of mass destruction by target countries or end-users, how broadly or narrowly should proliferation technologies be defined?

If the purpose of non-proliferation export controls is to deny access to technologies that contribute to proliferation, should restrictions be directed mainly at groups of commodities or technologies that could make a direct contribution to the acquisition or use of a weapon of mass destruction? Or should controls also target products that are of direct military use or that may enhance military capabilities, such as a modem telecommunications systems, high-speed computers, sophisticated machine tools, or other products that contribute directly or indirectly to such weapons programs? Some argue that controls should cover any product where an end-use is related to proliferation. In this context, controls would be broader, extending to commonly available goods that do not usually require a validated license, such as pencils, calculators, or other items that pose no direct proliferation risk. The question here is: what are the objectives of export controls and what is the likelihood that such controls can be successfully implemented?

The ability of the United States to generate multilateral support for controls on exports of proliferation-related technologies to specified target countries, which pose a proliferation threat, may be directly related to how widely or narrowly tailored such controls are. Partner - country support for export controls ranges from support for controls on technologies that contribute directly and materially to proliferation to support for controls on any or all goods that might find their way to a proliferator country or end-user.

Tensions within multilateral export control regimes can arise from legitimate differences over how to define a particular threat, or whether exports should be controlled to a country with a project that poses a potential proliferation threat (i.e., should the country be identified as a target for export controls?), or which technologies should be controlled. During the Cold War, the determination of what constituted a strategic threat, a target, or a technology of concern was not subject to the discretion of individual COCOM member-countries.

But post-Cold War threats, targets, and technologies appear to be different -- if only because countries that belong to nonproliferation regimes appear to be unwilling to assign their decision-making powers to such regimes, or allow one or more other members of such a regime to exercise a veto over national (export) decisions. The participants in proliferation regimes have demanded that licensing decisions be left largely to the discretion of *national* licensing authorities.

If the post-Cold War regimes are indeed different, and national discretion does seem to represent a significant break with past practice, then US policy-makers may find that it is difficult to impose (or achieve) multilaterally agreed export controls over a wide (as opposed to a limited) range of technologies, or to achieve unanimous agreement as to who is a target for the imposition of export controls. Although the dangers of proliferation are well understood, multilateral regime members may not be able to agree as to the source of the threat or how best to address the threat. If preventing the proliferation of unconventional weapons is a primary goal of export controls, the selection of technologies to be controlled also poses major challenges because of the rapid pace of technological change. Another problem is that many proliferation-related technologies are low-level and static. In developing an export control system, one of the most important elements to consider is how best to match technologies to threats and targets.

Approaches to Export Controls: Multilateralism

The success or failure of proliferation controls is an issue of great importance to the Clinton Administration and to many Members of Congress. It is a concern because a failure of such controls could, in the extreme, be catastrophic. A lesser failure might take the form of an inability to agree on effective international controls, which might tend to undermine efforts to build regimes capable of countering proliferation. Some Members of Congress have expressed the concern that a failure to make the transition from an effective, strategic export control regime (COCOM) to a post-Cold War regime (or regimes) that is equally effective may harm US security and US exporters.

The transition from a system primarily designed to deny strategic exports to the USSR and its allies to one designed to deny exports to countries seeking to acquire goods or technologies that could contribute to weapons proliferation has not been smooth. The rapid demise of COCOM and the failure of COCOM members to agree on a replacement regime has fueled concerns about security, as well as giving rise to fears among exporters that the application of US controls could be more stringent than those applied by foreign governments. COCOM, for all intents and purposes, went out of business on March 31, 1994.

In addition to COCOM, several regimes already exist to control exports of proliferation-related goods and technologies, although none of these require unanimous approval for exports of concern. The nonproliferation regimes include the Missile Technology Control Regime (MTCR), the Nuclear Suppliers Group (NSG), the Australia Group (chemical and biological weapons), and the Supercomputer Regime. They work on the basis of national discretion, rather than consensus. Consensus exists in such regimes only in the context of modalities and procedures, but not for license processing. National discretion means that national export control authorities make licensing decisions without the prior approval of other regime members. There is no prior approval of licenses and no requirement that license approvals be shared with other member countries after the fact. Only license disapprovals are shared, and these provide regime members with an important source of information for processing license applications.

National discretion decisionmaking differs significantly from decision-making under the COCOM regime, which required a review of license applications by all member countries and allowed a one-country veto. Two of the non-proliferation regimes, the Nuclear Suppliers Group and the Australia Group have no undercut policies. No undercutting means that if one member country denies a license and notifies the regime, other countries agree not to sell the product to that customer either.

The elimination of COCOM and the possibility of its replacement by another regime raises a number of interesting possibilities and potential problems for the United States. The successor regime to COCOM will be significantly different than COCOM in terms of its purpose, membership, and operating rules. The East-West (strategic) orientation of the regime will be dropped, Russia may be a founding member of the new organization, and national discretion will likely be the basis for decisionmaking. The new regime will probably not replace or otherwise affect any of the existing non-proliferation regimes, although it is likely that membership in the COCOM-successor regime will require membership in the other non-proliferation regimes.

A successor regime to COCOM -- if agreed to -- is unlikely to have license processing policies similar to the consensus process used by COCOM. That process required countries to submit license applications to COCOM for approval. Any single country could veto an application, and many of the COCOM partner countries accused the United States of abuse of process in its willingness to exercise its veto. The failure to achieve a successor regime comparable to COCOM, or to get the nonproliferation export control regimes to adopt COCOM-like procedures, is viewed by some as the penalty the United States is now paying for forty-plus years of COCOM -- a regime that is now widely credited as being an effective tool against the Soviet Union.

With respect to the threats, targets and technologies discussed above, harmonizing the use of national discretion in licensing and enforcement, as suggested by Bertsch and Cupitt,[16] may be an effective means for regime members to promote non-proliferation, reduce regime friction, and level the playing field for exporters without increasing the risk of proliferation. For such harmonization to occur, however, widespread agreement must be reached on threats, targets, and technologies. To take one example, if one country believes Iran is a threat but other countries believe that it is not, or that the proposed controls go too far, then the system will probably work badly or even fail. Even if there is complete agreement about which countries are valid targets, there may be no agreement as to the goods and technology to be controlled.

An export control system that does not prevent target countries (including rogue states as well as other countries with ambitions to possess weapons of mass destruction) from acquiring dual-use goods or technology will undoubtedly be called ineffective, despite the fact that export controls are among several types of instruments that might be used to curb proliferation. Reliance on export controls alone cannot guarantee that proliferation will not occur. The United States may have to combine export controls with other foreign policy initiatives to achieve non-proliferation goals. The focus of export control regimes appears to be shifting from curbing proliferation to preventing the use of weapons of mass destruction. Where such weapons have spread, curbing the behavior of target countries is, for many policy-makers, a desirable goal of export control policy. Will export control policy again become a cornerstone of a wider strategy of containment (in this case of rogue regimes)?

Approaches to Export Controls: Unilateral Controls

Unilateral controls have been an important element of US export control policy since the passage of the Export Control Act of 1949. The continued use of unilateral controls in the post-Cold War period is a major sore-point for many exporters, who complain that unilateral controls place them at a competitive disadvantage and achieve little more than to display US disapproval. Many Members of Congress have also expressed similar concerns about the continued use of such controls. Proponents of unilateral controls argue that such controls may be warranted even if other countries disagree, and that other countries will, as in the past, never adopt similar controls if the United States does not take the lead. Unilateral controls have been imposed for reasons of national security and foreign policy (including proliferation, international terrorism, regional instability, and human rights).

Non-Proliferation And High Technology Exports

The fundamental issue that will arise in the debate over export control re-authorization is how to liberalize controls to achieve economic objectives while furthering non-proliferation goals. Advocates of strong non-proliferation export controls have argued that denial of exports provides leverage to induce countries to cooperate with export control regimes, while liberalization (whether of control lists, foreign availability, sanctions, or control regimes) tends to reduce the effectiveness of such regimes. Additionally, the use of unilateral controls may be the only hope for keeping pressure on other regime members to adopt such controls. Membership in regimes becomes less meaningful, they argue, when the benefits of membership are granted to countries that "adhere" or "cooperate," but who do not belong. The result is that the goal of stopping proliferation will rapidly be eclipsed by another goal: preventing the use of nuclear and other weapons of mass destruction. Thus, non-proliferation advocates insist that a "target country" approach that denies exports primarily to a few rogue regimes will likely fail, and fail with disastrous consequences.

Advocates of export control liberalization suggest that multilateral controls that target specific countries and technologies provide the best chance to halt or slow the spread of unconventional weapons. Controls that are maintained unilaterally by the United States cannot be effective, they argue, unless they are promptly adopted by multilateral regimes. In addition to not promoting non-proliferation objectives, unilateral controls disadvantage US exporters. Liberalization, coupled with greater multilateralism, is viewed by business and other advocates of liberalization as the carrot that will attract new members to multilateral control regimes.

Ultimately, the debate over the re-authorization of dual-use export controls will probably turn on the issue of non-proliferation. The cost of export controls is an obvious factor in the debate, but the decision on how and to what extent to liberalize may require careful consideration of non-quantitative factors.

Notes

1. Dual-use exports are goods or technology that are essentially commercial in nature, but which may also have military uses.

2. In this report, 'national security' export controls refer specifically to controls imposed under section 5 of the Export Administration Act of 1979, as amended. Controls under that section are intended primarily to prevent exports of strategic goods to Communist countries.

3. For a discussion of the shift from containment to prevention of weapons proliferation, see: Gary K. Bertsch and Richard T. Cupitt, "Nonproliferation in the 1990s: Enhancing International Cooperation on Export Controls." *The Washington Quarterly* Vol. 16, no. 4 (Autumn 1993), pp. 53-70; Brad Roberts, "From Nonproliferation to Antiproliferation," *International Security* Vol. 18, no.1 (Summer 1993), pp. 139-173; Aaron Karp, "Controlling Weapons Proliferation: The Role of Export Controls," *Journal of Strategic Studies* Vol. 16 (March 1993), pp. 17-45.

4. Studies by J. David Richardson, the National Academy of Sciences, the Competitiveness Council, the Center for Strategic and International Studies, and the Trade Policy Coordinating Committee have either generated or disseminated estimates of the costs of export controls. See Trade Policy Coordinating Committee, *Toward a National Export Strategy* (Washington, DC: U. S. Govt. Printing Office, September 30, 1993); National Academy of Sciences. *Balancing the National Interest* (Washington, DC: National Academy Press, 1987); J. David Richardson. *Sizing Up U.S. Export Disincentives* (Washington, DC: Institute for International Economics, 1993); Council on Competitiveness. *Economic Security: The Dollar$ and Sense of U.S. Foreign Policy* (Washington, DC.: Center for Strategic and International Studies, February 1994). *Breaking Down the Barricades: Reforming U.S. Export Controls to Increase U.S. Competitiveness* (Washington, DC: CSIS, 1994).

5. *Balancing the National Interest*, p. 264. The annual job loss figure of 188,340 was based on a ratio of 25,800 jobs per $1 billion of lost exports. The direct export loss associated with U.S. export controls was found to be $7.3 billion. p. 275. The source of the NAS estimate is: Davis, Lester A. "Contribution of Exports to U.S. Employment" in *Trade Performance in 1985 and Outlook*, pp. 92-94.

6. Wisconsin Project on Nuclear Arms Control. *25 Myths about Export Control.* March 1994. 1 Op.
7. Richardson, pp. 125-126.

8. The goal of nuclear non-proliferation has been a long-standing objective of U.S. policy. Nuclear export controls, which date back to the Atomic Energy Act of 1946, the Atomic Energy Act of 1954, and the Nuclear Non-Proliferation Act of 1978, were distinct from the containment policies of the Cold War. Nuclear non-proliferation controls have a basis in the Nuclear Non-Proliferation Treaty. Treaties also provide a basis for chemical weapons and biological weapons controls. There is no international treaty on missile nonproliferation.

9. Testimony of Lawrence Eagleburger before the Subcommittee on Economic Policy, Trade and the Environment of the Committee on Foreign Affairs, September 22, 1993.

10. There are continuing concerns with Russia and the other former Soviet republics that retain a nuclear capability (Ukraine, Belarus, and Kazakhstan), and there are concerns about acquisition of sensitive goods and technology by the Russian military.

11. Non-proliferation regimes include the Nuclear Suppliers Group (NSG), the Missile Technology Control Regime (MTCR), the Australia Group, and a U.S.-Japan agreement to control supercomputer exports. Although these regimes pre-date the Gulf War, the non-proliferation issue loomed much larger as the Soviet Union dissolved and International Atomic Energy Agency inspectors began to investigate Iraq's nuclear program.

12. The EPCI was announced in 1990 after President Bush pocket-vetoed the Export Administration re-authorization bill, which included export control provisions and sanctions for violators. The EPCI has been implemented through a series of regulations that have, in the absence of legislation, gradually refashioned the U.S. export control system.

13. In numerous speeches, President Clinton and other officials of his Administration have discussed the dangers posed by proliferation of weapons of mass destruction and efforts being made to prevent proliferation. See, for instance: The White House. Office of the Press Secretary. Address by the President to the 48th Session of the United Nations General Assembly. September 27, 1993. The United Nations. New York, New York; The White House. Office of the Press Secretary. Remarks by the President to a multinational audience of future leaders of Europe, Gothic Room, Hotel De Ville. Brussels, Belgium, January 9, 1994; and the Trade Promotion Coordinating Committee. *Toward a National Export Strategy.* Report to the Congress, September 30, 1993. p. 54.

14. However, North Korea, which is usually identified as a rogue nation, is not

included on the special country list for nuclear non-proliferation.

15. Notwithstanding the general shift in policy, the focus of nuclear controls has always been nonproliferation.

16. Bertsch and Cupitt, *Washington Quarterly*, vol. 16:4, 1993, pp. 60-61.

Chapter 9

The Reform of Export Controls in the Post-Cold War Era

Thomas J. Schoenbaum

As the United States considers establishing a new export control regime, the familiar tension exists between the view that export controls place American industry at a disadvantage and the idea that security and strategic imperatives must prevail over commercial considerations. The purpose of this paper is to explore the impact export controls in the Post-Cold War world and to propose principles that may point the way toward a solution.

To set the stage, it is necessary to review the present export control system.

U.S. Export Controls

The principal export control regime under current U.S. law is, of course, the Export Administration Act (EAA), U.S.C. App. §2401 et seq. Export controls are generally divided into three categories: national security, foreign policy, and short supply controls.

Under current law, the U.S. controls exports through the use of licenses. In the United States, there is neither a constitutional nor a statutory right to export goods. The EAA targets both countries and products for controls. The Commerce Department maintains a list for this purpose designated as the Commerce Control List (CCL). The Bureau of Export Administration within Commerce implements United States export licensing requirements for commercial goods and technology; interagency cooperation is carried out with the Department of Defense and the Department of State. Since 1950, the U.S. has also coordinated its export controls with fifteen NATO allies through a "Coordinating Committee" based in Paris, commonly known as COCOM.

An exporter is required to have either a general license or a validated license before exporting a particular good. There are over twenty categories of general licenses and four main types of validated licenses. General licenses are self-certified by the exporter and no application is necessary. A validated license requires application; the exporter must receive a validated license before exporting the product. There is also a special license which is issued to cover a range of exportations by a particular exporter. The process of applying for an export license requires the following steps:

1. Looking up the Export Commodity Control Number. This determines what kind of license is required.

2. Filing the application, if necessary.

3. Preliminary Review of the Application by the Office of Export Licensing.

4. Final Review of the Export Commodity Control Number, the Country of Destination; the Users of the Product, the End-Use of the Product.

5. Referral to other agencies.

6. COCOM review.

7. Foreign Availability Determination.

There is a very limited appeal of a denial of a license. An affected party may appeal to the Assistant Secretary for Export Administration

Figure 9.1:

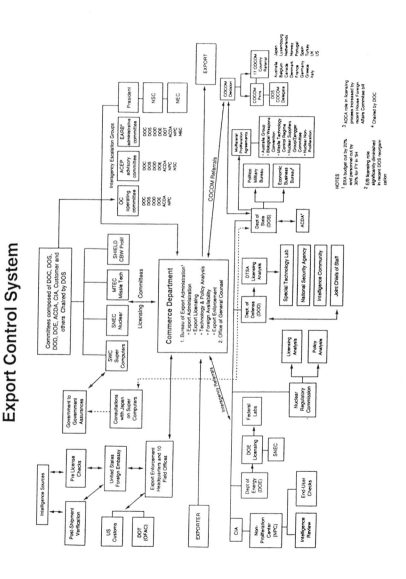

for reconsideration (15 CFR §789.2). An appeal may also be made to an administrative law judge, but only to determine whether the item is in fact on the control list (EAA §12). There is no judicial review.

Export Control Reforms

In the post-Cold War period, there have been calls for relaxation of export controls by American industry. The National Association of Manufacturers (NAM) conducted a survey in 1992 resulting in a finding that $15 to $20 billion in lost exports each year can be attributed to export controls.[1] Up to fifty percent (by value) of US exports is subject to export control approval.

Two important changes in export controls have already occurred. First, in response to the momentous changes in Eastern Europe and the breakup of the Soviet Union, COCOM overhauled the International Industrial List (IIL) and developed a new "core list" of dual-use controlled items. Thirty items were removed from the IIL, especially in three areas: computers, machine tools, and telecommunications.

The US responded to this initiative by removing twenty-two of the thirty items from the Commerce Control List (CCL). In August of 1991, the US published a revised and greatly liberalized CCL. However, the changes do not go far enough to suit many US companies who still contend export controls unnecessarily restrict the export of civilian high technology.

Moreover, the system of multilateral cooperation to control exports is breaking apart, creating more concern among US companies. The NATO allies agreed to dismantle COCOM by March 31, 1994. Negotiations to replace COCOM by a new weapons-related export control organization have proved difficult.

A second important development in the post-Cold War period is renewed emphasis on export controls over items that are potentially useful in the manufacture of weapons of mass destruction. With the demise of the bi-polar world dominated by the US and the Soviet Union, there is particular need to control the spread of nuclear, chemical, and biological weapons, as well as missile delivery systems.

President George Bush began this new emphasis on nonproliferation export controls by issuing Executive Order No. 12735 on November 16, 1990, which established the so-called Enhanced Proliferation Control Initiative (EPCI) to impose:

1. controls on items useful in chemical and biological, weapons manufacture;

2. controls on exports of chemical facilities;

3. controls on exports when a US export knows or has "reason to know" that a proposed export is for proscribed activities; and

4. restrictions on activities of US persons who knowingly assist in proscribed activities.

In addition, the Export Administration Act was amended in 1990 to add export controls on items useful for missile delivery systems. In December 1991, the President signed the Chemical and Biological Warfare Elimination Act of 1991, 50 U. S.C. App. § 2401 et seq., which provides additional sanctions and export controls on chemical and biological warfare items.

As a result of these US initiatives, the CCL identifies certain goods, software, and technical data as being elements of missile technology or nuclear, chemical, or biological weapons, including a number of "dual-use" items. For the most part, these controls are a unilateral effort by the US, but they are coordinated internationally with various multilateral groups, such as the Missile Technology Control Regime (MTCR), the Australia Group, and the Nuclear Suppliers Group.

Potential Problems

There is an urgent need both to overhaul the existing US export control regime and to establish a viable multilateral successor to COCOM to deal with post-Cold War problems of the proliferation of weapons of mass destruction. A new multilateral export control regime should be established that does not place a disproportionate competitiveness burden on US exporters, who should not have to contend with restrictions greater than are placed on companies from other industrialized nations. Thus the United States re-authorization of the EAA should de-emphasize unilateral controls and initiatives in favor of reflecting multilateral agreement on a new export control regime. International agreement on export controls should also minimize the potential extraterritorial application of the US EAA, which posed so many problems in the early 1980s.

The new EAA should have the following features:

1. The establishment of a new international successor to COCOM, which should include China and Russia as well as NATO and OECD countries;

2. A simple control list identifying critical technologies as well as countries and end-users of concern;

3. The monitoring of conventional weapons exports;

4. Harmonized export licensing procedures;

5. Transparency, including the application of the Administrative Procedure Act and judicial review.

Finally, nonproliferation of weapons of mass destruction should be addressed not only by the use of export controls, but also by other governmental initiatives, such as restrictions on imports, denial of airport landing rights, prohibitions on government loans and financial assistance, and various diplomatic means.

Appendix 9.1: The Export Administration Act Of 1995 (Administration Proposal)

In drafting its proposal to re-authorize the Export Administration Act, the Clinton Administration has six key objectives:

1) Encourage more effective multilateral regimes;

2) Increase discipline on unilateral controls;

3) Improve our ability to deal with nonproliferation;

4) Simplify and streamline the export control system;

5) Increase transparency in the process;

6) Strengthen enforcement.

Encourage More Effective Multilateral Regimes

• Remove Cold War distinction between national security and foreign policy controls and focus on new control regimes.

• Provide a clear preference for multilateral controls over unilateral controls.

• Encourage multilateral control regimes to adopt Common Standards of Effectiveness, such as agreements on uniform lists of controlled items and aggressive enforcement programs, in order to promote " effectiveness."

Increase Discipline in Unilateral Controls

• Enhance the analysis and reporting required before the imposition or extension of unilateral controls, including a requirement that, among other things, the

• Ensure that economic interests are considered.

• Maintain the contract sanctity provision of current law.

Improve Our Ability To Deal With Nonproliferation

• Provide nonproliferation as a distinct basis for controls, and encourage other countries to develop the same objectives.

• Provide incentives for countries to join nonproliferation regimes.

Simplify and Streamline The Export Control System

• Ensure that all licensing decisions will be made within 90 days even if escalated to the President, with the vast majority decided at lower levels in less time.

• Establish a clear "default to decision" process run by the Commerce Department for licensing decisions at the working level.

• Specify the interagency dispute resolution process for cases that go to the political level, which is chaired by the Commerce Department. Cases may be escalated to the President if necessary.

• Require clearer and more complete statements of the reasons why controls are imposed.

• Create a more accessible and balanced process for determining whether items should be on the Munitions List or the Commodity Control List by maintaining the State Department's leadership in dispute resolution but including defined roles for Commerce and other agencies.

Increase Transparency in the Licensing Process

• Give industry broader new rights to petition for the elimination of controls when they have an "unfair impact," defined to include foreign availability, as well as other factors that place US companies at a competitive disadvantage.

• Provide a clear process and time frame for determining whether relief is appropriate.

• Add the concept of forward-looking foreign availability, so that evaluations are not limited to current market availability but can consider prospective conditions, so American businesses can stay ahead of demand rather than behind it.

Strengthen Enforcement

• Codify appropriate provisions of the Commerce-Customs Memorandum Of Understanding on the division of enforcement authorities agreed to in 1993.

• Increase penalties and enhance enforcement authority

• Provide authority for forfeitures and undercover operations.

• Change the standard for issuance of a temporary denial order to "reasonable cause" when Commerce believes that there is probable cause to do so.

Notes

1. International Trade in Arms Regulations, Jan. 26, 1994, Vol. 11, p. 152

Chapter 10

From Containment To Counter-Proliferation: US Export Control Policy In The Post-Cold War

Richard T. Cupitt

Introduction

In 1984, the National Academy of Sciences (NAS) created a panel to study US export controls, in order "to achieve a desirable balance among the national objectives of military security, economic vitality, and scientific and technological advance."[1] In narrowing their focus the panel chose to examine only national security controls on dual-use exports, that is, US and COCOM controls on goods to communist states.

In a follow-on study mandated by the 1988 Omnibus Trade and Competitiveness Act, a new NAS panel chose to examine "all aspects of the US national security export regime."[2] They did so because the nature of the threat and the balance of interests relevant to US export control policy had changed fundamentally. No longer did the study focus on the costs and benefits of restricting trade with the Soviet Union and its allies. The panel recommended that US export controls, while still constraining the Soviet military threat:

• encourage, or not impede, stable political, and military reform in the Soviet Union Europe; and
• refocus US and multilateral efforts on controlling the proliferation of missile, nuclear, chemical, and biological weapons.[3]

As much as any other foreign policy, US export controls on dual-use items (goods, technologies, and services with primarily commercial uses that also have military applications) reflects the profound changes in the definition of US national security interests. Where conflict predominated, cooperation flourishes. Where neglect and lethargy reigned, interest and energy rule. These changes represent no less than a fundamental re-conception of US national security policy, unlike any in over four decades.

This reformation breeds tremendous uncertainty among policy makers and industry leaders alike. In a recent survey of forty-two companies with extensive export control experience prepared by the National Association of Manufacturers (NAM), business executives identified licensing delays and uncertainty as their most important problems, regarding export controls.[4] The NAM found that industry concerns over export controls increased in recent years, as export controls have became more complex and their future more uncertain.

The global economic and military capabilities of the United States make it the only superpower in the world. Its array of military and dual-use items and its overall economic, military, and political resources means that however US export controls on dual-use items develop, these decisions will affect the shape of international affairs in the next century.

Export controls on dual-use items also have a significant impact on the United States. The NAS reported that national security export controls affected forty percent of all US exports of manufactured items, not including arms, in 1985 at a cost of $9.3 billion.[5] In the NAM survey, on average, the companies had twenty-four employees working in their export control program at an average annual cost of $1.3 million.[6] Most recently, J. David Richardson found that export controls were the largest disincentive to US exports.[7]

Will the US continue to liberalize controls on exports to post-communist states? Will the US continue to harmonize its controls with those of Japan and the members of the European Union (EU)? Will the US tighten controls on dual-use items exported to developing countries with projects and policies that potentially threaten US interests? How will US policy makers balance its economic and security interests?

In this chapter the author examines recent efforts to reformulate US export control policy. The conclusion will make a preliminary recommendation about the need for better decision criteria to shape and evaluate policy.

Crafting Export Control Policy in Uncertain Times

Congress began to hold hearings in anticipation of re-authorizing the Export Administration Act in early 1990. In a somewhat surprising development, former Assistant Secretary of Defense Richard Perle, the guiding force behind much of the effort to tighten export controls in the 1980s, testified in January in favor of relaxing controls on high-tech exports to Eastern Europe.[8] In February, officials from Commerce, Defense, and State told the House Foreign Affairs International Economic Subcommittee, then chaired by Sam Gejdenson (D-CT), that controls on exports to Eastern Europe, even the Soviet Union, should be eased.[9]

Emblematic of this shift was the agreement that controls on personal computers, including 80386 machines should be decontrolled. Export controls on telecommunications equipment and computers were widely seen by US industry as damaging US economic competitiveness. Though controls on telecommunications items, particularly fiber-optics equipment, would remain controversial, decontrolling many computer exports was both a symbolic and substantive policy transformation.

Gejdenson, who took the lead on export control issues in the House, found an unusual degree of bipartisan support for his bill, the Export Facilitation Act. The Act would have: created a license free zone among COCOM and 5(k) countries; required an indexing provision that would remove restrictions from items as technology threshold increased; liberalized controls on exports to Eastern Europe and reduced sharply the number of dual-use items subject to controls (including telecommunications items); made Commerce responsible for all controlled items other than those specifically military in nature, which State would continue to oversee, and given Commerce representation at COCOM; and placed a sunset provision on restrictions on dual-use exports to countries other than the Soviet Union and its allies unless Commerce, in consultation with Defense, explicitly justified their retention.[10] By May 1990, the act had won approval from the full House Foreign Affairs Committee, such that the "markup was remarkable chiefly for its brevity and the lack of objection from committee conservatives."[11] By June the bill won House approval by majorities of both parties, despite opposition from the Bush administration.

In the Senate, the Banking Subcommittee on International Finance and Monetary Policy, then chaired by Paul Sarbannes (D-MD) held oversight hearings in March 1990, where administration officials reemphasized the new direction in US policy. A bill came out of committee in July, followed by approval on the Senate floor in September 1990. By that time, the invasion of Kuwait fully-alerted members of Congress to the, dangers of proliferation. Consequently, in addition to calling for sanctions on Kuwait, the Senate version included tough provisions on the transfer of missile, chemical, and biological items. This included mandatory sanctions on persons that knowingly contribute to chemical or biological weapons programs and countries that use such weapons, introduced by Senator Jesse Helms (R-NC) and Claiborne Pell (D-RI). In October of 1990, the conference report on the Export Administration Act passed both houses of Congress.

In the meantime, the administration had already moved beyond many of the provisions of the legislation. In COCOM, for example, US proposals helped spur immediate reductions in the Industrial List in June 1990 and shaped the narrower focus of the Core List. Some of these changes were already part of the Export Administration Regulations (EAR) before the re-authorization bill left the Senate floor.

Nonetheless, President Bush chose not to sign the re-authorization bill, using a pocket veto.[12] According to the veto message, President Bush opposed the mandatory sanctions imposed under the chemical and biological provisions of the bill. In the same message, under the authority in the International Emergency Economic Powers Act, the President ordered implementation of many of the provisions of the bill. In December President Bush revealed six specific measures to strengthen proliferation controls under the rubric the Enhanced Proliferation Control Initiative (EPCI).

Overall, the Bush administration substantially revised US export control policy in 1991. The newly renamed Commerce Control List (CCL), was streamlined and came to incorporate the COCOM Core List. The Nuclear Referral List (NRL) was revised considerably (twenty-five deletions, twenty-three additions, and twenty-six revisions leaving a list of seventy-nine items).[13] Many reexport controls on shipments to COCOM and 5(k) destinations were removed. Jurisdictional disputes between Commerce and State regarding the CCL and the US Munitions

List were resolved (without undermining the reductions in the CCL by expanding the Munitions List). Finally, industry representation in the Technical Advisory Committees (TACs) nearly doubled.

Besides these revisions in the management of export controls, the direction of US policy changed in six crucial ways:

- proliferation threats acquired at least equal status with the strategic threat posed by the former Soviet Union;
- supporting economic and political reform in post-communist states (and even some communist states) became an objective of export control policy;
- though not a prerequisite, achieving multilateral cooperation became a condition for tightening or extending US controls;
- more importance was placed on cooperating with communist and post-communist states on proliferation export controls;
- increasing safeguards of commercial exports against diversion to military end-use or end-users became as important as proscribing entire categories of items to proscribed countries; and
- instituting a "know" standard, where persons who knowingly export or otherwise contribute to a for a proscribed end-use or a proscribed under are subject to sanction.

Congress continued to lag behind actions by the executive branch. New measures to re-authorize the Export Administration Act languished in the House well into 1995. After resolving controversies over controls on telecommunications items and mass-market software and with a last minute agreement to remove a provision on mandatory sanctions on countries that did not abide by strict safeguards, for example, House and Senate conferees were able to craft a bill in September of 1992. The House leadership, however, choose not to bring the conference report up for a floor vote, ending the chances for re-authorization until the next session, when little progress was made in building a new legislative consensus.

Developing a New Model of US Export Control Policy Formation

Uncertainty over export control policy can inhibit the efforts of United States business and work to the detriment of the overall attempt to improve the trade balance of the United States.[14] High levels of policy uncertainty may be the norm for periods of global political transition, as decision makers struggle to adapt and create new policy tools for their new environment. When a large number of new countries emerge on the political scene, each must discover their own national interests and their place in the globe. Sufficient confusion now exists at the international level that governments need to minimize uncertainty on the domestic policy making level.

Since 1989, US export control policy has been in the early stages of melding two distinct policy communities --- the national security export control community and the nonproliferation community. These communities not only have different, even contradictory, points of view in some issue areas, their terms of reference are very different. Mixing the political assessments of nonproliferation and arms control issues with the technical aspects of export controls has been difficult. A policy making model for the next century is needed, and few in the US government have the time, energy or inclination to prepare it. What will the arms control community do, with lots of resources, as the US-Soviet rivalry fades into memory? What does the national security export control community do, with its expertise and relatively small budgets, as post-communist states become integrated into export control arrangements?

One of the most consistent complaints about US export control policy is that the bureaucratic arrangements are too complex and ill-suited to balancing various national interests. Numerous departments or offices are directly involved in licensing dual-use items, under the auspices of at least six major pieces of legislation, including the Export Administration Act, the Arms Export Control Act, the Atomic Energy Act, the Nuclear Non-Proliferation Act, the Trading with the Enemy Act, and the International Emergency Economic Powers Act.[15]

Even within departments, responsibilities for export controls may be fragmented. In late 1992, the Central Intelligence Agency moved to create the Center for Non-Proliferation, consolidating and re-targeting some of its resources previously aimed at the Soviet Union to focus on proliferation of weapons of mass destruction. At Defense and State, however, plans for reorganization were considered, though the transition to the Clinton administration slowed their formulation and implementation.

In early 1993, for example, officials at the Department of State struggled to revamp the disparate bureaucratic paths taken in export control policy: COCOM affairs controlled by the Bureau of Economic and Business Affairs (EB); Nuclear controls in the Bureau of Oceans,

Environment and Science (OES); controls on missile, chemical, and biological weapons, foreign policy controls, munitions controls in the Bureau of Politico-Military Affairs (PM). By 1995, Secretary of State Christopher united these functions in PM. Reportedly, this approach met opposition from inside the department, where experienced officials feared they would be cut off from the policy making process and that PM might grow into an unwieldy mess, as well as opposition in industry circles, where executives fear that PM will not represent commercial interests sufficiently in its decision making process.[16]

Coordinating the bureaucratic jumble has proven difficult in practice, in no small part because State faces so many policy requirements. Export to Iran, for example, may run afoul of general foreign policy considerations, specific foreign policy concerns regarding missiles, chemical, and biological items, munitions controls, nuclear controls, and COCOM controls (for diversion risks). While the BXA must handle many of these issues, it has more resources devoted to export controls and does not have to implement the International Trade in Arms Regulations (ITAR), where the number of license applications now double that going to BXA.

At Defense, plans were also made to redesign its approach to export controls. Ashton Carter was appointed Assistant Secretary for Strategic Security and Counter Proliferation.[17] The new organization consists of about 150 people working in the Pentagon. The organization has four groups:

- a group to manage the multilateral regimes and related the international agreements (including perhaps two dozen bilateral);
- a group to review all forms of export controls, including controls on munitions and dual-use items;
- a group to provide analytic support, including some independent policy research that links international conflicts with export control policies;
- and technology group that would not only consider technological aspects of licensing, but also about when technology matters, such as the relationship to military doctrine and training.

Under the old arrangement, the Defense Trade Security Agency, which has expertise in reviewing export controls, was separated from the Office of Non-Proliferation Policy. Officials in the Department felt the need to address proliferation threats more seriously, without losing sight of the strategic and proliferation threat still posed by Russia. Consolidating DTSA with the Office of Non-Proliferation Policy might achieve this objective.

Some defense officials hoped that reorganization would strengthen the voice of Defense in export controls. In particular, reorganization could make it easier for Defense political appointees to make trade-offs in interagency decisions. It also might get proliferation concerns treated as a national security matter rather than a foreign policy issue (which would give Defense a greater voice in the license review process). The Department of Commerce also reorganized the Bureau of Export Administration. Three new licensing offices were created, the Office of Nuclear and Missile Technology Controls, the Office of Chemical/Biological Controls and Treaty Compliance, the Office of Strategic Trade and Foreign Policy Controls. In addition, Commerce established an Office of Strategic Industries and Economic Security and an Office of Exporter Services.

Whatever intra-departmental reorganization occurs, inter-departmental conflicts have been the source of concern to most critics. Under the Export Administration Act, Commerce and Defense share information on dual-use proliferation cases through at least five interagency groups: the informal Missile Trade Advisory Group (MTAG); the informal Missile Technology Export Control Group (MTEC); the Subcommittee on Nuclear Export Coordination (SNEC); the Nuclear Export Violations Working Group (NEVWG); the chemical weapons group, SHIELD.[18] Lately, interagency referrals from Commerce have increased from twenty percent of the license applications to nearly fifty percent (though, overall, the number of license applications remains about the same), suggesting that the potential for interagency conflict may not have been reduced by liberalizing the CCL. As of early 1995, there appears to be no consensus about how the interagency process will work especially as Commerce and other actors may be abolished.

If anything, a new arrangement may elevate more agencies in the policy process. Allegedly, the CIA only had a dozen or so people working on proliferation issues a few years ago (not counting the personnel working on East-West technology transfers), but more than one hundred will work in the Non-Proliferation Center. The National Security Agency is now concerned about the spread of supercomputers, fiber-optics equipment and software encryption capabilities which may diminish their capacity to gather electronic intelligence. The Arms

Assess the strength of the importer's "commercial military-industrial"
base

The increase in weapons' systems requiring dual-use technologies
suggests that military strength increasingly rests on the civilian
industrial base. But throughout the Cold War, Soviet capability for
civilian technological innovation, diffusion, and adaptation lagged
further and further behind that of the West. And since there were few
backward and forward linkages among industries, few networks between
engineers, scientists, and military technicians and a rigid divide between
civilian and military industries, the Soviets had great difficulty adapting
commercial western technology to military purposes.[9] This partly
explains why the military technology gap remained large in favor of the
West, despite the legal and increasingly illegal import of dual-use
technologies.

In the current period, Third World country purchases of advanced
Western technology are likely to go the way of Soviet purchases. The
successful utilization of technology within any country depends on the
extent to which its positive effects can be diffused throughout an
industry, sector, or the economy as a whole. The success of commercial
technology transfer depends on the nation's industrial structure and
whether that structure provides for strong linkages among related
industries through which the positive effects of innovation (whether
domestic or imported) can spread. And the speed at which commercial
innovation can be translated into weapons' systems seems to depend on
the strength of the networks between scientists, engineers, and defense
contractors in military and civilian industries and policy-makers in
government.[10] Within a state that has a "commercial/military-industrial
complex" these networks are both tight and stable. But in weak
countries, these linkages do not exist, and the positive effects of
commercial technology imports on military strength will be nil. Finally,
if scarce resources are invested in military technology, third world states
today, much like the Soviet Union during the cold war, will undercut
their ability to innovate and develop economically, perpetuating their
dependence on the international market. This does not mean, of course,
that they cannot develop weapons of mass destruction with a weak
industrial base. The cases of India and China and even Iraq suggest
otherwise. But it is unlikely that they will be able to develop the
sophisticated support and delivery systems necessary to make the
weaponry wholly effective.[11] Indeed, the Gulf War demonstrated that

this was the case with Iraq.

Assess business strategies for the sale of dual-use technologies

A third vulnerability assessment technique involves a careful examination of the business strategies of commercial exporters of dual-use technologies. Widespread publicity over the Toshiba case, Imhausen Chemie's sale of a chemical weapons plant to Libya, and the discovery that Iraq's 1991 invasion of Kuwait was assisted by military equipment and technology developed largely with illegal western assistance, have all bolstered recent calls for stepped up government enforcement of export controls. Given the potential gravity of the consequences of illegal exports, there is general agreement that such enforcement provisions are necessary. But practitioners must recognize that the vast majority of firms do not cheat and in fact have their own strategies for withholding high technology that could be adapted to military use.

Again, the Soviet case is illustrative. During the cold war, the pattern of business involvement combined with Western corporate strategy worked to ensure Soviet dependence on western technology rather than provide the means to build up the Soviet industrial base.[12] Western private investment was targeted primarily for extractive industries and commodity production, and most industrial cooperation agreements and joint ventures were in services and the marketing of Western imports. Investment targeted for manufacturing industries was largely confined to assembly operations, adding little value to the goods produced and intended for the Soviet market rather than for export. Component parts for Soviet plants were sourced in the West, inhibiting the creation of linkages between the joint venture and the rest of the economy. Corporate officials believed that transfer of obsolete technology through these ventures was sufficient to capture domestic market share. Contractual provisions ensured that the most advanced Western technologies were withheld from the Soviet economy. Technology transfer was used as a "hook" in order to get a foot into the Soviet market, and "core" technologies were rarely included in joint venture agreements.[13]

A knowledge of these business strategies in particular transactions involving questionable dual-use technologies is likely to be a useful contribution to an overall assessment of the contribution a particular technology transfer will make to the closing of the technology gap

bought dual-use space technology and planned in early 1992 to sell it in global markets.[17] Although Yeltsin threatened to impose sanctions of such activity, it was entirely unclear whether his government had the power to do so.

In order to prevent this technology exodus from the former USSR to other dangerous countries, the Bush Administration initially provided $25 million to help finance international science and technology centers supporting former Soviet scientists and engineers so that they could redirect their talents to non-military endeavors.[18] But by mid-1994, these centers had not yet been established, and at the same time that the US provided funding for them, it blocked the purchase of missiles, rocket engines, satellites, space reactors, spacecraft and other aerospace technology from the former Soviet Union in order to force the decline of the Russian space and military industry so that it would pose no future threat to the US. Many argued that this embargo would further force former Soviet scientists to sell their knowledge to potential military rivals in the Third World.[19]

Before Russia and the other Newly Independent States can begin to enforce the export controls they have now established, the West must assist these new nations in strengthening their states and their science and technology infrastructure. We once feared both a strong state and scientific and technological advance in the region. Now, states must be strengthened or incidents like the above will proliferate. The current dominance of market logic, however, mitigates against strong states. It calls for "state shrinking" so that the domain of the market can expand. What those who call for state shrinking forget, however, is that is the state that must establish and protect legal and rational markets, and it is the state that must enforce new market-oriented laws. At the present time, market-oriented laws initiated by the central government of the Russian Federation are often ignored or opposed in regional and city governments; a weak central state has found it close to impossible to enforce market reforms.

If the coordinating states want these new states to cooperate in multilateral export control, they must be prepared to provide ample financial and technical assistance in these countries to strengthen the state in the ways discussed above. Assistance in strengthening export control laws in these states alone will not help, because the problems affecting export control are both deeper and more widespread than export controls themselves.

In an environment in which all technology supplying states are both under tremendous economic pressure and are unsure about the direction of post-Soviet political developments, obtaining more multilateral aid agreement to strengthen the state, the economy, and science and technology establishments in the NIS will be the most difficult task set forth in this essay. Raising export control issues to prominence in debates over economic aid will help. And clear vulnerability assessments will help to legitimize export control issues and place them on the aid agenda.

Conclusions

I have argued here that despite the new, uncertain, and tumultuous security environment of the post-cold war world, there are important lessons to be learned from the cold war experience for cooperation in multilateral non-proliferation export control regimes. The cold war taught us that--with regard to dual-use export controls-the construction of a grand strategy to guide joint decisions may actually do more harm than good. Because restricting dual-use technologies is highly controversial, it is best to pursue flexible and incremental decision-making procedures. Flexible typologies of states in their relation to the export of sensitive dual-use technologies, their own security strategies, and potential strategies to be pursued toward them may be an important beginning.

A second lesson from the cold war is that in lieu of grand political guidelines to guide export control, restrictions should be based on specific, case by case vulnerability analyses. The assessment should answer the following questions: 1) Does the potential sale of dual-use technology close the military gap between exporter and importer, negating the exporter's advanced weapons' systems? 2) Does the importing state possess the infrastructure, policy and technical networks, and industry linkages to adapt advanced civilian technology to military purposes? 3) What is the corporate strategy with regard to technology transfer in this case? Does the strategy provide for the withholding of key sensitive technologies? Certainly there are many more ways to refine a vulnerability analysis. These questions are merely suggestive and provide a first cut at the problem. But their answers can yield valuable data on the danger of any specific technology transfer to the exporting state's relative capabilities.

Finally, chaotic events in the former Soviet Union in the aftermath of the cold war have exposed entirely new export control problems, not

10. This argument is made persuasively by Philip Gummett and Judith Reppy, "Military Industrial Networks and Technical Change in the New Strategic Environment," *Government and Opposition* Vol 25, No. 3 (Summer, 1990), pp. 287-303.

11. See, for example, Future Security Environment Working Group, *The Future Security Environment* (Washington, D.C.: Commission on Integrated Long-Term Strategy, October 1988).

12. This argument about dependence was made by Timothy W. Luke, "Technology and Soviet Foreign Trade: On the Political Economy of an Underdeveloped Superpower," *International Studies Quarterly,* Vol. 29, 1985.

13. See Beverly Crawford *Economic Vulnerability in International Relations* Chapter Three.

14. See, for example, Kenneth Waltz, "The Case for Nuclear Proliferation," Steven Miller, "Western diplomacy and the Soviet nuclear legacy," in *Survival,* vol. 34, no. 3, (Autumn 1992); Barry R. Rosen, "The Security Dilemma and Ethnic Conflict," in *Survival* Vol. 35, no.1 (Spring 1993), pp. 27-47.

15. See "U.S.-NIS Dialogue on Nonproliferation Export Controls," Conference report, June 15-17, The Airlie Center, Virginia for specific country problems in the NIS.

16. See Eric Schmitt, "U.S. worries about spread of arms from Soviet sales," *The New York Times*, November 16, 1991, p. 5.

17. See "Russia to fight Private Sell-offs by Ex-Officials," *The New York Times,* February 29, 1992, p. 4.

18. The European Community and Russia also promised to assist in financing. See "Baker and Yeltsin Agree on U.S. Aid in Scrapping Arms," *New York Times,* February 18, 1992, pg. 1.

19. Opponents claimed that the acquisition of Moscow's best technology could save Washington and American industry many billions of dollars in development costs, ease Russia's economic woes, discourage the spread of Russian scientists to the third world, and help the US compete with foreign rivals. See "US Moves to Bar Americans Buying Soviet Technology," New *York Times,* March 1, 1992, pg. 1. In response to both of these moves, a

panel of 120 scientists and engineers from the National Academy of Sciences recommended that the United States provide $150 million to support Russia's scientific elite. The panel also called on the US to open its markets to Soviet high technology in order to create more revenue in the Soviet Union and discourage the exodus of Russian scientists, See "Panel Calls for Wider Help for Ex-Soviet Arms Experts," *New York Times,* March 14, 1992, pg. 3.

"Economic Cold War", which is an exception in international trade regimes. Therefore, trade relations with reference to COCOM control were called "strategic trade", and have been differentiated from general free trade relations.

Consequently, it is natural that COCOM controls have been rapidly relaxed since 1990, following the US-Soviet summit talks held at Malta in December 1989. COCOM's objective was to fight the economic Cold War against the Soviet Union. One of the confronting military blocs disappeared on account of the dissolution of the Warsaw Treaty Organization (WTO) in 1991, thus dissolution of the "hidden" regime COCOM, which has been supporting the "official" regime NATO was only a matter of time.

However, it took more than 3 years since the WTO dissolved for COCOM to break up. Moreover, during this period, some of the Western states, particularly the military establishment in the US, strongly opposed the proposal to break up COCOM. This is because they still perceived the threat of the Soviet Union as a nuclear super power even after the Cold War had ended. As a result, they persistently resisted relaxing controls on technology transfer to the Soviet Union concerning "C^3I" (command, control, communications, and intelligence), which are the key technologies for the global military strategy of the US. Therefore, COCOM controls to Eastern European countries such as Hungary and Poland, that have rapidly shifted to the market economy system, were relaxed immediately. On the contrary, strict controls to the Soviet Union were laid down with respect to information and telecommunications equipment, and the so-called "two tiers" of regulations were promoted.

Undoubtedly, there are many other reasons why the "two tiers" of regulations, differentiating the Soviet Union from Eastern Europe, were generally adopted. Such factors as economic confusion before the demise of the Soviet Union, a delay in the shift to a market economy, and the vulnerability of President Gorbachev's leadership were also influential. Nonetheless, it was mainly because the Soviet Union still possessed nuclear forces exceeding those of the US, particularly in the strategy nuclear forces, that COCOM has treated differently the Soviet Union.

Nevertheless, export controls to Russia, were promptly relaxed after the demise of the Soviet Union and the shift to a market economy in January 1992. This followed the abortive coup d'etat in 1991 and in addition, the signing of the Strategic Arms Reduction Treaty (START

1) in 1991 and START II in 1992. These events were supported by the G-7's support for democratization and economic reforms executed by President Boris N. Yeltsin. Additionally, the COCOM Co-operation Forum (CCF) was organized, including Central and Eastern Europe and the CIS states, and held the first meeting in November 1993. This gives an impression that COCOM is losing its original character as the coordinating committee for the export control to the Communist Bloc. At this stage, COCOM secretly entered discussions when to exclude Russia from the list of states subject to export control.

Finally, deciding to dissolve COCOM means that Russia, after the demise of the Soviet Union, is no longer perceived to be a military threat to the West and that the Cold War has in a strict sense ended. In addition, the West now intends to include the CIS states, Central and Eastern Europe, and China in the New COCOM, which suggests that the term "strategic trade" is obsolete. Needless to say, Russian and Chinese participation in a New COCOM is necessary, if a renewed COCOM plans to change into a regime controlling conventional arms export and technology transfer to some concerned countries or regions.

2) Chinese participation in the New COCOM is needed

COCOM, which had started to function as an organization to control export to the Third World in the 1990's, has been promoting its cooperation with international export control regimes concerned with weapons of mass destruction, such as the Missile Technology Control Regime (MTCR), the Australian Group (AG), and the Nuclear Suppliers Group (NSG). That is to say, COCOM has been the core of this linkage structure. For example, through the CCF, Russia has received assistance and support to strengthen its own export control system, which also, bolsters its attempts to prevent technologies related to weapons of mass destruction from being transferred to countries in a conflict or potential conflict situation.

However, US-Japanese differences in views on Chinese participation in the CCF imply the possible re-occurrence of a dispute between the US and Japan on the process of including China in the New COCOM. The post Cold War relationship between the US and China seems tenuous, considering the US imposed economic sanctions on China in August 1993 over the export control issues surrounding the transfer of the M-11 missile and related technologies to Pakistan. As a result, it is difficult to predict whether China can participate in the

order to maintain production lines. In fact, in 1992 the US increased its share of the arms market in the Third World up to 60 percent, and became the principal arms supplier, surpassing Russia.

In addition, US weapons manufacturers requested support from the Senate for government loan guarantees. Thus, the Senate adopted an amendment to offer their loan guarantees for overseas arms sales, in response to the request.[2] This decision may facilitate arms races in the Middle East and Asia owing to the export subsidy policy, which will be adopted by such competing states as the UK and France. Although conditions surrounding the US and Russia are different, the US, facing difficulties in conversion as much as Russia, is going to accelerate overseas arms sales. The US diplomacy no doubt lacks logic, showing its leadership as a builder of the New COCOM to control arms and technology transfer on the one hand, and promoting arms sales from the viewpoint of economic security on the other.

This "double standard" diplomacy, more critically, "the forked-tongue diplomacy" is not new. The US-Japan conflict in 1981 over the export of Hitachi computers to China was a typical example. That is, the US protested the Hitachi computer export on account of possible. dangers of diversion to military use, while immediately after that rejection it showed its intention to permit IBM to export larger computers to China. Consequently the Japanese government was enraged. It is better to assume that the US will not always put its policy principles into practice after shifting to the New COCOM. The dilemma which the New COCOM will face can be easily imagined.

5) How to cope with the "dual use threats"

With regard to arms exporting and the transfer of dual use technologies, Chinese exports of M-11 missile parts to Pakistan were sanctioned by the US. The sanctions were applied by invoking the Helms Amendment of the Arms Export Control Act of 1990. Then immediately afterward, the US Government permitted supercomputer exports amounting to 8 million dollars to China in November. It was alleged that the US government allowed the sales to give relief to Cray Research, which was facing management crisis.[3]

This case recalls the another episode in August 1972 when the Nixon administration permitted Bryant Co. to export ball bearing grinding machines to the USSR, justifying it by claiming that it was a proof of detente. The true intention was to give relief to Bryant Co., which was in the midst of a financial management crisis, however, the Soviet Union consequently diverted them to military use and succeeded in converting the SS-19 missiles to multiple independently targetable re-entry vehicles (MIRV). Because supercomputers are the typical dual-use technologies, an emerging supercomputer export control regime has already been formed between the US and Japan.

What is more, the US promised Israel to sell her a new type of fighter aircraft, when Prime Minister Itzhak Rabin visited Washington in November 1993. Israel is still a country of proliferation concern in the Middle East. The US always justifies its overseas arms sales to conflicting regions on the grounds of maintaining or recovering the "regional military balance".

Japan is the rare state which has not exported arms since the end of the Second World War. Accordingly, Japan should show political initiative in opposing these contradictory tendencies as much as possible at any high level meeting in COCOM. Moreover, since it is reported today that Japan is trying to form an Asian export control regime, Japan has become the focus of attention on how it will deal with the "dual use threat" increasing in Asia.[4]

6) Chinese arms build-up and Western countries' dilemma

The most noticeable change among international military developments after the end of the Cold War is the Southeast Asian and Chinese intentions to expand their armaments. Besides, there are a lot of sources which will cause regional conflicts; for example, conflict over territory of the Spratley Islands in the South China Sea. Above all, in China a policy to increase the defense expenditure of 1994 by 22.4 percent compared with that of 1993 was announced at the National People's Congress held in March, which may raise other nations' fear of Chinese arms build-up. The Japanese Prime Minister Hosokawa's anxiety about Chinese arms built-up, expressed during the Chinese Deputy Prime Minister's visit to Japan in February 1994, is an illustration of these fears in the region.

In addition, there is still a possibility that a problem of sales of weapons of mass destruction and related technologies will recur, such as the previously mentioned problem of Chinese missile export to Pakistan. China already officially announced that it will observe the MTCR guidelines and increase its involvement in the non-proliferation export control regimes when the former US Secretary of State James

7) Is it possible to establish an Asian regional export control regime?

Is it possible to establish a sub-regime in East Asia, to support global export control regimes? And if it is possible to do so with all difficulties concerning Chinese participation in the international export control regimes, then under what conditions?

The unstable situation in East Asia after the Cold War is not only made more uncertain by the Chinese arms build-up. It is well known that the Korean Peninsula, which is the last seat of the Cold War left in East Asia, the tension between both Koreas has been mounting since North Korean nuclear activities aroused international scrutiny. Moreover, the tension intensified through North Korean success in launching the ballistic missile 'Nodong-1'. Thus, the Korean Peninsula becomes the test site for forming a regional nonproliferation regime. In that case, not only South and North Korea, but also the U.S, Russia, China, and Japan, which are formally or informally participating in multilateral non-proliferation regimes, will play important roles. In addition, Taiwan, Hong Kong, and Singapore will be involved to some extent.

Needless to say, North Korea has been a target state for COCOM regulation not only as a remaining socialist state but also as a state in a potential conflict situation. Even after COCOM transforms itself to a conventional arms and related technology transfer control regime, the present control framework including nonproliferation regimes will not change much, as long as the Kim regime continues. Therefore, if China formally participates in the non-proliferation regimes or the post-COCOM regime, a regional regime targeting North Korea will, in practice, start to function.

However, the problem is how a regional regime, whose purpose would be controlling export to North Korea, should be organized. North Korea has rapidly become isolated from the rest of the world since the Cold War system was dissolved. Accordingly, it is the best way to avoid isolating North Korea further and forcing it to pursue a nuclear potential. Since the export control regimes targeting North Korea, such as the non-proliferation regimes or COCOM, are already working, it is unnecessary to create an additional regional export control regime.

Though there had been no regional export control regime, the newly industrialized economic states (NIES) became more careful in transferring military related high-technologies. This is because since the mid-1980s the US, led by Assistant Secretary of Defense Richard N. Perle under the Reagan administration, urged the Asian NIES that are not members of COCOM to organize and intensify their own export control systems. In addition, the US informal announcement of establishing an Asian COCOM had a great influence in that respect. As a result, sensitivity to militarily related high-tech export has dramatically risen. In fact, Taiwan, Hong Kong, South Korea, and Singapore, have started to establish their own export control system since the last half of the 1980s. It can be said, therefore, that these countries and areas are already involved in the non-proliferation export control regimes or a COCOM-like regime to a large extent.

With reference to militarily related high-tech led by electronics technologies, the NIES had made such remarkable progress that they have almost caught up with states that are COCOM members or other participants in the non-proliferation export control regimes. Therefore, role of the NIES in preventing proliferation of sensitive technologies related to weapons of mass destruction and conventional arms become logically important. It is quite natural that the Asian NIES should increase their involvement in the nonproliferation export control regimes or in the New COCOM. On the contrary, whether it is necessary to establish a new regional export control regime, including all these countries and areas, taken charge of by the U.S and Japan is a serious matter.

To sum up briefly, as previously noted, further isolating North Korea should be avoided. What is more, with the Taiwan issue, no policies that might arouse Chinese offensive posture are advisable from the viewpoint of stability in East Asia. Judging from the present strategic environment in Asia, it would be a better scenario to establish a soft system aiming at loose cooperation of concerned states than a hard system of export control.

more technologies that are developed in the commercial sector.

The second part is an economic analysis of export controls. Export control regimes are analyzed applying simple cartel theory and differences between COCOM and nonproliferation regimes are examined. I will point out some of the difficulties facing non-proliferation export control from economic perspectives.

In the last section, the above two analyses are combined and implications for non-proliferation export control of dual-use technology are examined. The main conclusion drawn from the examination is that the cost-benefit relationship of nonproliferation export control is worsening. In order to increase effectiveness of the control under these circumstances, three possible approach to the problems are suggested.

Although analyses here have limitations in incorporating such concept as power distribution among countries that are used frequently in international relations, they would provide different perspectives on the working of interactions between dual-use technology and export controls.

Economic Analysis of Dual-Use Technologies

A Framework for Analyzing Dual-Use Technologies

Analytical approaches to dual-use technology seem to be lagging behind considering the great amount of literature available on this subject.[2] One of the reasons that dual-use technology is a politically controversial issue related to both military and commercial industries, and thus, it induced more policy-oriented studies rather than the analytical ones.

In Japan, government policy also seemed to impede the development of studies on the transfer of dual-use technology. The Japanese government adopted a policy to separate national security issues from economic and trade issues. This policy indirectly influenced Japanese scholars to concentrate only on commercial aspects of technology studies. The national security aspects of technology transfer are neglected in academic research and issues concerning military aspect of dual-use technology have been only mentioned in the media rather sensationally. As a result, serious academic studies on dual-use technology totally divorced from the study of technologies in the Japanese academic world.[3]

In this chapter, I will employ analytical approaches to dual-use technology from two dimensions. They are, first, the degree of technology duality and second, the direction of dual-use technology development.[4]

Each technology has its own unique degree of duality. Here high technology duality refers to the situation where technology can be converted from commercial to military applications easily and *visa versa*. For instance, semiconductor memory is judged to have high technology duality because they can be incorporated both in military and commercial use without major changes. In the research and development (R&D) stages, the technology duality tends to be higher in basic research in comparison with applied research. This is because the development path to a final product, which is either commercial or military, has not been clarified in basic research stage. However, as the research goes into the application stage, a specific final product is in sight in, utilizing the research, therefore, technology duality tends to be lowered on this state.

At a product level, technology duality tends to be lowered as we advance from materials and parts to final products. It is obvious that as we advance to a final product, its use tends to be limited toward either military or commercial use. The reason why above-mentioned semiconductors have high technology duality is that they are electronics components, therefore, they can be used both in military electronics product such as missiles and in consumer electronics product such as VCRs. The similar distinction also can be made between product and process technologies, in which the latter technology's duality tends to be higher. Machine tools are a good example of the latter case.

Technologies with high duality tend to develop toward military applications in one time and toward commercial applications in another time. Because of these tendencies, it looks as if the nature of technology in terms of military and commercial applications changes over time. However, the dual-use capability of each technology does not change but direction of dual-use technology development is the one that changes over time.

In order to examine the direction of dual-use technology development, we have to look into cost-benefit environments in military and commercial markets for companies that produce dual-use technology products. In capitalist countries, dual-use technologies are usually developed by private companies. If we suppose that there is no coercion from government on private company's activities, companies

An Economic Analysis of Export Control Regimes

Export Control as an Extreme Case of a Cartel

Export control regimes can be considered as a kind of a cartel. In general, a cartel is formed to raise the price of a product or commodity by cutting the amount supplied to a market. Participating members of a cartel can get extra benefit due to the increase in the product price. In order to cut the supply, it is necessary for the members to collude and assign the amount of available to each of them. As such, an export control regime is an extreme case of cartel; that is, it tries to eliminate supplies to a certain number of countries, rather than limiting them. This kind of cartel does not make economic sense since members can not get any economic profits from this kind of cartel. Obviously, the purpose of forming an export control cartel is to get benefits in the national security area. By controlling the flow of technologies to undesirable countries, member countries can reduce the threat from these countries, and thus, obtain national security benefit by paying the economic cost of reduced supplies.

A simple economic theory implies that a cartel tends to break down under free competition. Since participating members are assigned a quota of supplies that are less than the amount without the cartel, they always have incentives to increase the amount supplied and obtain more profits. This incentive is especially strong because of the higher price set by the limited amount supplied to the market. If one member breaks the agreement of the cartel and increases the amount supplied to the market, other members, who perceive unfairness in the agreement, could follow the cartel breaker and the whole cartel would break down eventually.

This implies that in order to maintain a cartel under market pressure there must be an effective mechanism of monitoring each member's ill or deviant behavior and enforcing the agreements to prevent the members from increasing the amount supplied. Therefore, a maintainable cartel requires an effective system of monitoring and enforcement and it has to be provided at a low cost. The same line of the argument can be applied to export control regimes. That is, export control regimes are always in danger of breaking down from market pressure. However, only if the regime establishes effective means of monitoring member's less than prudent behavior and provides an effective method of enforcing agreements at a low cost, will the regime have the possibility of survival. It is important to start from the possibility of break down, rather than taking the persistence of a cartel for granted, as the basis for establishing an effective export control regime.

An Ideal Export Control Regime

Let us examine factors that are essential for maintaining effective export controls. In terms of the monitoring and enforcement aspect of maintaining effective cartels, the following six points can be considered as such factors (see the Table 1):

(1) Small number of member countries ----- It becomes less costly to monitor each other's behavior and enforce agreements as the number of member countries decreases;

(2) Small number of countries to which technology flow is controlled ---- It becomes less costly to control and monitor the flow of technology;

(3) Small number of items to be controlled ----- It becomes less costly to control and monitor flow of technology;

(4) High world market share of controlled technologies by member countries ----- If there are countries outside the regime that have the capacity to supply controlled technologies, these countries are happy to provide controlled technologies to undesirable countries. This incentive is especially strong because price of controlled technologies are set artificially higher due to the limited supply of technologies imposed by the export control;

(5) Strong common ideology among member countries ----- If the member countries share a common ideology, it becomes more difficult to break the agreement. This is because if one country breaks it, it would lose other member's confidence in that country and the country would worsen its position in international relations. Therefore, the ideological factor puts additional cost on breaking the agreement; and

Chapter 12

Japan And The Korean Peninsula: The Idea of a 'Northeast Asia Nuclear Non-Proliferation Zone'

Hajime Izumi

The March 12, 1993 announcement that North Korea would withdraw from the Nuclear Non-Proliferation Treaty (NPT) was a shock to the peoples of the world. Then after four sets of high-level talks, North Korea and the United States released a joint statement on June 11, 1993. This statement said, "The DPRK (Democratic People's Republic of Korea) has decided unilaterally to suspend as long as it considers necessary the effectuation of its withdrawal from the Treaty on the Non-Proliferation of Nuclear Weapons.[1] But Pyongyang has yet to show any sign of a turnaround or any attempt to stay in the NPT framework and allow the International Atomic Energy Agency (IAEA) to inspect the full scope of its nuclear materials and facilities.

A worst-case scenario would be North Korea really withdrawing from the NPT and declaring its policy to develop nuclear weapons as defensive measure in response to pressures and a threat of sanctions from the international community. There is another scenario where North Korea may resort to "military resources" to cope with sanctions of the international community. We must avoid such possibilities.

With Pyongyang's decision to withdraw from the NPT, the sense of urgency increased in efforts to work for a non-nuclear Korean Peninsula by preventing nuclear development in North Korea. For the moment, the United States is negotiating with North Korea on behalf of the international community, aiming at the realization of a non-nuclear Korean Peninsula, and the Japanese government welcomes these efforts of the United States and shows strong support for them. The position adopted by Japan is consistent: nothing has been changed even after the Liberal Democrat cabinet was replaced with the Hosokawa coalition cabinet in August 1993. Foreign Minister Tsutomu Hata of the new administration often expresses the government's support of US efforts before the press.

Around the time when US-North Korea high-level talks started in June 1993, there was anxiety in Japan that Japan might miss the bus, that is, improvement of Japan-North Korea relations would be delayed while US-North Korea negotiations proceed, and normalization between the United States and North Korea would eventually come earlier than between Japan and North Korea. This anxiety, however, has vanished by now. Rather, the general way of thinking is that the precedence of US-North Korea normalization should be reasonable consequence, because there will be no more big obstacles in relational improvements between the United States and North Korea if the nuclear issue is solved. Between Japan and North Korea, however, there will still be the question of "compensation" for the past colonial rule by Japan. It can be said that most of the Japanese people now have a good understanding that many difficulties exist still remain in the relationship with North Korea, compared to that between the United States and North Korea.

At any rate, Japan has high expectations for the solution of problems through diplomatic negotiations between the United States and North Korea. There is of course the perspective in Japan that the 'stick' and not the 'carrot' should be used to deal with North Korea, and there are many who side with this view. If diplomatic efforts to solve problems do not succeed and the international community faces the need to apply sanctions against North Korea, then Japan would play an important role.

When Foreign Minister Hata and Director General of the Defense Agency Kazuo Aichi met with U.S. Secretary of State Warren Christopher and Undersecretary of Defense Frank Wisner in the first US-Japan Security Consultative Committee meeting (referred to as the "two plus two" talks) on March 11, 1994, the two sides reaffirmed that a diplomatic solution is the best means of resolving the North Korean nuclear issue.[2] Both the United States and Japan thus completely agree to giving priority to the diplomatic efforts to solve this dilemma. There is no change in Japan's posture of support toward US negotiations with North Korea.

North Korea's decision to withdraw from the NPT has revealed the difficulty of achieving a nuclear-free Korean Peninsula through the efforts of only the two Koreas. This is also clear from the fact that the North-South Joint Declaration on Denuclearization of the Korean Peninsula is still not implemented despite its validation more than two years ago. In this context, the United States has begun high-level talks with North Korea and made strong calls to Pyongyang for a complete implementation of the North-South Joint Declaration.

Briefly, for the Korean Peninsula to become denuclearized, the neighboring major powers must play an increasingly important role. After the high-level consultations between the United States and North Korea, held in New York and Geneva in 1993, the question of implementing the Joint Declaration has changed in nature: it is no longer a "local issue" between North and South Korea but an "international issue" to which the United States is committed as a leading major power.

One should be cautious, however, not to immediately conclude that this shift represents a step forward toward a nuclear-free Korean Peninsula, because, as has been touched upon, this worst-case scenario must not be disregarded. While North Korea continues to refuse full-scope inspections of its nuclear materials and facilities by reason of the IAEA's "lack of impartiality," South Korea may start reconsidering policies unless Pyongyang moves to dissolve nuclear development suspicions of itself. This might lead both Koreas to eventually choose the nuclear option. Since this 'vicious circle' possibility exists, the role of the surrounding major powers really does have significant weight.

The obvious reasons for North Korea (and potentially for South Korea as well) to possess a nuclear capability are to (1) guarantee its own security and (2) gain political leverage in dealing with the other side and with neighboring countries. To kill the feasibility of nuclear proliferation on the Korean Peninsula, the neighboring countries should provide strong assurance for the security of both South and North and, the international community should establish an environment in which North and South will never think of nuclear weapons as an attractive tool for wielding political leverage. What is really important is to remove the basis for any excuses that may possibly justify either side in developing their nuclear weapons.

To do so, plans for a nuclear-free Northeast Asia deserve consideration. But to begin with, let's not mean "nuclear-free" in the strict sense of the word that not a single nuclear weapon is used nor 0 ed. I should rather like to recommend the use of the term 'Northeast Asia Nuclear Nonproliferation Zone' in line with the spirit of the Nuclear Non-proliferation Treaty (NPT). This would be a transitional state before declaring the entire region to be an absolutely nuclear-free zone, the non-nuclear nations would permanently renounce any kind of "nuclear options," while the nuclear powers are not only pledge no use of nuclear arms against non-nuclear states, but would also vow to actively work toward nuclear disarmament.

To be more specific, North Korea, South Korea, and Japan must approve of forever institutionalizing their status as being "non-nuclear" and the three nuclear powers the United States, China, and Russia, on the other hand must completely renounce a first strike against the former three, besides limiting their deployment of nuclear forces wherever possible and devoting maximum effort to overall nuclear disarmament in the region. This will remove, for the most part, the nuclear threat on the Korean Peninsula coming from the nuclear powers, and fears about Japan's going nuclear will be reduced.

The idea of a "Non-proliferation Zone" will not only guarantee the security of the Korean Peninsula, but leaves no room for justifying any plans to develop nuclear arms and technologies. It would also be instrumental in moving China along a course toward nuclear disarmament.

It will take some time before the international community comes to trust in denuclearization of the Korean Peninsula, and the path leading to that goal will not be a smooth one. However, not denuclearizing and firmly establishing the non-nuclear status of the Korean Peninsula with all possible speed would strengthen the fears that Japan might react by developing a nuclear capability of its own. These fears will certainly hang over Japan for the years to come. For example, when questioned in the 4 July 1993 interview with the *Asahi Shinbun,* US President Bill Clinton stated as follows on the possibility that possession of nuclear weapons by North Korea would lead to Japan's acquiring nuclear capability:

Let me say that I think the Japanese concerns would be legitimate about North Korea going nuclear. This is not a frivolous issue, that is a serious issue. On the other hand, I think it would be better if, we had no more nuclear powers. And I think that Japan would be better off economically, politically and militarily in a world in which would not go nuclear and Japan would not have to spend, invest scientific and technical energy and deal with all of the ions that go with being a nuclear power. The United States will have to work very closely on the issue, because what North Korea affects, at least potentially, Japan's security and Japan's economic and political activities throughout the region.[3]

Although indirectly, President Clinton expressed his concern that the development of nuclear weapons by Pyongyang might instigate the possibility of nuclear weapons possession by Japan. When President Clinton met with a group of American journalists on the eve of his first overseas trip as president on 2 July 1993, he commented on this concern much more directly, "'my gut feeling' is that the quest for nuclear weapons by Iran and Iraq may confront him some day, but he quickly added it would be 'our biggest nightmare' if 'a regime like North Korea that is prepared to use them acquired that capacity.' Even the possibility of such a development, he said, could prompt Japan to abandon its non-nuclear policy and enter an arms race that could destabilize all of Asia. "That would be a very serious thing."[4]

For Japan the days when simply declaring the three non-nuclear principles was sufficient to dispel fears of other countries are now gone. It is most urgent that a new approach, including efforts directed toward establishing a Northeast Asia Nuclear Non-Proliferation Zone, be taken. The way to a Non-Proliferation Zone, I should stress, matches the course of policies that the Hosokawa Administration has adopted as the new Japanese government. The following is a part of the address that Prime Minister Morihiro Hosokawa delivered to the United Nations General Assembly on 27 September 1993:

The Nuclear Non-Proliferation Treaty is the centerpiece of efforts to prevent the spread of nuclear weapons. I wish to affirm that Japan supports the indefinite extension of that Treaty beyond 1995. It is critically important that countries which have not yet acceded to the Treaty will do so to enhance its universality. At the same time, the indefinite extension of the NPT should not

mean to perpetuate the possession of nuclear weapons by the
nuclear weapon state.[5]

Addressing Japan's future role in nonproliferation efforts he continued:

> Japan thus welcomes the progress made toward nuclear
> disarmament made by the United States and Russia, and
> emphasize that all nuclear states must work in earnest to achieve
> further progress in nuclear disarmament. We hail the decision to
> commence substantive negotiations aimed at a comprehensive
> nuclear test ban. For its part, Japan will work actively to help
> reduce world stockpiles of nuclear weapons. For example, we
> are ready to assist in the dismantling of nuclear weapons in the
> former Soviet Union. We also strongly urge North Korea to
> dispel international concern about its developing nuclear weapons
> by, for example, fully implementing the safe, agreement with the
> IAEA.[6]

By mentioning its decisive support for the indefinite extension of
the NPT and urging that all nuclear countries should dare to tackle the
issue of nuclear disarmament, the Hosokawa Administration has
apparently re-affirmed the will of Japan that it shall carry out its 'non-
nuclear' policy, along with its wishes for a realization of a nuclear-free
Korean Peninsula.

On February 11, 1994, Prime Minister Hosokawa also stated as
follows in his address at Georgetown University:

> One of Japan's major goals is to strengthen the NPT system for
> preventing the spread of nuclear weapons. That is why one of
> the first international policy decisions I made after becoming
> Prime Minister asserted Japan's strong support for the indefinite
> extension of the NPT beyond 1995. There have been reports in
> the last few days that Japan might change its policy should North
> Korea arm itself with nuclear weapons. I wish the people who
> write such reports would come to Japan and talk to our people.
> Then the would realize how deeply we feel about this issue. Let
> me be very clear on this point: I see no possibility that Japan
> would become a nuclear power. Such a policy would be against
> Japan's national interest. We, like you, are very concerned about
> the current situation on the Korean peninsula. And we are
> determined, working closely with government leaders in the
> Republic of Korea and America, to help settle this issue.[7]

This stance by Japan will certainly provide a base for structuring a Non-Proliferation Zone in Northeast Asia in the future. To create this "Nuclear Non-Proliferation Zone", both North and South Korea are being strongly urged to completely implement the Joint Declaration on Denuclearization of the Korean Peninsula, which is aimed, not only at realizing a Korean Peninsula without nuclear weapons, but also at prohibiting the production of nuclear materials on either side that could be used for nuclear weapons.

On July 10, 1993, President Clinton addressed before the National Assembly of South Korea, stating, "The future of this is for you and North Korea to shape. The South-North nuclear accord you negotiated goes even further than existing international accords. It not only banishes nuclear weapons from the peninsula, it also bans the production of nuclear materials that could make those weapons. We urge full implementation of this path-breaking accord, which can serve as a model for other regions nuclear tension."[8]

Providing a "model" for other regions, a North-South dialogue --for discussing nuclear issues should be begun as soon as possible. But prospects for this are weak and, even if held, no substantial results might be expected for the time being.

If the North-South dialogue does not make progress, it may be better to convene "North-South talks limited to nuclear issues' in the form of "tripartite talks" including the United States. With the US-North Korea high-level talks already held, the Joint Declaration on Denuclearization of the Korean Peninsula is now an "international issue" as has been mentioned. It is therefore worth considering that the talks include the United States and that these talks will include a discussion of North-South mutual inspections, dismantling of North Korean facilities seen as nuclear fuel reprocessing plants, and the means of guarantee for prohibiting the North's and the South's production of nuclear materials and securing their relief from nuclear threats instead. Anyway the United States has already promised that, once North-South mutual inspections were realized, it would open its military bases in the South to inspection by North Korea. Even thinking of this alone, the United States will be instrumental with the implementation of the Joint Declaration between North and South.

In this context, Japan may have to start considering seriously the construct and operation of a nuclear fuel recycling center in Japan within the framework of this and other international nonproliferation and security arrangements, to undertake all such processes as reprocessing the used nuclear fuel or enriching uranium in order to meet the demand for peaceful use of nuclear energy among the Northeast Asian countries inclusive of North and South Korea.

Moreover, Japan should not only begin the process outlined above, but should also offer to participate along with the United States in the discussions to put the North-South Joint Declaration into practice. As has been argued, it is an essential condition for achieving denuclearization of the Korean Peninsula that Japan remain "non-nuclear," and does so convincingly. In addition, the two Koreas should approve of the status that Japan will be continuously permitted to produce nuclear materials, whilst they will be prohibited from it. Whatever plans may be discussed in the tripartite discussions, they would be difficult to implement without consultation with Japan. It is to be earnestly desired that Seoul and Pyongyang ask for and accept both US and Japanese participation in implementing their Joint Declaration on Denuclearizing the Korean Peninsula.

On January 17, 1994, quoting a high-ranking South Korean government source, the *Donga Ilbo* reported that the United States was demanding that the South agree to making the Joint Declaration on Denuclearization of the Korean Peninsula an international treaty, where the two Koreas would be guaranteed of a stable supply of nuclear fuel in return for their giving up nuclear reprocessing facilities.[9] Of course the truth of what was reported is unknown. According to the *Korea Herald,* a South Korean Foreign Ministry official said that this plan was discussed among some US officials soon after the North Korean announcement to withdraw from the NPT, but Seoul and Washington have never discussed the plan together, formally or informally.[10] I personally think that the plan of turning the Joint Declaration on Denuclearization into an international treaty is a positive proposal. If the United States and Japan join in the process of fulfilling the Joint Declaration on Denuclearization, it will be possible to develop the Declaration into an international accord. Once the outlook for a continued Washington-Pyongyang negotiation is established, we should discuss the plan in real earnest, seeking participation from China and Russia, as well. This will then open the way to a Non-Proliferation Zone in Northeast Asia.

Notes

1. *Joint Statement of the Democratic People's Republic of Korea and the United States of America*, New York, June 11, 1993, p. 1.

2. See *Asahi Shinbun*, March 11, 1994.

3. Yoichi Funabashi, "Clinton says Japan must make change," *Asahi Evening News,* July 6, 1993.

4. David S Broder, "Clinton Warns Summit," *Washington Post*, July 3, 1993.

5. "Full text of Hosokawa's speech at U.N. General Assembly," *Daily Yomiuri*, September 28, 1993.

6. *Ibid.*

7. Speech by H.E. Mr. Morihiro Hosokawa, Prime Minister of Japan, at Georgetown University on February 11, 1994, p.5.

8. President Clinton, "Fundamentals of Security for A New Pacific Community," Address before the National Assembly of the Republic of Korea, Seoul, South Korea, July 10, 1993, *U.S. Department of State Dispatch*, Vol.4, No.29 (July 19, 1993), p.510.

9. See *Donga Ilbo,* January 17, 1994.

10. See "U.S. Studied International Treaty on Korean Denuclearization," *Korea Herald*, January 18, 1994.

Chapter 13

Theory and Practice Of China's Export Controls

Zachary S. Davis[1]

The steady growth of China's power makes it essential to the success of regional and global nonproliferation efforts. Yet China's nonproliferation policy is an enigma. On one hand, China's nonproliferation policy has evolved from outright opposition to the nonproliferation regime to partial membership. If this evolution continues, China could become a senior partner in the regime. On the other hand, China has not yet become a full partner in the regime because it has continued to export nuclear and missile technology in contradiction to the norms of the regime and in contradiction to its own nonproliferation policy. Beijing can not close the gap between its declarations of support for nonproliferation and its continued pattern of controversial exports without implementing effective export controls on sensitive technologies.

This study examines the gap between China's declared nonproliferation policy and its failure to put an end to controversial exports. The gap, I argue, can be explained by examining China's nascent export control system and the way it differentiates among export commodities. Political and military officials regulate exports within the limits of their authority. In effect, two export control systems have evolved -- one for civilian commodities and conventional arms, and another for sensitive exports. Continued evolution of China's nonproliferation policy depends on bridging the gap between these two systems.

I. Three Stages of Evolution in China's Nuclear Nonproliferation Policy[2]

Throughout the most tense periods of the Cold War, the United States and the Soviet Union cooperated to build the nonproliferation regime.[3] China, however, remained isolated from nonproliferation and arms control diplomacy. Whereas Washington, Moscow, and most all other nations perceived mutual interests in controlling the spread of nuclear weapons, China rejected the nonproliferation norm and refused to cooperate with the institutions and practices which constitute the nonproliferation regime. That policy has evolved, however, as Beijing has gradually accommodated the regime to further its foreign policy interests.

The Chinese attitude of exceptionalism toward nonproliferation is yielding to a policy of differentiation among nonproliferation commitments. A selective nonproliferation policy enables the Chinese government to deflect criticism of its nonproliferation behavior through partial acceptance of certain nonproliferation commitments while keeping others at arms length. By signing the Nuclear Nonproliferation Treaty (NPT) and agreeing to abide by the Missile Technology Control Regime (MTCR) guidelines, China moved closer to the nonproliferation regime. However, continuing reports of Beijing's nuclear and missile exports and its refusal to adhere to the Nuclear Suppliers Group (NSG) guidelines for nuclear exports or to require full-scope safeguards on its nuclear exports suggest that China is not yet ready to fully support the nonproliferation regime.

China's nonproliferation policy has evolved through several stages. From its outright condemnation of the NPT in 1968, China has gradually accommodated Western interests in nonproliferation. How far this evolution can progress depends on Beijing's calculation of the costs and benefits of regime membership. If there is to be another stage of development toward full regime membership, China would have to upgrade its export control system.

Stage One: 1968-1981 During the initial stage, Beijing condemned the NPT because it bestows a nuclear monopoly on five declared nuclear weapons states and relegates other nations to permanent non-nuclear weapons status. Seeking to lead the Third World and chart an independent foreign policy course, China repudiated such discrimination as a vestige of colonialism and advocated the overthrow of the NPT regime. As part of its modernization program, Beijing began to convert its primarily military nuclear program to include peaceful applications of nuclear technology. China declared it would not export nuclear weapons to non-weapon states, but neither would it condemn or interfere with other nations attempting to acquire nuclear arsenals. Deng Xiaoping himself proclaimed the anti-NPT policy, saying that "the nuclear powers have no right to prevent non-nuclear countries from possessing nuclear weapons" unless the nuclear armed nations disarmed.[4] Other components of China's early arms control strategy included a no-first-use policy and support for regional nuclear weapons free zones.[5]

The Chinese government adopted a declared policy of not assisting other countries in acquiring nuclear weapons. However, during its post-1978 economic modernization drive, China established a pattern of exporting nuclear materials and technology to a variety of nations known or suspected to have secret nuclear weapons programs. Examples of such sales have included exports of heavy water to India and Argentina, nuclear technology to Brazil, nuclear technology and bomb design to Pakistan, possible nuclear cooperation with Iraq, Syria, and South Africa, a secret reactor sale to Algeria, and nuclear cooperation with Iran.[6] During this stage China had no nonproliferation export controls. However, its exports during this period provide clues for understanding more recent developments.

Stage Two: 1981-1991 China's bid for nuclear cooperation agreements with the United States and other countries in the early 1980s marked the beginning of a second stage in its nonproliferation history. In 1985, President Reagan submitted to Congress a proposed agreement for nuclear cooperation with China. However, it has not been implemented due to the failure of Presidents Reagan, Bush and Clinton to provide the required "peaceful use" certifications to Congress.[7] Evidence of a change in policy included Beijing's statement of support for the norm of nonproliferation in 1982, its joining the International Atomic Energy Agency (IAEA) in 1984, and its endorsement of IAEA safeguards for its nuclear exports in 1985. Beijing continued to oppose the discriminatory aspect of the NPT, but coupled its criticism with occasional praise for the objective of nonproliferation and with denials of aiding proliferation. Beijing's denials of contributing to proliferation came in response to growing concern in the United States and elsewhere that Chinese nuclear transfers offered an alternative source of supply to nations that refused to join the NPT and allow inspections by the IAEA.[8] China adopted a policy of providing assurances that it would not assist proliferation and stating its agreement "in principle" to adhere to internationally accepted nonproliferation norms and guidelines.[9] These statements, however, were not always consistent with China's nuclear export behavior.

China's nuclear relationship with Pakistan has often been at odds with its declared policy of not aiding proliferation, and this was particularly evident during the 1980s. The Reagan administration reportedly had evidence that China was helping Pakistan operate its Kahuta uranium-enrichment plant, and that Beijing provided Islamabad with a design for a 25 kiloton implosion device along with enough weapons-grade uranium to build two nuclear weapons.[10] Chinese scientists have regularly visited the Kahuta complex (in which gas centrifuges are used to produce weapons-grade uranium). As evidence of Islamabad's nuclear intentions accumulated during the 1980s, China expanded its nuclear cooperation with Pakistan. In 1989, China helped Pakistan build a research reactor (PARR-2) which uses highly enriched uranium fuel and assisted in fuel fabrication for the rebuilt and upgraded PARR-I research reactor, whose capacity was doubled from five to ten megawatts in 1991. After Japanese, German, and French firms denied supporting systems and components for a power reactor, China signed a contract to build a 300 MW reactor.[11]

China's nuclear cooperation with Iran also raised questions about Beijing's commitment to the norm of nonproliferation. According to published reports and Chinese admissions, China -- Iran's largest arms supplier during the Iran-Iraq War -- concluded covert agreements in 1989 and 1991 with Tehran to provide nuclear technology. Iran also is believed to have nuclear collaboration with Pakistan.[12] Such cooperation raises the issue of third-party transfers among recipients of Chinese nuclear and missile technology. Third-party transfers are either prohibited or tightly restricted by most other suppliers.

China's Foreign Ministry probably exacerbated the problems caused by these controversial nuclear exports by denying the existence of any Sino-Iranian nuclear cooperation, despite the fact that US and European intelligence sources had disclosed that: Iranian nuclear engineers from Iran's nuclear research center at Isfahan were secretly trained in China, that China transferred technology for reactor construction and other projects at Isfahan, and that China had signed a secret nuclear cooperation agreement with Iran.[13] The Chinese embassy on July 2, 1991 issued a statement asserting that "China has struck no nuclear deals with Iran." During that same month Chinese Premier Li Peng visited the Isfahan complex, where he reportedly promised expanded nuclear cooperation during a meeting with Chinese and North Korean missile experts.[14] When a report said that China Nuclear Energy Industry Corporation experts were building a nuclear research reactor in Iran as part of a secret weapons program, the Chinese Foreign Ministry, on October 21, 1991, denied the story as "groundless."[15]

China finally admitted its nuclear cooperation with Iran following a spate of media reports that Iran was trying to build a nuclear bomb and that China was secretly providing a calutron (electromagnetic isotope separation equipment) for uranium enrichment, a nuclear reactor, and training for Iranian nuclear engineers.[16] (Bush administration officials testified in June 1991 that they had "no reason to conclude that the Chinese are assisting Iran in developing nuclear weapons," despite warnings from the intelligence community about the risk of diversion associated with China's nuclear technology transfers to Iran.)[17] China's Foreign Ministry acknowledged the existence of Sino-Iranian nuclear cooperation on November 4, 1991, explaining that Chinese and Iranian companies had signed commercial contracts in 1989 and 1991 for an electromagnetic isotope separator (calutron) and a small nuclear reactor, for peaceful purposes.

These episodes during the 1980s drew attention to the widening gap between China's words and deeds. The Ministry of Foreign Affairs increasingly depicted Beijing as a reliable member of the regime, but China's state-owned nuclear industry continued its controversial export behavior.

A Third Stage: 1991 - ? Despite continued nuclear cooperation with Pakistan and Iran, Beijing's policy toward the NPT showed signs of entering a third stage in 1990. In trying to improve its tarnished international image after the June 1989 Tienanmen Square crackdown on pro-democracy protesters, China sent officials to observe the Fourth Review Conference of the NPT (and other international arms control meetings) and issued favorable statements about the treaty. Three factors added to scrutiny of China's nonproliferation policy: worldwide nonproliferation sentiment stirred by the 1990-91 confrontation with

Iraq, the April 1991 revelations about China's secret reactor project in Algeria, and the announcement by French President François Mitterrand in June 1991 that France would join the NPT. These events factored into a contentious congressional debate over China's most favored nation (MFN) trade status. The Chinese Foreign Minister and the Premier signalled the change, stating that "China has not yet decided whether or not to join the Nuclear Nonproliferation Treaty," but was continuing to study the question of participating.[18]

The turning point came in August 1991 when Premier Li Peng announced China's decision "in principle" to join the NPT. Chinese leaders promised Secretary of State Baker during his November 1991 trip to Beijing that China would join the NPT by April 1992.[19] Although some observers expected China to delay its accession to the treaty, the Standing Committee of the National People's Congress approved the treaty at the end of 1991, and on March 9, 1992 China became the fourth acknowledged nuclear weapon state to accede to the NPT.[20]

Why did China finally join the NPT? In a broad sense, signing the NPT was a cost-free step which enabled Beijing to gain legitimacy and status as a great power with little risk to its diplomatic, economic, and strategic interests. Possible motivations for signing the NPT include the following:

1. By joining the NPT, China hoped to deflect criticism of its nuclear export policy, especially in the aftermath of the Tienanmen Square massacre. In signing the NPT, China committed to few, if any, new constraints on Chinese policy or behavior, but muted criticism that Beijing was leading a Third World revolt against the nonproliferation regime.

2. Signing the NPT was a step towards securing normal MFN trade status from the United States. Joining the NPT removed the possibility that MFN could be denied if Congress were to link MFN with NPT membership. In trying to promote a constructive bilateral relationship, President Bush cited China's accession to the NPT and its increased support for global nonproliferation efforts when he recommended normal trade tariffs for China in June 1992 and vetoed legislation to tie conditions to MFN status in September 1992.[21]

3. NPT membership would secure the ability to purchase nuclear goods and services, particularly from France and other countries increasingly unwilling to sell nuclear technology to non-NPT states.

4. Without signing the NPT, China would remain the only

acknowledged nuclear weapon state not a party to the treaty, and would continue to share non-NPT status with threshold nuclear states such as India, Pakistan, and Israel. Not only did this association equate China with lesser powers in a general sense, it linked Beijing with arch rival New Delhi as the main critics of the treaty. With world interest in nonproliferation growing, and the 25-year NPT Review Conference on the horizon in 1995, the prospect of attending the Review Conference with the same observer status as India was distasteful. Beijing found the marginal rewards of joining the NPT as a nuclear weapon state preferable to continued isolation.

5. China accepted the rationale that nuclear proliferation could threaten its interests, and that the NPT could contribute to China's security.

China's Missile Exports

In addition to joining the NPT during the third stage of its nonproliferation policy, China also began to accommodate Western interests in halting the spread of missiles and missile technology throughout the world. Beijing is not a full member of the Missile Technology Control Regime, and Washington has not pressed for China to become a member, in part because of its weak export control record. Beijing began to adjust its claim of being exempt from the voluntary guidelines of the MTCR by issuing statements supporting the principle of missile nonproliferation. During his November 1991 visit to Beijing, Secretary of State Baker announced that Chinese officials had verbally agreed to observe the MTCR guidelines and that "this applies to the M-9 and M-11 missiles." The M-9 (600 km) and M-11 (300 km) ballistic missiles are considered capable of delivering nuclear weapons and would be controlled by the MTCR if China were a member or adhered to the MTCR guidelines.[22] In return for its promise of adherence to the MTCR, China required that the United States lift the sanctions imposed earlier in 1991 on two Chinese defense industrial companies in retaliation for China's export of missile technology to Pakistan.[23] The Bush administration effectively waived those sanctions on March 23, 1992 to secure Chinese nonproliferation commitments.

Beijing's informal promise to abide by international missile nonproliferation norms contrasted with its formal accession to the NPT, but resembled the NPT commitment insofar as Beijing's MTCR statements did not end its controversial missile exports. China's foreign minister gave no joint press conference with Secretary Baker, but instead issued a series of statements through the official news agency. Premier Li Peng gave no written assurances when he met with President Bush at the United Nations on January 31, 1992, nor did Li personally state China's position on the MTCR.[24] Instead, the Bush administration received a letter the next day that reportedly confirmed the November 1991 promise in writing. Since then, there have been numerous reports that China continued to transfer M-9 and M-11 missile components.

During the 1992 presidential campaign, candidate Clinton favored taking a tougher approach toward China's nonproliferation and human rights behavior. Once in office, however, President Clinton did not seek a radical departure from the Bush policy of combining targeted sanctions with conditional extensions of China's MFN status. Indeed, the Clinton administration muted Congressional debate over China's MFN status in 1993 by agreeing to link future MFN decisions to a requirement that China demonstrate "significant progress" on human rights, but did not condition MFN on China's nonproliferation behavior. The administration instead vowed to "pursue resolutely all legislative and executive actions" to ensure that China abides by its NPT, MTCR, and other nonproliferation commitments.[25]

After months of reviewing the evidence, the Clinton administration determined in August 1993 that China had transferred missile-related equipment to Pakistan in violation of MTCR guidelines and reimposed sanctions on eleven Chinese and one Pakistani arms exporting enterprises.[26] The government of China called the US sanctions "a naked hegemonic act" that "puts Sino-US relations in serious jeopardy." In his protest to U.S. Ambassador Stapleton Roy, Chinese Vice Foreign Minster Liu Hauqiu maintained that "China has honored its commitment to act in accordance with the MTCR guidelines and parameters and has done nothing in contradiction of that commitment." Accordingly, China threatened to "reconsider its commitment to MTCR.[27] Several months after the sanctions decision, the Clinton administration attempted to soften the impact of the sanctions -- both on Sino-US relations and on US high-tech firms doing business in China -- by offering to waive the sanctions banning the export to China of commercial satellites which were to be launched on Chinese rockets.[28]

It may be too soon, and the proliferation issue may be too interrelated with other considerations, to assess the influence of Washington's carrot and stick approach to China's nonproliferation behavior. During the third stage of its nonproliferation policy, China accommodated certain Western interests in maintaining and strengthening the nuclear and missile regimes, although it did not end its controversial exports. Beijing adjusted its declared nonproliferation policy, but its behavior remained inconsistent with nonproliferation norms in the post-Cold War period. To what extent the gradual progress of China's nonproliferation policy is related to Western diplomacy is unknown. But for China to enter the next stage of progress it must close the gap between its policy and behavior. This will depend on Beijing's ability to upgrade its export control system.

II. The Evolution of Export Controls in China: Different Rules for Different Exports

Export controls serve multiple purposes in China, as they do in the United States and other countries. They can be a useful tool for achieving domestic as well as international objectives. For example, the US controls exports for national security, foreign policy, short supply, and nonproliferation reasons. Beijing's introduction of export controls was initially motivated by domestic objectives, foremost of which was the desire to retain enough centralized command of the economy to enable it to implement long-term, macroeconomic policies. China's economic modernization over the last decade required decentralization of some economic decisionmaking authority. However, successful economic liberalization policies also brought political and economic problems, most of which are beyond the scope of this paper. What is important for understanding export controls in China is that they originated as part of an effort to bring a measure of accountability to the booming economy. Specifically, central planners viewed export controls as a way to measure economic activity in order to control and tax it. These export controls originally had no connection with nonproliferation policy. Nevertheless, their past and present operation could determine the future of China's nonproliferation behavior.

Exports From China's Military Industrial Complex

A significant proportion of China's major industrial centers were established in the interior regions of the country by the People's Liberation Army (PLA) as part of Mao's "Third Line" strategy.[29] The strategy called for dispersing strategic assets to make them less vulnerable to invading forces. These industries with close ties to the

PLA were critical to China's economic development. Through the 1970s, collegial relationships between political and military leaders assured that decisions on arms exports were made at the highest levels and were made primarily to advance Beijing's strategic interests.[30] However, Deng Xiaoping's reforms in the 1980s called for rapid economic development -- even if such development required sacrifices from the military. This butter over guns policy required China's military-industrial complex to provide the backbone for a new phase of economic development, but at the same time left the PLA to fend for itself to provide the resources needed to sustain its forces. Arms sales enabled the military to provide for its own self-preservation while it carried out Deng's orders to harness Chinese industry for a new phase of economic growth. PLA-run arms manufacturers -- notably New Era and Poly Technologies -- made a virtue of a necessity by becoming profitable. The PLA's success as a global arms merchant, however, weakened the Communist Party leaderships' direct involvement in and influence over most non-sensitive arms exports, which were increasingly viewed as normal business transactions.

While extensive blending of the public and private sectors may have been new to America when President Eisenhower issued his warning about the military-industrial complex, no similar institutional barriers ever separated China's military-industrial complex from the political process. Thus, the PLA took the lead in implementing Five Year Plans and exercised considerable autonomy over how it achieved results, but without calling into question the political leadership's ultimate authority over the military. Over time, arms industries that were started to provide supplemental income to the military budget became increasingly successful and independent, but retained their links to top military and political leaders. The connections among the various state-owned defense-industrial entities and top Communist Party officials are well documented. The evolution of these collegial and familial networks helps to explain the independence and entrepreneurship that have become characteristic of China's military industries.[31] PLA-run industries perform many functions, including: spearheading economic and technological modernization; providing for the national defense; generating profits for Party leaders and their families.

The PLA industries' brand of entrepenureship, however, is increasingly at odds with efforts by the Ministry of Foreign Economic Relations and Trade (MOFERT) to impose a degree of order on China's phenomenal economic growth. Export controls are one of MOFERT's main tools for reigning in free-wheeling military-industrial enterprises. But MOFERT policies have been motivated mainly by economic planning and management considerations, not by foreign policy, and least of all nonproliferation.

Central planners in China have used export controls primarily to reduce supplies of exports in which China has a large market share, to increase the availability of goods needed for its economic development, and to impose order on the unruly transition to a market economy.[32] During the early 1990s MOFERT promulgated new export control regulations affecting a wide range of civilian commodities. The purpose of the new controls was to reform a two-level system of controls in which licensing authority was shared between MOFERT and the provincial authorities. MOFERT promulgated the new regulations because provincial licensing departments "often overstepped their power, exceeded their jurisdiction, and have issued more licenses than the state plan and the quota allow." According to MOFERT, this misuse of licensing authority by local officials "exacerbated the already chaotic export order."[33] The government laid out a series of reforms in 1991 and 1992 to clarify export licensing responsibilities and procedures.[34]

China's main interest in export controls has been to assert a measure of accountability on exporters. Controlling, or at least monitoring, the exports of foreign-owned joint venture companies has been a particular concern. Increased accountability supports efforts to manage China's trade and investment policies, including efforts to cultivate lucrative high technology industries. In addition to boosting exports, high tech joint ventures also play an important role in China's technology acquisition policy. Economic planners will not want to restrict export activity in ways that discourage the influx of new technologies. Consequently, Beijing's export control efforts have been tentative, and enforcement appears to be at an early stage of development. It seems likely that even if China established a formal system of controls for sensitive goods and technologies, it may be some time before a reliable level of enforcement is achieved.

Nonproliferation was not among the motivations for establishing export controls in China. Moreover, there are few signs that China is adapting its existing export control system to include nonproliferation objectives. If China wants to improve its nonproliferation credentials, it will have to control exports of a wide range of dual-use commodities (such as computers, machine tools, and chemicals) in addition to restraining sales of missiles, reactors, and directly useable technologies. A major overhaul of China's export control system would be required for China to meet the standards of the Nuclear Suppliers Group, the MTCR, and the Australia Group.

Export Controls for Politically Sensitive Items

Economic reforms have reinforced China's defense industry's tradition of independence. Defense conversion -- which in China often means using factories to produce military and civilian products -- has bolstered this tradition. The independence of defense industries and the weakness of export controls shed considerable light on China's exports of commercial commodities and conventional weapons. However, these explanations alone do not fully satisfy questions about China's exports of sensitive goods and technologies.[35] Do the defense industries that produce sensitive nuclear and missile technologies operate with the same independence as those that produce other commodities, or are they subject to special foreign policy and nonproliferation considerations? If nuclear and missile producers operate with the same freedom as conventional arms dealers associated with New Era and Poly Technologies, the question arises whether China's nuclear and missile exports are beyond Beijing's control. This would explain the gap between declarations by the Foreign Ministry supporting nonproliferation and China's export behavior. However, if there is a special process for evaluating sensitive transfers, we can view such transfers as representing official policy decisions.

There is little evidence that Beijing has promulgated nonproliferation export controls to regulate sensitive transfers. However, there is evidence that sensitive exports are given special consideration. This special consideration is conducted through the informal clan networks to which the heads of the relevant industries and the top Communist Party officials belong.[36] Most sensitive conventional arms transfers are handled by Poly Technologies through its ties with top Party officials. Industries that produce sensitive exports such as China Nuclear Energy Industrial Corporation (CNEIC), Great Wall Industrial Corporation, China Precision Machinery Import Export Corporation (CPMIEC) -- which makes the M-series missiles, China North Industries Corporation (NORINCO), and several others, are affiliated with the New Era Corporation, the sister organization of Poly Technologies. Like Poly Technologies, New Era and its affiliated industries have institutional and personal ties with the Commission of Science, Technology and Industry for National Defense (COSTIND), the Central Military Commission of the Communist Party, and the State Council.[37] Members of these institutions reportedly meet regularly to discuss export policies. Products produced by New Era companies can be evaluated for their political or technological sensitivity through the same type of networks that oversee Poly Technologies' weapons exports.

It is not necessary to know the precise bureaucratic structure of China's defense industries to conclude that top leaders are not normally excluded from decisionmaking on sensitive exports; they are in the loop. In contrast with civilian commodities and conventional arms -- which may not register as a top priority for policy-makers -- nuclear, chemical, missile, and some conventional arms exports are usually scrutinized by top Party officials. These officials have in many cases been made aware of US and other countries' concerns about such transfers, and presumably take these into consideration when they weigh the probable costs and benefits of particular exports. Factors such as short-term profit, political consequences, risk of sanctions, and strategic benefit probably weigh into the consideration just as they do in other countries. Thus, decisions on sensitive exports are traceable to China's top leadership. The process may be ad hoc and follow different bureaucratic pathways for different exports. Not all leaders are informed about all decisions on controversial transfers. But responsible officials either know, or have reason to know, about significant breeches of nonproliferation norms and commitments.

Silent Partners: The Roles of the Ministry of Foreign Affairs and the Ministry of Foreign Economic Relations and Trade

The existence of a decisionmaking process for sensitive exports raises questions about the role of the Ministry of Foreign Affairs (MFA) in nonproliferation policy. The MFA is mainly responsible for articulating Beijing's declared nonproliferation policy. Thus, its statements contribute to the perception that a gap exists between China's words and deeds on nonproliferation. There are several possibilities that could explain the MFA's position. First, the MFA may be out of the decisionmaking loop. In this case, the MFA may simply follow orders to issue declarations about China's nonproliferation policy, regardless of whether or not they reflect actual policy. A second possibility is that the MFA may be in the decisionmaking loop, but either its positions carry little weight, it takes no position, or endorses certain sensitive transfers. It is difficult to know if the MFA is in the loop on controversial transfers, or if MFA knowingly or unknowingly spreads misinformation about Beijing's nonproliferation behavior. It is worth noting that China would not be the only country in which foreign ministry declarations were not always consistent with actual behavior. Nevertheless, the MFA is the primary point of contact for nonproliferation diplomacy; its role in the decisionmaking process has implications for US and international nonproliferation policy.

The decisionmaking process also raises questions about the role of the MOFERT, which is conspicuously absent from the scholarly and policy literature on China's defense industries and nonproliferation policy. It does not appear on organizational charts depicting China's military industrial complex. The MOFERT does have a role in technology acquisition and science and technology development strategy, and probably has some experience with policy issues stemming from the military applications of certain technologies.[38] Officials of the MOFERT are aware of nonproliferation issues and questions related to China's export of sensitive technologies.[39] So far, MOFERT may not be directly involved in the decisionmaking process for sensitive export policy. However, like the US Commerce Department, it could have important responsibilities if China decides to upgrade its export control system to improve its nonproliferation credentials. MOFERT would probably take the lead in efforts to retrofit existing controls to accommodate nonproliferation objectives. Consequently, MOFERT must be included in domestic and international efforts to close the gap in China's nonproliferation policy and behavior.

Both the MFA and MOFERT are relatively weak institutional actors in the nonproliferation decisionmaking process. While the organization of the PRC government may have some unique characteristics, it is fair to assume that the economics and foreign ministries would both play important roles in carrying out the nonproliferation policies of any major country. The weakness of these ministries and their marginal roles in the policymaking process probably reflect the low priority of nonproliferation. But it may also reflect the lack of statutory authority for nonproliferation and other policies. The high level yet informal decisionmaking process for sensitive transfers is not accountable to anyone. This situation suggests several policy prescriptions for countries interested in working with China as a partner in nonproliferation.

Conclusions and Recommendations

A top priority for regime leadership is to bring China fully into the nonproliferation consensus. The United States and other countries should engage MFA, MOFERT, and PLA officials on a broad range of proliferation issues. Frequent contacts are useful for communicating the importance of nonproliferation for bilateral relations. In addition to raising nonproliferation issues with the top Chinese leaders, MFA, MOFERT, and PLA officials should be accountable for China's nonproliferation behavior. It is not necessary to identify key behind-the-scenes policy-makers; bureaucrats at all levels should understand that reckless exports threaten world security. One way to promote nonproliferation is through confidence building measures such as military exchanges, semi-official meetings of mid-level officials, and seminars which build a foundation for more substantive cooperation. Many Chinese officials are not familiar with Western thinking on nonproliferation, and Americans may not appreciate the difficulties of China's position.

For its part, the United States should clearly identify its own priorities and discontinue vague linkages to numerous issues. If nonproliferation is a top priority for Washington, this message should be clearly articulated, with linkage limited to predictable consequences for violations of specific commitments. Targeted sanctions such as those triggered by MTCR violations would be consistent with this approach, but perennially holding MFN hostage to undefined progress on multiple issues would not. On conventional arms, China's arms exports are small in comparison with other major arms exporters, such as the United States, that view the arms trade as a legitimate industry.[40] United States policy should engage China as a great power with which Washington shares a high-priority security interest in stemming the spread of the world's deadliest weapons. A model can be found in US-Soviet cooperation in arms control and nonproliferation, which usually transcended other issues. In fact, progress on nearly every major arms control and nonproliferation issue facing the world today hinges on Sino-US cooperation.

There is considerable room to expand cooperation between Beijing and Washington to advance their mutual nonproliferation interests, assuming that China continues to move toward full regime membership.

Starting with export controls, the United States and other countries could offer technical assistance to help China modernize its export control system. This could include computer-based export licensing to improve monitoring and enforcement. The United States is already providing such assistance to Russia and several of the former Communist bloc nations. China's eventual membership in a replacement institution for COCOM could provide opportunities to bring China's export controls into conformity with regime standards. China could attend MTCR and NSG meetings in preparation for joining both regimes when its export control system has developed. It may be useful to recall that nonproliferation export control policies have evolved over time in all other major supplier nations, and occasional lapses have not been uncommon. Beijing's formal and actual adherence to the MTCR and the NSG would be a major step forward. However, the task of persuading China to upgrade its export control system will be much more difficult if the United States and other regime members are moving in the opposite direction of relaxing their own controls. Beyond export controls, Beijing and Washington can cooperate on a broad range of regime-strengthening initiatives. In fact, as mentioned above, the lack of such cooperation could jeopardize the future of the nonproliferation regime. Sino-American cooperation to bring North Korea into compliance with its nonproliferation commitments provides a good starting point; both countries should highlight the contributions of the other in seeking solutions to the problem. In the long run, China's security would decrease if North Korea's bomb program instigates a nuclear arms race in Asia. China should support the assertion of International Atomic Energy Agency inspection rights and United Nations Security Council actions against North Korea, including sanctions.

The standoff with North Korea could also affect the 25 Year Review Conference of the NPT in April 1995, where NPT members will vote on the future of the treaty.[41] China and the United States should join forces to ensure a strong endorsement of the treaty. The key to strong endorsement, of course, is a comprehensive nuclear test ban (CTB). All nuclear weapons states except China are observing a moratorium on nuclear testing. Negotiations are underway, but it is probably unrealistic to expect an agreement on a CTB by April 1995. It will nevertheless be crucial to demonstrate significant progress toward a CTB at the Review Conference. Continued Chinese testing -especially close to the date of the Conference -- will severely undermine efforts to show that the weapons states are taking seriously their commitments under Article VI of the NPT "to pursue negotiations in good faith on effective measures relating to the cessation of the nuclear arms race at an early date and to nuclear disarmament..."

There are several other initiatives that could be incorporated into a Sino-US nonproliferation strategy. President Clinton's proposed global cutoff of production of fissile material for weapons is one possible avenue for cooperation. More generally, joint statements by the nuclear weapons states regarding the non-use of nuclear weapons against non-- weapons NPT states (negative security assurances) could help to delegitimize nuclear weapons and reinforce the norms of non-use and nonproliferation. Such an approach might use China's no-first-use policy as the basis of a Security Council resolution on the future of nuclear weapons. Finally, Washington and Beijing have mutual interests in promoting regional arms control and security arrangements to prevent arms races in South Asia and the Pacific.[42]

The evolution of China's nonproliferation policy is not unlike that of other countries, including the United States. Effective export controls begin by halting sales of actual weapons, components, and materials, and gradually expand to include a wider range of dual-use goods and services. Implementation and enforcement have often lagged behind declared policies, and violations of regime guidelines by regime members have been regrettably common, as Iraq's nuclear program demonstrated. Moreover, it has not been unusual for governments to be selective in the implementation and enforcement of their nonproliferation policies; nonproliferation has not always been the top foreign policy priority. From a comparative and historical perspective, China's nonproliferation policy is not unique, but it is at an earlier stage of development than the nonproliferation policies of the established members of the regime. The challenge for the United States and other proponents of nonproliferation will be to foster rapid progress to the next stage of China's nonproliferation policy. The success or failure of China's export controls could determine the fate of the nonproliferation regime.

Notes

1. The views expressed are the author's and do not necessarily reflect the views of the Congressional Research Service or the Library of Congress.

2. This section draws from a chapter by Zachary Davis and Shirley Kan, "China's Nonproliferation Policy and Behavior: Challenges for the United States," in Mitchell Reiss, ed. *Nonproliferation in the 1990s* (Baltimore: Johns Hopkins University Press, forthcoming).

3. On different uses of the term "regime" see Zachary Davis, "The Realist Nuclear Regime," in Zachary Davis and Benjamin Frankel, eds., *The Proliferation Puzzle: Why Nuclear Weapons Spread* (London: Frank Cass, 1994).

4. Vice Premier Deng Xiaoping, *Xinhua* (New China News Agency), February 14, 1979, "Chinese Statements on Proliferation Issues - 1979-1991," FBIS Special Memorandum, December 18, 1991, p. 1.

5. China's arms control policy emphasized support for measures that would restrict U.S. and Soviet capabilities. Robert Sutter, *China's Nuclear Weapons and Arms Control Policies: Implications for the United States* (Washington: Congressional Research Service, Report for Congress, 1988), p. 22-23; Dingli Shen, "The Current Status of Chinese Nuclear Forces and Nuclear Policies," Center For Energy and Environmental Studies, Princeton University, February 1990, p. 15; Richard Fieldhouse, *Chinese Nuclear Weapons: A Current and Historical Overview,* Natural Resources Defense Council, March 1991.

6. On Chinese nuclear exports see: Timothy V. McCarthy, *A Chronology of PRC Missile Trade and Developments* (Monterey: Monterey Institute of International Studies, 1992); R. Bates Gill, "The Challenge of Chinese Arms Proliferation: U.S. Policy for the 1990s," U.S. Army War College, Carlisle Barracks, PA, August 1993; "Bending Rules," *Far East Economic Review,* May 16, 1991; Gary Milhollin and Gerard White, "A New China Syndrome: Beijing's Atomic Bazaar," *Washington Post,* May 12, 1991; Mark Hibbs, "Despite U.S. Alarm Over Algeria, Europeans Won't Blacklist China," *Nucleonics Week,* May 23, 1991; Hibbs, "Bonn Will Decline Teheran Bid To Resuscitate Bushehr Project," ibid, May 2, 1991; Hibbs and Ryan, "Official Says China Developing Ability to Supply Entire PWRs," and "Sensitive Iran Reactor Deal May Hinge on MFN for China," ibid, October 1, 1992.

7. Warren Donnelly, *Implementation of the US-Chinese Agreement for Nuclear Cooperation,* Congressional Research Service, September 28, 1989. The Clinton administration signalled a change in U.S. policy banning all nuclear trade with China when it allowed U.S. companies to sell power reactor equipment to Beijing in March 1994. See Daniel Kaplan, "Commerce to Lift Ban on Nuclear Power Exports to China," *Energy Daily,* March 7, 1994, P. 1.

8. Emerging Nuclear Supplier Project, *Eye on Supply,* Number 4, Spring 199 1; Ram Subramanian, "Second-Tier Nuclear Suppliers: Threat to the NPT Regime?" in Rodney Jones, Cesare Merlini, Joseph Pilat, William Potter, eds., *The Nuclear Suppliers and Nonproliferation* (Lexington: D.C. Heath, 1985), p. 97-100; Charles Van Doren and Rodney Jones, *China and Nuclear Non-Proliferation: Two Perspectives,* Programme for Promoting Nuclear Non-Proliferation, Occasional Paper Three, July 1989.

9. "Facts About Some China-Related Issues of Concern to the American Public," Factsheet from the Embassy of the People's Republic of China, Washington, D.C., May 1991, p. 13.

10. Leonard Spector, *Nuclear Ambitions* (Boulder: Westview Press, 1990), Chapters 7 and 4 ; Leslie H. Gelb, "Pakistan Links Peril U.S.-China Nuclear Pact," and "Peking Said to Balk at Nuclear Pledges," *New York Times,* June 22 and 23, 1984; *Nucleonics Week,* May 23, 1991; Zachary Davis and Warren Donnelly, *Pakistan's Nuclear Status,* Congressional Research Service, July 1992; Gary Milhollin and Gerard White, "A New China Syndrome: Beijing's Atomic Bazaar," *Washington Post,* May 12,1991. See also Seymour Hersh, "On the Nuclear Edge," *The New Yorker,* March 29, 1993, P. 56.

11. *Nucleonics Week,* August 9, 1990; ibid, January 24, 199 1; Tai Ming Cheung and Salamat Ali, "Nuclear Ambitions," *Far East Economic Review,* January 23, 1992; Leonard Spector, *Nuclear Ambitions,* Chapter 7, P. 89.

12. Zachary Davis and Warren Donnelly, *Iran's Nuclear Activities and the Congressional Response,* Congressional Research Service, 1993; R. Jeffrey Smith, "Officials Say Iran is Seeking Nuclear Weapons Capability," *Washington Post,* October 30, 1991-1 Elaine Sciolino, "Report Says Iran Seeks Atomic Arms," *New York Times,* October 31, 1991.

13. Mark Hibbs, "Bonn Will Decline Tehran Bid to Resuscitate Bushehr Project," *Nucleonics Week,* May 2, 1991.

14. "PRC Agrees to Complete Construction of Nuclear Reactor," *Sawt Al-Kuwayt Al-Duwali* (London), July II, 199 1; in JPRS-TND, August 8, 1991.

15. Bill Gertz, "Chinese Build Reactor for Iranian Program," *Washington Times,* October 16, 1991.

16. R. Jeffrey Smith, "Officials Say Iran is Seeking Nuclear Weapons Capability," *Washington Post,* October 30, 1991, P. Al.

17. R. Jeffrey Smith, "China-Iran Nuclear Tie Long Known," *Washington Post,* October 31, 1991, p. Al.

18. Qian Qichen, interview with reporters during a visit to Japan, June 27, 1991; Li Peng, interview with Chinese and Iranian journalists during a visit to Iran, July 10, 1991, both in *Chinese Statements on Proliferation Issues,* ibid, p. 6-7.

19. T.R. Reid, "China Plans to Sign Pact on A-Arms," *Washington Post,* August 11, 1991; Mark Hibbs, "Chinese Signature on NPT May Pressure North Korea," *Nucleonics Week,* August 15, 1991.

20. France acceded to the NPT on August 3, 1992, five months after China.

21. White House Statement, Letter to Congress, and Report to Congress on Extension of MFN Status to China, *Department of State Dispatch,* vol. 3 no. 23, June 8, 1992, p. 452.

22. The MTCR guidelines were revised on January 7, 1993 by the United States and 21 other members to cover all missiles capable of delivering weapons of mass destruction (chemical, biological, and nuclear), regardless of range and payload. *Department of State Dispatch,* vol.4, no. 3, p.41.

23. Those sanctions were required by Chapter 7 of the Arms Export Control Act, P.L. 90-629, "Control of Missiles and Missile Equipment or Technology." On Chinese missile proliferation and the U.S. response see Shirley Kan, *Chinese Missile and Nuclear Proliferation: Issues for Congress,* Congressional Research Service, 1993.

24. Don Oberdorfer, "China to Reinforce Pledge on Missiles," *Washington Post,* February 2, 1992, p. A17.

25. "China: Most-Favored-Nation Status," Statement released by the White House, May 28, 1993; Executive Order on Conditions for Renewal of Most Favored-Nation Status for the Peoples's Republic of China in 1994; and Statement by Winston Lord, Assistant Secretary of State for East Asian and Pacific Affairs before the House Ways and Means Committee, Subcommittee on Trade, June 8, 1993, in *US Department of State Dispatch,* June 14, 1993,

vol. 4, no. 24, P. 425.

26. Statement by State Department spokesman Michael McCurry, August 25, 1993; "US Punishes China Over Missile Sales," *Washington Post,* August 26, 1993, Al; Shirley Kan, *Chinese Nuclear and Missile Proliferation,* op. cit.

27. Embassy of the People's Republic of China, Press Release, August 27, 1993. See also, Ambassador Li Daoyu, "Foreign Policy and Arms Control: The View From China," *Arms Control Today,* Dec. 1993, p. 11. Both official statements deny that China transferred M-11 components to Pakistan.

28. R. Jeffrey Smith and Daniel Williams, "US Offers to Waive China Trade Sanctions," *Washington Post,* Nov. 11, 1993, A39; Elaine Sciolino, "US and China Try to End Bar to High-Tech Trade," *New York Times,* Nov. 12, 1993, A10. The satellites reportedly contain sensitive components, but were to be launched without revealing information about those components.

29. John Lewis, Hua Di, and Xue Litai, "Beijing's Defense Establishment, Solving the Arms-Export Enigma," *InternationalSecurity,*Spring 1991, Vol. 15, No. 4, P. 99; John Frankenstein, "The Peoples Republic of China: Arms Production, Industrial Strategy, and Problems of History," in Herbert Wulf, ed., *Arms Industry Limited* (New York: Oxford University Press, 1993), P. 280; Barry Naughton, "The Third Front: Defense Industrialization in the Chinese Interior," *China Quarterly,* September, 1988, P. 352.

30. Richard Bitzinger, "Chinese Arms Production and Sales to the Third World,," RAND Note N3334-USDP, 1991, P. 3; Bates Gill, "The Challenge of Chinese Arms Proliferation: U.S. Policy for the 1990s," ibid, p. 23.

31. John Lewis, Hua Di, and Xue Litai, "Beijing's Defense Establishment," op. cit., Figure 1, "Organization of China's Military System Related to Arms Sales," p. 89; and John Frankenstein, "The People's Republic of China: Arms Production, Industrial Strategy and Problems of History," op. cit., Table 14. 1, "China's Military-Industrial Commercial Complex in the 1990s, P. 276-277; R. Bates Gill, "The Challenge of Chinese Arms Proliferation: U.S. Policy for the 1990s," op. cit., P. 20-23; Ronald Humble, "Science, Technology, and China's Defense Industrial Base," *Jane's IntelligenceReview,* v.4, January 1992, p. 5-6.

32. *China Foreign Trade Reform: Meeting the Challenge of the 1990s,* World Bank Report No. 11568-CHA, June 18, 1993, p. 68.

33. "New MOFERT Regulations on Export Control Explained," *Hong Kong Ching-Chi Tao-Pao (Economic Reporter),* Jan. 22, 1990, p. 15. Translated in

JPRS-CAR-90-023, March 29, 1990.

34. Interview with MOFERT officials; "Temporary Regulations on Export License System," *Beijing Guoji Shangbao,* Dec. 21, 1991, p. 2, translated in JPRS-CAR-92-006, *Trade Transparency: MOFERT Regulations,* Feb. II, 1992; and JPRS-CAR-92-057, *Trade Transparency: MOFERT's Third Set of Regulations on Foreign Trade and Investment,* July 30, 1992.

35. An export may be considered to be sensitive by virtue of its potential to aid the development or acquisition of weapons of mass destruction, or by its destination. For example, the US Commodity Control List restricts exports of specific items and restricts exports to certain countries for security and foreign policy reasons. See Glennon Harrison, *Export Controls: Background and Issues, CRS Report,* January 1994.

36. Lewis *et al.* describe the networks as based on a "lingering clan mentality." Lewis et al, ibid, p. 91.

37. See note #32; "China's Defense Industrial Trading Companies," DIA Reference Series UP-1920-271-90.

38. "MOFERT Regulations on Trade-Related S&T," Beijing *Guoji Shangbao,* April 18, 1992, p. 2, in *Trade Transparency: Mofert's Third Set of Regulations of Foreign Trade and Investment,* JPRS-CAR-92-057, July 30, 1992, p. 14; Ronald Humble, "Science, Technology and China's Defense Industrial Base," *Jane's Intelligence Review,* ibid.

39. Discussion with MOFERT officials.

40. Richard Grimmett, *Conventional Arms Transfers to the Third World, 1985-1992,* Congressional Research Service, July 1993.

41. Zachary Davis, *The Nuclear Nonproliferation Treaty: Preparations for a Vote on Its Extension,* CRS Issue Brief, March, 1994.

42. This point is elaborated by Robert Manning in *Back to the Future: Toward a Post-Nuclear Ethic - The New Logic of Nonproliferation,* Progressive Policy Institute, January 1994.

Chapter 14

The Challenge of Nonproliferation Export Control in the Former Soviet Union

Gary K. Bertsch

Introduction

The disintegration of the former Soviet Union (FSU) raises the threat of what US Senator Sam Nunn has referred to as "the danger of the largest [weapons] proliferation in the history of the world."[1] The FSU was a nuclear and military superpower. The successor and newly independent states (NIS) of the FSU have inherited vast stockpiles of conventional and non-conventional weapons, including nuclear weapons, and the industrial and technological capacity to build more.[2]

The weapons supply is great in the NIS and so are the economic incentives to sell. Financially strapped states, enterprises, groups, and individuals in the FSU can make considerable money by selling weapons and weapons related materials and technologies. There will always be some who are willing to do so even when such sales violate national policy and international norms. The demand is also considerable and comes from many dangerous states including North Korea and China in the East Asia and Iran, Iraq, and Libya in the Middle East. Political instability in many of the NIS has severely weakened governmental authority. The development of effective export controls is a low priority in the present NIS environments of economic and political crisis. Furthermore, there is no export control experience or expertise in these states, with the exception of Russia. With the growth of privatization, reduced governmental control, and a "sell anything" mentality among many of the new marketeers, the challenge of NIS nonproliferation export control in the 1990s is extraordinarily acute.

Export controls can make and have made a difference. A Russian company's attempt to export a banned chemical to Libya was blocked by Ukrainian customs officials in April 1993.[3] German officials have blocked a host of dangerous transfers of NIS origin including enriched uranium and other weapons related technology and materials.[4] Police in Finland and Germany arrested seven persons, including two Russians, in August 1993 who were carrying small quantities which they hoped to sell of the isotope californium-252, obtained from the Russian nuclear complex Tomsk-7. In June 1994, the Russian press reported that the St. Petersburg branch of the Federal Counterintelligence Service arrested three individuals and confiscated 3.05 kilograms of enriched uranium. The material was reportedly stolen from a plant in the Moscow area.[5] German authorities seized weapons grade plutonium on a Lufthansa flight from Moscow to Munich in August of 1994. German Chancellor Helmut Kohl called the nuclear smuggling a "grave danger" and Foreign Minister Klaus Kinkel called for a new comprehensive system of export controls and urged the Russians and governments in neighboring states to improve their export controls.[6] NIS, European, and international export control officials and systems working in harmony can help stop the dangerous exports that nations have agreed to control.

Underdeveloped and ineffective controls as exist in most of the NIS, on the other hand, will allow a considerable amount of dangerous exports to pass through national borders. Because of the need for export earnings, NIS government officials are often more sensitive to export promotion than export control. This point of view was expressed by Russian Prime Minister Victor Chemomyrdin when he told Russian exporters: "I am all for selling military goods, but the problem is no one is buying them; if you manage to find a client I am ready to sign *any* export license" (italics mine).[7]

Scientific experts and government export control officials themselves are sometimes more sensitive to making money than to controlling proliferation. Gennady Mesyats, Vice President of the Russian Academy of Sciences and the Academy's representative to the

Russian Export Control Commission, has described his efforts to work around controls in order to arrange export control agreements.[8] Mesyats claimed that directors of Russian scientific institutes have the right to negotiate technology transfers and make assessments as to the dual-use (and proliferation) potential of transfers. Mesyats noted that if a conflict arises "I make a few calls and the [Export Control] Commission will look the other way."

There is also a disturbing denial and "everything is under control" attitude surrounding Russian export controls. When the numerous reports on nuclear leaks were made in summer of 1994, the dominant response in the Russian bureaucracy was denial, rather than this is something that needs to be investigated. Experts in Russia and abroad are well aware that the Russian system of nuclear materials accounting is deficient and makes the denial or verification of reported leaks very difficult. A Russian response in 1994 that "this is a deficiency that we are addressing or will address" would have been more assuring than the flat denials coming from most official quarters.

What is and can be done to deal with such problems? What export control policies, rules and regulations exist in Russia and the other NIS? What policies have been implemented to address these issues, and with what effects? Furthermore, what is the West doing to help the NIS develop more effective export controls? What should be done in the future?

Nonproliferation Export Control in Russia

The FSU developed a weapons industry that was, with the exception of the United States, unequaled in the world. With the collapse of the Soviet state, Russia inherited most of this industry and military-industrial know-how. In the present environment of economic hardship, individuals can benefit economically by exporting the products of and technology related to this industry. Russian exporters and government officials are confronted daily with reconciling the competing interests of weapons and weapons-related *sales* and nonproliferation *export control*.

Unlike the other NIS, Russia inherited considerable experience in both these activities (i.e., *exporting and controlling)* from its Soviet predecessor. While export promotion is an important activity deserving attention, we will focus here on the issue of *export control*. We will, however, acknowledge the obvious; that is, that Russia commands considerable export potential in conventional and non-conventional weapons.[9] It is Russia's desire and ability to *control weapons of mass destruction and their associated technologies and materials* that will concern us here.

There are a complex set of forces affecting the development and implementation of nonproliferation export controls in Russia. Some forces are "enhancing" the development of controls and others appear to be "impeding," or making controls more difficult. Unfortunately, as Figure 15.1 indicates, there appear to be more forces impeding than facilitating the development of Russian controls. Let us begin with the "good news," the enhancing factors.

With the collapse of the USSR in 1991, the government of the Russian Federation inherited the export control policy, personnel, and bureaucracy of its Soviet predecessor.[10] Because the Soviet communist state maintained a centralized foreign trade monopoly, the function of export control was relatively simple and effective. The Export Control Commission of the State Planning Committee (GOSPLAN) carried out export control in line with Communist Party policy. Although the Soviet state was a major exporter of conventional weapons, it strictly controlled the export of nuclear related goods and technologies. The considerable stability and power of the Soviet government allowed it to implement its nonproliferation export controls authoritatively and relatively effectively. These factors--the inherited control tradition, the foreign trade monopoly, and the governmental institutions and personnel who carried it out--are forces which may influence export control development and make implementation easier in Russia than in the other NIS.

There are other factors facilitating Russian nonproliferation export control. High level officials like Boris Yeltsin have declared their support for nonproliferation and have worked with the relevant ministries to push through a series of presidential decrees and government resolutions which form the legal basis for Russian export controls today. (See Appendix 14.1 for a listing of many of these decrees.)

Decree No. 388 ("On Measures for Creating an Export Control System in Russia") provides the present basis for nonproliferation export control in the Russian Federation (see Appendix 14.2 for this 1992 decree).

Figure 14.1:
Forces Affecting the Development of Nonproliferation Export
Control in Russia

Enhancing Development
1. Soviet tradition of nonproliferation with weapons of mass destruction (WMD)
2. inherited governmental institutions and personnel with export control experience
3. high level political support and declaratory policy in the form of decrees, resolutions, etc.
4. Russian security concerns resulting from the possible spread of WMD
5. Western pressure, encouragement, and assistance
6. desire to be recognized as a civilized, democratic state and to create a favorable trade and investment climate

Impeding Development
1. disorder and confusion resulting from the breakup of the Soviet Union.
2. diminishing governmental authority and growth of organized crime and corruption in the weapons trade
3. increasing regionalization and decreasing central control
4. growing Russian nationalism critical of submission to Western interests
5. bureaucratic politics placing export promotion over export control and intragovernmental rivalry over cooperation
6. shortage of funding for export control personnel and policy implementation
7. overmilitarized economy and industrial pressures for military exports
8. slow pace of defense conversion and continuing military production
9. porous borders and lack of customs control and enforcement
10. less than ideal coordination and cooperation with neighboring NIS countries
11. tradition of economic and technological cooperation with problem countries

Source: Expanded and adapted from Mike Beck, Gary Bertsch, and Igor Khripunov, "The Development of Nonproliferation Export Control in Russia," *World Affairs*, 157:1 (Summer 1994): 17.

The decree calls for an interagency Export Control Commission to implement Russia's export control policy. This body is not autonomous, however, and is buffeted by other (and often higher level) bodies such as the Security Council and the Presidency, and independent governmental institutions such as the Russian Parliament, the Foreign Intelligence Agency, and the military industrial complex (see Figure 14.2). However, the high level political support, decrees and administrative structure, taken together, give the Russian Federation some of the necessary ingredients for policy success.[11]

There are also other "enhancing" factors that deserve mention. Number 4 in Figure 14.1 calls attention to the Russian security concerns that result from the possible spread of weapons of mass destruction. Mr. Yevgeniy Primakov, Director of the Russian Foreign Intelligence Service has expressed the concern this way: "The problem of the proliferation of weapons of mass destruction affects the immediate interests of Russia. A situation in which new states possessing weapons of mass destruction on the perimeter of Russian borders looks unacceptable."[12] The former director of export controls in the Russian Ministry of Foreign Affairs expressed Russia's national security concern similarly:

> We should underline that Russia is developing its national export control system not as a favor to Western countries but for its own national sake. Russia has inherited from the cold war perhaps the worst periphery. All the would-be proliferators are there. In case of failure of Russian export controls, Russia would be the first and major victim of potential proliferation. That is why setting up an effective export control system is a strategic imperative for this country, a matter of vital importance and even national survival.[13]

It is clear to Russian policy-makers and officials that powerful weapons can spread to neighboring states and be targeted at Moscow. Russia's more cooperative post-Cold War relationship with the West also has an "enhancing" impact on her nonproliferation and export control policy. At present, Russia is receiving assistance, encouragement, and pressure from the United States and other industrial democracies to do all that it can to control dangerous exports. The Russian government appears to be trying to cooperate because it desires to be recognized by the Western democracies as a cooperating, civilized state that deserves normalized trade and technological relations with the post-industrial democracies. It also appears to be cooperating because it desires the economic "carrots" these post-industrial economies are linking to Russian cooperation.

Unfortunately, there is a longer and troubling list of "impeding factors" in Russia (see Figure 14.1). First is the disorder and confusion resulting from the breakup of the USSR. The disintegration of the Soviet state had a powerful deleterious impact upon proliferation and export controls in Russia and the region. Following the Soviet collapse, there is diminished governmental authority and control. The central government is losing power while organized crime is gaining power. According to the Russian Ministry of Internal Affairs, there are 91 organized criminal groups in Russia with foreign connections.[14] One day before Prime Minister Chernomyrdin's 1994 visit to Italy, Russian television reported documented evidence of cooperation between Italian, South American, Chinese and Russian organized criminal elements in trading of weapons and weapons-related materials and technologies.[15]

Diminishing authority of the central government is also marked by the growing power and activity of regional governments and military industrial enterprises in conducting foreign trade and weapons and weapons-related commerce. There is much money to be made in some local areas. There is decreasing deference to Moscow and almost "anything goes" in the new quest for *"free"* trade and *"private"* enterprise.

Another trend is that related to Russian nationalism and international cooperation. In the present environment of economic hardship, a "Russian interests come first" point-of-view is on the rise. Many Russian leaders feel that the promotion of exports and protection of Russian economic interests can not be subordinated to international cooperation on nonproliferation. It is increasingly difficult for moderate leaders like President Boris Yeltsin or Foreign Minister Andrei Kozyrev to argue for Russian export control given the rise of ultra-nationalist leaders such as Vladimir Zhirinovsky. This trend in national politics is also apparent in the increase in bureaucratic politics. The Russian Ministry of Foreign Affairs and its support for international export control cooperation may be losing ground to export-oriented economic agencies of the Russian government. In this bureaucratic environment, government funding for export control

Figure 14.2

Organizational Chart of the Russian Federation (RF) Export Control System

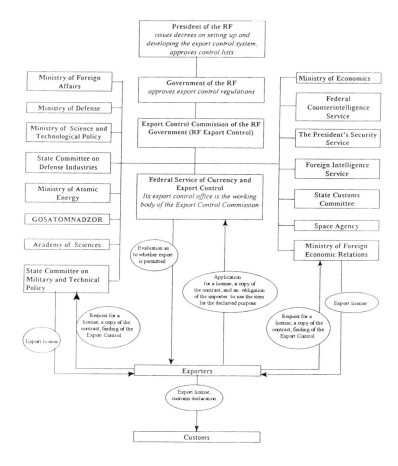

programs and personnel is a low priority resulting in the employment of less than a hundred officials in the Russian government handling the same export control functions that are handled by what must be over a 1000 in the United States. Little money exists in the Russian export control community for additional staff, computers, traveling to and participating in international programs to deal with export control and nonproliferation initiatives and the like.

In this competitive environment of nationalistic and bureaucratic politics, there appears to be a rise in conflictual relations among the Russian governmental agencies that must work together to control proliferation. On February 24, 1994, *Rossiiskaya Gazeta* reported that Minister of Atomic Energy Victor Mikhailov sent a letter to Minister of Internal Affairs Victor Yerin requesting him to take necessary measures that would prevent reports by his employees based on "inventions and fantasies,"[16] Minister Mikhailov claimed that employees of the Ministry of Internal Affairs were regularly speaking to the media about cases of stolen weapons-grade uranium and plutonium, and even cases of nuclear warheads, being taken from the facilities of the Ministry of Atomic Energy. Minister Mikhailov said he knew of no such cases and asked the Minister of Internal Affairs to produce evidence if he knew. Bureaucratic frictions such as this do not bode well for inter-agency export control implementation.

There is also unfortunate conflict within organizations responsible for export controls. Differing interests and views on export controls within the Ministry of Economics resulted in the 1994 movement of the Export Control Office to a new (and much lower status) agency, the Federal Service of Currency and Export Control. Personal ambitions and petty organizational politics is rampant in the bureaucracy and is having a significant impact on the implementation of export control policy in Russia.

The overly militarized Russian economy also affects the domestic politics of Russia and thereby impedes the establishment and implementation of effective export control policies. With the powerful political pressures coming from the military industrial complex, the considerably weaker export control lobby is likely to lose. This is the situation today and is bound to continue in the future in view of the slow pace of defense conversion and continuing military production. If the military industrial enterprises could convert to non-military production, a major factor contributing to proliferation would be reduced.

The problem of export control is worsened by the political and economic relations Russia has with other states in the region. With the disintegration of the USSR, the once secure Soviet border dissolved into a complicated and porous confusion of Russian and NIS borders. The director of Russia's Foreign Intelligence Agency characterized the situation this way:

> Russia has proved to be a country with transparent borders. The military industrial complex is on the verge of collapse. The financial situation is grave in "closed" cities, where a high level of secrecy has been traditionally maintained. Today the entire system of control over the maintenance of secrets is cracking at the seams and becoming warped as is the military-industrial complex.[17]

Customs control and enforcement in this environment are considerably weakened. Furthermore, with the tradition of economic and technological cooperation among the former Soviet republics, a high level of commerce moves through these borders. Thus far, there is less than ideal customs and export control cooperation among these states, and the potential for considerable illicit trade in weapons and weapons-related materials and technologies is great.

To deal with this problem Russia has attempted to promote export control cooperation within the Commonwealth of Independent States (CIS). The Russian government was instrumental in bringing most CIS governments together in Minsk in June of 1992 to sign an export control cooperation agreement. (See Appendix 14.3 for the text of this agreement.) The agreement was to encourage efforts to develop coordinated export control lists and systems, to share information and experience, and to promote the implementation and enforcement of export control policies. Unfortunately, the level of CIS cooperation and coordination thus far has been discouraging.[18]

Finally, the former Soviet Union had a tradition of economic and technological cooperation with many of the countries (e.g., Iraq, Iran, and North Korea) that are considered among the "problem proliferant states." The potential for illicit transfers to these states is considerable given this tradition, the economic incentives involved, and the difficulties of export control.

When taking all of the "enhancing" and "impeding" forces into account, it is clear that Russia is finding, and will likely find in the future, the implementation of nonproliferation export control to be a considerable challenge.[19] Although the declaratory policy for export control represented by the Russian leadership's policy pronouncements and promulgated decrees is impressive, it should not be confused with effective policy implementation. Research in both East and West should give more attention to the implementation component of the policy process and to the policy outcomes that result.

Nonproliferation Export Control Development in the Other NIS

Belarus, Ukraine and Kazakhstan

Without the export control tradition and inheritance that Russia received from the USSR, other NIS had to build their export control systems from scratch. Belarus is actively engaged in this process. Contemporary Belarusan nonproliferation export control policy reflects the government's commitment to denuclearization. In October of 1991 the Belarusan government decreed (No. 386) that weapons and weapons-related materials, technology, and equipment must be licensed for export by the State Committee for Foreign Economic Relations (see Appendix 14.4). A subsequent decree (No. 516) in August of 1992 defined more clearly the export licensing procedures and responsibilities of respective ministries and departments for controlling weapons and military hardware, nuclear materials, and dual-use items. The decree banned altogether the export of such items to zones of conflict and allowed only duly authorized companies to engage in such business.

In 1993 the Belarus government gave more attention to export control issues and licensing. A decree (No. 344) of Council of Ministers in May 1993 implemented a common export administration procedure applying to all enterprises in Belarus. This regulation is the main act for export administration in the country. An October 1993 regulation (No. 733) of the Council of Ministers specified how export control violators would be punished. A December 1993 regulation (No. 82) of the same Council addressed the transfer of dangerous items and materials across the borders of Belarus. The regulation approved a list of controlled items including weapons and ammunition, explosives and explosive devices, and radioactive and nuclear materials. In 1995 Belarusan authorities were considering the drafting and implementation of a comprehensive export control law.

Like Russia, the Belarus export control mechanism involves numerous governmental agencies. These include a Council of Ministers Commission which issues permissions for significant foreign trade operations, the Economic and State Planning Committee, the Ministry of Foreign (or sometimes called External) Economic Relations, the Ministry of Foreign Affairs, the Ministry of Defense, the State Customs Committee, Border Guards, and the State Security Committee (KGB). The Ministry of Foreign Economic Relations plays a leading role in developing export control policy and in export administration.

Export licensing is based upon seven control lists: No. 1 - nuclear weapons, material and equipment related to nuclear weapons, and relevant dual-use technologies; No. 2 - chemical weapons and equipment for their production; No. 3 - bacteriological (biological) weapons and equipment for their production; No. 4 - delivery means for nuclear, chemical and bacteriological weapons; No. 5 - conventional weapons; No. 6 - raw materials, equipment, inventions, technologies, services, and know-how which can be used in manufacturing weapons and military hardware; and No. 7 - dual-use items of use in weapons.

The Belarusan government has established an Export Control Commission to coordinate state policy and licensing. The Ministry of Foreign Economic Relations handles day to day licensing matters. Licenses may be denied for items included in lists 1-7 if official information from relevant bodies reveals that the export violates international nonproliferation agreements, or if there are substantiated facts of clandestine or illegal acquisition or use by the importer of such items for manufacturing weapons of mass destruction. Decisions to deny licenses are to be communicated to the applicant in writing and include reasons for denial.

The principal export control problem for Belarus is the transshipment of sensitive goods through Belarus. Transshipment problems require close export control cooperation with other countries in the region. Although Belarus is a signatory to the June 1992 CIS Export Control Cooperation Agreement, it has not taken an active role in advancing the cooperative work called for in the agreement.

In October of 1992 the Belarus Ministry of Defense signed an export control related agreement with the US Department of Defense "Concerning the Provision of Assistance Related to Establishing an Export Control System to Prevent Proliferation of Weapons of Mass Destruction from Belarus." This agreement has resulted in a US program of export control assistance (financial and technical) in Belarus.

(This involves, among other things, the commitment of $16.26 million dollars of US assistance for export control development in Belarus.)

Belarusan experts indicate that the major need continues to be developing export control expertise and the training of export control officials.[20] The governmental Institute of the State Security Committee is involved in training such officials. A nongovernmental organization, the Minsk Center for Nonproliferation and Export Control (co-founded by two American institutions, the University of Georgia and the Monterey Institute of International Studies) is involved in a number of activities designed to promote export control and nonproliferation. Dr. Ural Latypov, former Director of Research at the Center, described these activities as follows:

• providing public information reflecting the modern experience of export control including the international nonproliferation regimes
• conducting international research on nonproliferation and export control issues
• preparing materials and manuals for exporters on export administration issues
• publishing periodicals on export control issues
• organizing seminars and conferences on export administration issues for specialists from Belarus and other NIS
• organizing short-term training courses for exporters
• supporting students and researchers dealing with export administration and export control issues[21]

Latypov believes that US assistance can be put to good use. The main use should be for personnel training and include:

• assistance in developing curricula on non-proliferation and export control
• assistance in the preparation of manuals, training aids, and materials for practical studies
• providing literature for specialized libraries and a database on export control issues
• delivery of computer and other hardware and software for application in training
• training of Belarus lecturers in the US and participation of American lecturers in training of national personnel in Belarus
• training of Belarus students in American educational institutions.[22]

Like their Belarusan counterparts, Ukrainian officials are also working hard to develop a viable export control system. And like Belarus, they too are still in the early stages of doing so. Presidential decrees define the current (1995) export control system. A Presidential decree (No. 3) of January 1993 established two new export control bodies. They are the State Commission on Export Controls and the Expert Technical Committee. A Cabinet of Ministers decree (No. 160) of March 1993 "On Establishing State Controls over Exports/Imports of Arms, Military Material, and Materials Needed for Their Production" was intended to implement the Presidential decree. Decree No. 778 (September 1993) outlined the roles and responsibilities of the Expert Technical Committee under the Cabinet of Ministers.

The State Export Control Commission has the function of issuing licenses for weapons and weapons-related and dual use exports. The decisions of the Commission are intended to be binding on all ministries and state agencies. The Export Control Commission was headed in 1994 by Vasily Ivanovich Yevtukhov, Deputy Prime Minister of Ukraine. As head of the Commission, his responsibilities include: securing control over exports in order to honor Ukraine's international commitments regarding the nonproliferation of weapons of mass destruction (WMD) and their delivery systems; coordinating the formulation of Ukrainian export control policy concerning dual-use items; overseeing intergovernmental agreements regarding the arms trade; undertaking improvements in the export control system; cooperating with foreign export control bodies and experts; developing and updating the control lists; and overseeing the functioning of the Expert Technical Committee.[23]

The Expert Technical Committee is the key body providing technical support to the State Commission. It also has the responsibility of overseeing the implementation of decisions of the Commission. Other governmental agencies are also involved. For example, the Ministry of Foreign Affairs coordinates Ukrainian policy with other states. Yet, there is considerable change and uncertainty regarding agency roles and responsibilities in the Ukrainian export control system. Agency roles are being continually redefined.[24] Like Belarus, much remains to be done to create and implement a comprehensive and effective national export control policy.

Of the four nuclear republics of the FSU, Kazakhstan has the farthest to go to establish a viable export control system. This is particularly troubling in view of Kazakhstan's extensive nuclear weapons related materials and technology.[25] Like in Russia, Belarus, and Ukraine, government decrees and resolutions currently serve as the legal basis for Kazakh export controls. For example, in February 1992 the President of Kazakhstan issued a decree (similar to that of Russia) on export licensing and quotas. In 1993 and 1994 the legal basis of Kazakhstan's export controls appeared to be the Cabinet of Ministers March 1993 decree (No. 183) "On Control of Export/Import of Nuclear Materials, Special Non-nuclear Materials, and Dual-Use Materials." A government resolution "On Export and Import of Nuclear Materials, Technologies, Equipment, Plants, Special Nonnuclear Materials, Sources of Radiation and Isotope Products," regulates nuclear weapons related trade. Article five of the resolution stipulates that nuclear exports to nonnuclear states will be granted only if there are assurances from the importing state that the imports will:

- not be used for producing nuclear weapons or pursuing military objectives;
- be under IAEA safeguards in accordance with a safeguards agreement between the recipient country and IAEA;
- be physically protected in line with IAEA standards and recommendations; and
- be reexported only on conditions specified by relevant Kazakh authorities (e.g., the Kazakhstan Atomic Energy Agency).

Like the other three nuclear successor states to the FSU, Kazakhstan has an interagency export control structure which includes the National Security and Defense Committee of the Kazakh Supreme Soviet, Kazakhstan Customs Service, Ministry of Foreign Economic Relations (renamed Ministry of Industry and Trade), Ministry of Internal Affairs, the Ministry of Economics, and Ministry of Foreign Affairs, and the Kazakhstan Atomic Energy Agency. The principal governmental bodies with responsibility for export control are the Ministry of Foreign Affairs, Ministry of Atomic Energy, and the Ministry of Industry and Trade. All of these agencies, however, have few who work on the issue of export control. For example, in 1994 the Ministry of Atomic Energy (the lead agency) had three officials with responsibilities for export control but all were involved with other responsibilities as well.

Nonproliferation export control in other NIS.

Export control is a low policy priority in most of the remaining NIS for numerous reasons. These states do not have nuclear weapons, have far fewer military (particularly nuclear) assets, and have not received as much external and internal pressures and support to control exports. They are also consumed by what their leaders and citizens perceive to be far more pressing issues (e.g., economic survival) and they consider export control to be a relatively esoteric policy issue (and one which appears to be counter to the imperative to *expand* exports). Finally, these new states are overwhelmed with the new responsibilities of governance and have far too few resources and competent personnel to handle the responsibilities of state.

Although these countries do not have the military capabilities of the four nuclear republics, they are not insignificant in terms of their potential for proliferation. The development of export controls and nonproliferation restraint is important for several reasons including: 1) they can be (and have been) involved in the transshipment of illegal exports from neighboring states; 2) some do have significant nuclear and other weapons related assets that can contribute to proliferation problems and should be subject to control; and 3) many represent unstable and desperate political environments that have been (or may be) the site of violent conflict. Advanced weaponry can be easily and destructively used in such environments of economic hardship, injustice, and conflict. Although of lesser significance than the four militarily advanced nuclear weapons states, the other NIS are still of considerable consequence when it comes to proliferation threats and export controls.

One country that is working to develop a viable export control system is Latvia. The Latvian Cabinet of Ministers passed a resolution in September 1994 "On Control System of Strategic Export and Import of Goods, Products, Services and Technologies." This resolution appointed the Control Committee of Strategic Export and Import. The Committee is composed of representatives of the Latvian Development Agency and the Ministries of Defense, Economics, Environment, Finance, Foreign Affairs, Interior, Regional Development, and Welfare. The Ministry of Foreign Affairs presides over the Committee. The committee is to prepare export control legislation for the Parliament; establish, appoint personnel, and administer an executive body, the

Export-Import Control Department; prepare export control lists and licensing procedures; represent Latvia in international export control regimes; and coordinate international assistance and cooperation.[26]

The specialist from the Ministry of Foreign Affairs went on to note that although the developments above are an important accomplishment, export control in the Baltic and newly independent states will face a variety of difficulties, including:

> It is no secret that in transition to the market economy there will always be a great number of large and small shady companies, some even with a criminal background, which will act on the principle to make quick money by any means possible and then disappear.[27]

The Latvian official concluded by calling for the exchange of confidential information and close cooperation among countries in the region.

What Is Being and Should Be Done to Promote NIS Export Control Development?

Deeply troubled about the potential for weapons proliferation from the territories of the NIS, most concerned governments and experts believe that considerable effort should be made to promote export control development in these states.   At the 1992 G-7 summit in Munich, for example, the representative declared that "We attach the highest importance to the establishment in the former Soviet Union of effective export controls on nuclear materials, weapons, and other sensitive goods and technologies and will offer training and assistance to help achieve this."[28] Unfortunately, too little has been and is being done to provide this assistance.   Two countries doing much, but still too little, are the United States and Japan.

The United States

Senator Nunn's concern about "the danger of the largest [weapons] proliferation in the history of the world" noted at the outset of this chapter is widely shared by many US governmental and nongovernmental experts.   The US Congress appropriated significant sums of money to address this threat and some of it was earmarked for promoting export control development in the NIS. For example, the so-called "Nunn-Lugar" appropriations provided millions of dollars of financial support. Basic Nunn-Lugar funding in 1993 provided a base of $2.26 million for export controls in the four nuclear republics, Belarus, Kazakhstan, Russia, and Ukraine. This base of support expands when the four republics meet certain conditions. After signing the bilateral agreement on export control implementation with the United States, and after reviewing Belarus' active denuclearization policy and practice, US officials expanded export control assistance to Belarus to $16.26 million.

In this context the US's Belarus Export Control Assistance Project outlined three important and interrelated areas for support: policy development, program development, and training and technical assistance. Numerous governmental groups traveled to Belarus in the early 1990s to put the project in place and to implement the assistance program. Both Belarusan and US governmental and nongovernmental experts characterize the implementation of the project as slow and disappointing and believe more can and should be done.

The Ukrainian government is also working to establish a viable export control system. Because Ukraine signed the bilateral export control agreement with the United States and demonstrated its commitment to export control development and cooperation, the United States raised Ukraine's "Nunn-Lugar" export control assistance base to $7.6 million in 1994. As in Belarus, however, the implementation of the US export control assistance program and the use of the funding has been slow and disappointing to all parties.

Perhaps the largest threat and most disappointing developments have been in Russia. The site of a massive nuclear, conventional, and unconventional weapons arsenal, too little has been done and is being done to support Russian export control development. There are many reasons for this. Russia had not signed the bilateral export control agreement with the United States (as of December 1994) and was therefore ineligible for "Nunn-Lugar" export control assistance. Russian officials generally contend that export controls are sound in Russia, that "everything is under control," and that they prefer export control "cooperation" rather than "assistance." They have been much more cautious in cooperating and in seeking US export control assistance than either Belarus or Ukraine. In fact, they have requested and received little export control assistance from either US governmental or nongovernmental sources.

At the same time, there appears to be considerable potential for both cooperation and assistance. Presidents Clinton and Yeltsin have discussed both issues on several occasions and their governments have released numerous memoranda and statements noting agreement and pledging cooperation (see the Joint Statement and Memorandum of Intent in Appendices V and VI). Although useful consultation and discussion has taken place, relatively little of consequence has been done to promote the development of more effective export controls in Russia.

Kazakhstan has signed the bilateral agreement and has sought US governmental and nongovernmental assistance. Thus far, it has received little. The other NIS states have received even less export control assistance from either US governmental or nongovernmental sources. They have requested it at various times and in various places but have received almost nothing of significance.

Japan

Japanese officials are troubled about military exports and export control, For example, Japanese officials are very concerned about Russian weapons exports to Iran. From their view, this problem must be addressed before Russia can fully participate in a new post-COCOM export control system. In addition, official assistance for Russian export control efforts is hampered by the territorial issues which divide the two countries. The Ministry of Foreign Affairs, the private Center for Information on Security Trade Controls (CISTEC), which works closely with the Ministry of International Trade and Industry (MITI) on these issues, and other organizations, however, are bringing delegations of Russian export control officials to Japan. For example, Russian officials participated in a meeting sponsored by the Japan Atomic Industry Forum in September 1994.

There are also important examples of governmental assistance. For example, Japan signed an accord in September of 1994 with the government of Kazakhstan to assist in the development of a Kazakh export control system. As with their efforts to assist Mongolia, this represents the Japanese regional policy focus on supporting Central Asian countries in the development of nonproliferation export controls, allowing other countries to take the lead elsewhere in the FSU. Japanese experience with the Central Asian republics was very limited under Soviet rule, so there is much to do to develop the appropriate contacts and resources for increasing their assistance role in the region.

Conclusion

The challenge of developing effective nonproliferation export controls in the NIS of the FSU is great. Because economic conditions are poor and likely to deteriorate further in the years ahead, there will be unusually strong economic incentives among governments, military industrial enterprises, and individuals to export conventional and nonconventional weapons and weapons related dual-use technologies and materials. Because of these strong economic incentives, political instability, and weak governments, NIS officials may not have the power and capacity to implement effective export control systems. If governments do not have the power and capacity to control the sale of weaponry, then significant proliferation is likely to occur. The United States, Japan, their governmental allies, and nongovernmental organizations should do everything possible to alter this dangerous chain of events.

Promoting nonproliferation and export control development in the NIS requires long-term, multifaceted, and coordinated efforts involving businesses, national governments, international and nongovernmental organizations. This complex collection of private and public organizations should develop a comprehensive plan to encourage desired outcomes. They should share information and coordinate their efforts. They should work together and avoid unnecessary duplication and waste.

Furthermore, foreign assistance should recognize the special conditions and needs in each NIS. Russian infrastructure and expertise with export controls is different than that of Belarus or Ukraine. That of Uzbekistan or Armenia is different from that of Belarus and Ukraine. Differentiated assistance programs should be designed and implemented for each state.

Export control development should be placed and pursued in the broader context of international economic and technological cooperation, defense conversion, and nonproliferation. NIS political leaders, officials, and citizens should be informed that the United States and Japan will be more inclined to encourage economic and technological cooperation with these NIS if they pursue defense conversion and implement effective export controls. Conversely, the United States, Japan, and others brand countries that expand defense production and allow the resulting weapons to be exported to undesirable parties as "pariahs."

The US, Japanese, and other foreign governments should take the lead in developing and implementing such assistance programs in the NIS. However, they should not attempt to meet this challenge alone. There are international organizations such as the International Atomic Energy Agency (IAEA) and Nuclear Suppliers Group (NSG), businesses such as IBM and Hitachi, and nongovernmental organizations such as the Center for Information on Security Trade Controls (CISTEC) and the Center for International Trade and Security (CITS) at the University of Georgia that have important roles to play. Meeting "the danger of the largest weapons proliferation in history of the world" will require a coordinated, multifaceted, and multiparty program.

Appendix 14.1
Russian Export Control Decrees and Resolution[29]

Decree No. 90: On Quotas and Licensing of Exports and Imports of Goods and Services in the Russian Federation. (December 31, 1991)

Decree No. 179: On Categories of Products (Works/Services) and Industrial Wastes, Sale of Which is Prohibited (February 22, 1992)

Decree No. 312: On Control Over Export of Nuclear Materials, Equipment and Technologies from the Russian Federation. (March 27, 1992)

Decree No. 388: On Measures to Establish an Export Control System in Russia. (April 11, 1992)

Government Resolution No. 366: Approval of Nuclear Supplier Guidelines Governing the Transfer of Dual-use Nuclear Related Equipment, Materials, and Technology. (May 29, 1992)

Government Resolution No. 469: Approval of the List of Individual Types of Raw Materials, Equipment, and Technology and Scientific and Technical Information Used in Developing Weapons and Military Hardware, whose Export is Controlled and Licensed During the Period of 1992-1993. (July 5, 1992)

Decree No. 508: Control on the Export from the Russian Federation of Chemicals and Technologies which have Peaceful Purpose but Can Be Used in Developing Chemical Weapons. (September 16, 1992)

Decree No. 711: Control on the Export from the Russian Federation of Pathogenic Organisms, Their Genetically Changed Forms and Fragments of Genetic Materials Which Can Be Used in Developing Bacteriological (Biological) and Toxin Weapons. (November 17, 1992)

Decree No. 1005: On the Procedure of Exports and Imports of Nuclear Materials, Technology, Equipment, Installations, Special Non-nuclear Materials, Radioactive Sources of Ionizing and Isotope Products. (December 21, 1992)

Decree No. 827: Control on the Export from the Russian Federation of Dual-Use Equipment and Materials and Relevant Technologies Used for Nuclear Purposes. (December 28, 1992)

Decree No. 20: Control on the Export from the Russian Federation of Equipment, Materials and Technologies Used in Developing Missile Systems. (January 11, 1993)

Government Resolution 1030: Control on the Implementation of Obligations Stemming from the Guarantees to Use Dual-use Imported and Exported Items and Services for the Declared Purposes. (October 11, 1993)

Appendix 14.2

Yeltsin Decree No. 388 To Create Export Control System

[Text] With a view to protecting the Russian Federation's state interests during the implementation of foreign economic activity and defense industry conversion, and also to observing international obligations regarding the nonproliferation of mass destruction weapons and other very dangerous types of weapons, I resolve:

1.   To create in the Russian Federation an export control system including state administration organs whose activity must be aimed at preventing harm to the Russian Federation's state interests as a result of the export (transfer, exchange) of certain types of raw and other materials, equipment, technologies, scientific and technical information, and services which are used or could be used in the creation of weapons or military equipment, and also of materials, equipment, technologies, and services which have a peaceful purpose but could be utilized in the creation of missile, nuclear, chemical, and other types of mass destruction weapons.

2.   To form the Russian Federation Export Control Commission (Eksportkontrol Rossii) under the Russian Federation Government to ensure a unified state policy in the said sphere and coordinate and provide organization and methodological support for export control work.

The commission's members will include the deputy leaders of the Russian Federation Ministry of Foreign Affairs, Russian Federation Ministry of Economics, Russian Federation Ministry of Defense, Russian Federation Ministry of Science, Higher Education, and Technical Policy, Russian Federation Ministry of Industry, Russian Federation Ministry of Foreign Economic Relations, Russian Federation State Customs Committee, Russian Federation Ministry of Security, Committee for Protecting Russian Federation Economic Interests under the Russian Federation president, State Committee for Oversight of Nuclear and Radiation Safety under the Russian Federation president, and Russian Academy of Sciences.

To entrust to the Russian Federation Ministry of Economics department for export controls over the defense industry complex and conversion the functions of a working organ for the preparation of questions relating to the activity of the Russian Federation Export Control Commission.

3. To appoint Ye. T. Gaydar, first deputy chairman of the Russian Federation Government, as chairman of the Russian Federation Export Control Commission, instructing him within a month to submit for approval to the Russian Federation Government a draft statute, coordinated in the prescribed manner, on the Russian Federation Export Control Commission and proposals on its personnel.

4. To instruct the Russian Federation Export Control Commission: To prepare and present in the second quarter of 1992 for adoption by the Russian Federation Government a draft list of raw and other materials, equipment, technologies, and scientific and technical information which are used or could be used in the creation of armaments and military hardware in 1992-1993 and whose export is controlled and carried out under license;

To prepare and present in the third quarter of 1992 for adoption by the Russian Federation Government schedules of materials, equipment, and technologies which have a peaceful purpose but which could be used in the creation of missile, nuclear, chemical, and other types of mass destruction weapons whose export is controlled with a view to observing the Russian Federation's international commitments on the nonproliferation of weapons of mass destruction.

To lay down that the list and schedules adopted by the Russian Federation Government shall be approved by the Russian Federation president and are binding on all juridical and physical persons on the Russian Federation's territory.

Amendments and additions to the list and schedules shall be made by the Russian Federation Government and subsequently approved by the Russian Federation president.

5. The Russian Federation Foreign Ministry, together with the Russian Federation Export Control Commission, shall conduct talks with the governments of CIS member states on the coordination on a multilateral basis of export control work with a view to the nonproliferation of weapons of mass destruction and also take part in the work of international organizations in preparing international harmonized control lists of materials, equipment, and technologies which have a peaceful purpose but may be used in the creation of weapons of mass destruction.

6. The Russian Federation Ministry of Justice together with the Russian Federation Export Control Commission shall within two months prepare proposals on the introduction of criminal and administrative liability for the

unlawful export of raw and other materials, equipment, technologies, and scientific and technical information and services included in the list and schedules.

7. The decree enters into force from the moment of signing. [Signed] B. Yeltsin, president of the Russian Federation Moscow, The Kremlin, 11 April 1992. No. 388. Source: *Rossiyskaya Gazeta* 4/16/92 Translation FBIS.

Appendix 14.3

CIS Agreement on Export Control Cooperation

On coordination of work on matters of export control issues, materials, equipment, technologies, and services that could be used for developing weapons of mass destruction and their missile delivery systems.

The governments of the state parties of this Agreement, further referred to as "state parties,"
-affirm their readiness to develop economic, scientific and technical ties among themselves and with other countries on the principles of equality and mutual benefit,
- realizing that at the present time the task of preventing the dissemination of the weapons of mass destruction and modern technologies that contribute to their development is acquiring special significance, -taking into consideration that uncontrolled export of some categories of raw materials, materials, equipment,technologies, and services can result in their use by some countries for developing weapons of mass destruction and their delivery systems, which can be used in regional conflicts and terrorist acts, -bearing in mind that the export controls of the above aforementioned products, technologies, and services are aimed at protecting the political, military, and economic interests of the state parties, -guided by the need of consolidating the efforts for creating a coordinated policy for nonproliferation of weapons of mass destruction and agreed upon actions in export controls implementation, taking into account the obligations undertaken by the state parties in accordance with the Alma-Ata and Minsk Agreements, agreed upon are the following :

Article I The State parties shall cooperate on the issues of export controls of some categories raw materials, materials, equipment, technologies, and services, which are used or could be used for development of weapons of mass destruction and their missile delivery systems, and shall carry out coordinated actions for this purpose.

Article 2 The Agreement does not intend to hinder international cooperation provided that such cooperation will not contribute to the development of weapons of mass destruction and their missile delivery systems.

Article 3 The state parties shall comply with the Agreement in accordance with their current legislation and obligations resulting from the Agreement.

Article 4 The state parties consider it necessary to immediately create national export control systems for the purpose of fulfilling the cooperation stipulated in this Agreement.

The principal tasks of these national export control systems will be to secure the export controls of some categories of raw materials, materials, equipment, technologies, and services used in development of weapons of mass destruction and of their missile delivery systems.

Article 5 The state parties shall execute the export controls by establishing licensing and customs controls, which will be based on uniform control lists of some categories of raw materials , materials, equipment, technologies, and services employed in development of weapons of mass destruction and their missile delivery systems. The control lists will be modeled after those used by existing international regimes(of export controls).

Article 6 The state parties will bring the uniform lists to (all) subjects carrying out economic activities, regardless of the forms of ownership existing in state parties' territories, in order to guide them in conducting their foreign economic activities. The state parties will organize suitable export controls enforced by national authorities.

Article 7 The state parties agreed to prevent reexport of raw materials, materials, equipment, technologies, and services covered by the control lists without a written consent of an authorized governmental body in the territory in which they (i.e. technologies, raw material, materials, equipment, technologies, and services) were produced.

Article 8 The state parties shall exchange information on previous export (operations covering the denied cases) of raw materials, materials, equipment, technologies, and services covered by the control lists and the state parties are committed to prevent circulation of any such information,received from the state-parties, to other countries or international organizations.

Article 9 The state parties will pursue coordinated export control policies, including application of sanctions against all economic subjects that violate the export control requirements. In this regard the state parties agreed to hold consultations.

Article 10 The state parties can cooperate with other countries in developing harmonized control lists and standardize export control regulations in the area of raw materials, materials, equipment, technologies, and services used for the development of various kinds of weapons of mass destruction and their missile delivery system.

Article 11 Each state party has the right to withdraw from this Agreement by notifying in writing the government of the Republic of Belarus and other state parties of its decision no less than 6 months prior to the presumed date of withdrawal.

Article 12 The Agreement can be modified or amended only with the mutual consent of the state parties.

Article 13 This goes into effect the moment it is signed.

Article 14 Done in the city of Minsk on the 26th of June 1992 in one original Russian language copy. The original is deposited at the Archives of the Government of the Republic of Belarus. The government of Belarus. The government of Belarus will send a certified copy to each government that signed this Agreement.

Minsk, June 26, 1992

Appendix 14.4

Belarus Export Control Decrees*

Decree No. 386: On Regulations Governing Exports and Imports. (October 16, 1991)

Decree No. 50: On Quotas and Licensing of Exports and Imports of Commodities on the Territory of Belarus. (February 3, 1992)

Decree No. 516: On Creating Controls in the Field of Exports and Commodities (Goods/Services) in the Republic of Belarus. (August 21, 1992)

Decree No. 573: On the Introduction of Changes to the Decree of the Republic of Belarus' Council of Ministers No. 386. (September 22, 1992)

Decree No. 782: On State Regulations and Control of Foreign Economic Relations. (December 28, 1992)

Decree No. 344: On a Unified System for Establishing Quotas and Issuing Licenses to Import and Export Commodities (Goods/Services) on the Territory of the Republic of Belarus. (May 25, 1993)

Decree No. 568: On Improvement of Foreign Economic Activities. (August 20, 1993)

Decree No. 733: On Violations of the Procedures for Establishing Quotas and Issuing Licenses to Import and Export Commodities (Goods/Services). (October 25, 1993)

Decree No. 82: On Transfer Restrictions of Dangerous Items and Materials Across the Border of the Republic of Belarus. (December 19, 1993)

Belarus currently is drafting an export control law.

*Source: Adapted from *Nuclear Successor States of the Soviet Union, No.* I (May 1994), p. 24.

Appendix 14.5

U.S.-Russia Joint Statement
On Issues of Export Controls and Policy in the Area of Transfers of Conventional Weapons and Dual-Use Technologies

The Secretary of State of the United States of America and the Minister of Foreign Affairs of the Russian Federation underscored the staunch commitment of their countries to efforts to curb the proliferation of weapons of mass destruction and to enhance global and regional stability. In keeping with the spirit of the new strategic partnership between the United States and Russia the Ministers have agreed on development of wide-ranging cooperation in the field of export control. Moreover, they have agreed that all necessary steps in this field be taken expeditiously, and have established a senior-level working group for this purpose, as well as to initiate bilateral cooperation in the areas specified in a Memorandum of Intent signed this day in Moscow.

The Ministers expressed satisfaction with steps taken since the last meeting of the President of the United States and the President of the Russian Federation to eliminate the vestiges of the Cold War, such as the Coordinating Committee for Multilateral Export Controls (COCOM), which according to the understanding reached by COCOM members will be terminated not later than March 31, 1994. They also welcomed the decision to establish a new multilateral regime for enhancing responsibility and transparency in the transfers of armaments and sensitive dual-use technologies. This new arrangement would not be directed against any state or group of states, and would prevent the acquisition of such items for military end uses if the behavior of a state is or becomes a cause for serious concern as determined by the participants of the new multilateral regime.

The United States and Russia, as leading exporters of conventional weapons, military equipment and dual-use technologies, are convinced that additional measures are needed on an international basis to increase responsibility, transparency and, where appropriate, restraint in this area. They expressed their willingness to work with other countries in bringing about the early establishment of a new multilateral regime in order to achieve these objectives, which would supplement existing non-proliferation regimes, in particular through arrangements to exchange information for the purpose of meaningful consultations.

14 January 1994
Moscow

Appendix 14.6

Memorandum of Intent
Between the Government of The United States of America and The Russian Federation on Cooperation in the Area of Export Control

The Government of the United States of America and the Government of the Russian Federation,

REAFFIRMING their desire to promote the strengthening of measures directed against the proliferation of weapons of mass destruction, their delivery systems, and other weapons, as well as the technologies and specialized experience relating to such weapons;

DESIRING to develop cooperation of the Russian Federation and the United States of America in the area of export controls;

NOTING that cooperation in strengthening the export control systems in the Russian Federation and the United States of America will promote the development of economic, scientific, and technological relationships between the two countries in accordance with principles of equality and mutual benefit;

INTEND TO COOPERATE IN ANY OR ALL OF THE FOLLOWING AREAS:

a. Conducting bilateral and multilateral discussions at the political and technical level on matters relating to the enhancement of export control systems;

b. Conducting bilateral consultations at the expert and government levels on obligations relating to non-use of export controlled items for unapproved purposes;

c. Conducting bilateral consultations on specific multilateral export control regimes and their implementation and on the technical parameters of the items and technologies covered by them;

d. Participating in seminars, conferences, and other multilateral meetings devoted to considering export control issues;

e. Discussing opportunities to train personnel involved with export control, the work of licensing and customs agencies; and

f. Joint efforts to expand cooperation in the area of export control.

The parties may establish expert working groups for the purposes of carrying out this Memorandum of Intent.

DONE at Moscow, this 14th day of January, 1994, in two copies, each in the English and Russian languages, both texts being equally authentic.

FOR THE GOVERNMENT
OF THE UNITED STATES:

FOR THE GOVERNMENT
OF THE RUSSIAN
FEDERATION:

Notes

1."U.S. Must Take Steps to Dismantle Soviet Arsenal, *The Atlanta Constitution*, November 29, 1991.

2. For details, see: William C. Potter, "Exodus: Containing the Spread of Nuclear Capabilities," *Harvard International Review* (Spring, 1992), P. 26; "Exports and Experts: Proliferation Risks from the Soviet Commonwealth," *Arms Control Today(1-2,* 1992), pp. 32-37; and *Nuclear Profiles of the Soviet Successor States* (Monterey, CA: Monterey Institute of International Studies, 1994).

3. Chrystia Freeland, "Russia and the G-7: Libya Shipment Barred," *Financial Times,* April 15, 1993.

4. Boston Globe, October 30, 1992; *Die Welt,* June 16, 1993; *Sueddeutsche Zeitung,* July 2, 1993; *Nucleonics Week,* September 2 and 9, 1993; *Nuclear Fuel,* September 13, 1993; and *Novoye Russokoye Slovo,* December 4-5, 1993.

5. Published in *Novaya Yezhednevnaya Gazetta* and reported in Steven Zaloga, "From Missile Busters to Manportables," *Armed Forces Journal International,* August, 1994, p. 43.

6. Nesha Starcevic (Associated Press) in the *Atlanta Journal-Constitution,* August 14, 1994, p. C4. Also, see other disturbing reports: Ferdinand Protzman, "Germany Reaffirms Origin of Seized Plutonium in Russia," *New York Times,* July 21, 1994 A6; "Black Market Weapons-Grade Plutonium Came From Russia," *The Korea Times,* July 19, 1994; "German Alert on Nuclear Smuggling," *International Herald Tribune,* July 18, 1994.

7. Stephen Foye, "Chernomyrdin Urges More Defense Conversion," *Radio Free Liberty/Radio Liberty Report,* July 28, 1994.

8. Interview with Gennady Mesyats at the University of New Mexico, Albuquerque, NM, August 9, 1993.

9. See, for example, Igor Khripunov, "Russia's Arms Trade in the Post-Cold War Period," *Washington Quarterly,* 17:4, 1994, pp. 79-94.

10. For details, see Elina Kirichenko, "The Evolution of Export Control Systems in the Soviet Union and Russia," in Gary Bertsch, Richard Cupitt and Steve Elliott-Gower, eds., *International Cooperation on Nonproliferation Export Controls* (Ann Arbor: University of Michigan Press, 1994), pp. 163-78.

11. For a Russian review of export controls in Russia, see A. Ponomarev, *et al.*, *Conversion in Russia* (Moscow: Interdepartmental Analytical Center,

12. Report prepared by the Foreign Intelligence Service of the Russian Federation, Moscow, 1993.

13. Sergei Kortunov, "National Export Control System in Russia," *Comparative Strategy*, 13 (May 1994), pp. 231-238.

14. *Novoye Russkoye Slovo*, October 2-3, 1993. Because of growing concerns with organized crime, the U.S. Government opened in 1994 an FBI office in Moscow. See the testimony of FBI Director Louis J. Freeh before the Permanent Subcommittee on Investigations, U.S. Senate Governmental Affairs Committee, May 25, 1994.

15. Ostankino (Moscow) Television, January 27, 1994.

16. *Rossiiskaya Gazeta*, February 24, 1994.

17. Vladimir Orlov, "Nuclear Analysis by General Yevstafyev of the Russian Intelligence Service," *Moscow News Weekly*, August 27, 1993.

18. See Michael Beck, Gary Bertsch, and Igor Khripunov, "The Development of Nonproliferation Export Controls in Russia" *World Affairs* 157,1 (Summer 1994), pp. 3-18, for more details on the CIS agreement and experience. Also see Gary Bertsch and Igor Khripunov, eds. *1994 Annual Report on Russia's Nonproliferation Export Control* (Athens, Georgia: The University of Georgia, 1994).

19. In testimony before the U.S. Senate in 1993, CIA Director James Woolsey put it this way: "Russia's ability to maintain control of its special weapons and associated technologies has somewhat weakened under the stresses and strains of the Soviet breakup." Hearing before the Senate Committee on Government Affairs, *Proliferation Threats of the 1990s*, February 24, 1993.

20. See, for example, Ural Latypov, "Export Control in Belarus: Trends of Evolution," unpublished paper, Minsk, Belarus, 1994.

21. Latypov, p. 24.

22. *Ibid.*, p. 22.

23. William Potter, *Nuclear Profiles of the Soviet Successor States,* pp. 92-3.

24. See the statement of Sergei Svistil of the Ukrainian Expert Technical Committee at the International Workshop on Export Controls in the NIS, Minsk, Belarus, October 3-4, 1994.

25. See Potter, *Nuclear Profiles of the Soviet Successor States,* pp. 16-32.

26. This information was taken from the written statement of Dr. Sc. Ing. Girts Krumins. Department of Foreign Economic Relations, Latvian Ministry of Foreign Affairs, at the International Workshop on Export Controls in the NIS, Minsk, Belarus, October 3-4, 1994, p. 2.

27. *Ibid,* p. 3.

28. "Full text of the political declaration issued at the Munich summit," *The Japan Times,* July 8, 1992: 19.

29. Decrees of the President are usually followed by government resolutions intended to implement the decree.

Chapter 15

Reducing Demand and Controlling Supply: CBMs, Export Controls and Integrated Strategies for Non-Proliferation

Cathleen S. Fisher

Like export controls, confidence-building measures (CBMs) were stepchildren of the Cold War, designed to address the principal security concerns of the East-West conflict. While export controls sought to restrict the transfer of sensitive technologies to the Soviet Union and its allies, technical confidence-building measures, such as secure communication lines or pre-notification and observation of military exercises, were designed to introduce greater openness, or "transparency", into the military activities of the East-West blocs, thus reducing the risk of inadvertent conflict, uncontrolled escalation and surprise attack.

With the end of the Cold War, export controls and CBMs have lost much of their traditional rationale. Rather than passing into obscurity, however, both policy instruments are being transformed to meet new security concerns and threats. Though originally designed to function as tools of East-West containment and conflict management, export controls and CBMs are finding new applications in international efforts to stem the proliferation of mass destruction weapons.

The problem of proliferation has taken on new urgency in the post-Cold War international system. The creation of "instant" nuclear powers through the dissolution of the Soviet Union, revelations regarding the Iraqi nuclear and chemical weapons programs, and suspicions surrounding North Korea's nuclear intentions raise the specter of an increasingly proliferated world, while highlighting the shortcomings of the existing non-proliferation regime.[1] Though steps have been taken at the national and international levels to enhance the effectiveness of export controls and the inspections regime of the Nuclear Non-proliferation Treaty, many analysts predict that restrictions on supply ultimately are doomed to failure. The only long-term solution, many believe, is to address the regional conflicts that motivate states to seek more destructive capabilities. In this view, the problem of proliferation will only be solved by reducing demand.[2]

This chapter will examine the potential role of confidence building measures as instruments of non-proliferation policy, and their relationship to "supply side" measures, such as export controls. It begins with a conceptual discussion of alternative approaches to non-proliferation. After a brief introduction to the theory of confidence-building, it reviews the application of CBMs to Europe and to regions of past and present proliferation concern, with special emphasis on the Korean peninsula. The paper concludes with some tentative observations regarding the non-proliferation function of CBMs, and the design of integrated non-proliferation strategies.

Two Approaches to Non-Proliferation: Supply and Demand-Side Strategies

Traditional approaches to non-proliferation have concentrated on constraining the supply of technologies relevant to the development and production of mass destruction weapons (see Table 15.1). The non-proliferation regime relies on a variety of supply-side tools, including international and regional treaties, multilateral export controls, sanctions, and military responses.[3]

Table 15.1: Alternative Approaches to Non-Proliferation

"Supply" Side Approaches	"Demand" Side Approaches
Function: constrain the flow of knowledge and supplies	Function: change perceptions of need and motivations
• Non-proliferation treaties and agreements	• Structural arms control agreements
• Export controls (national and multilateral)	• Confidence-building measures
• Sanctions	• Security assurances
• Military actions	• Regional or international security arrangements
	• New norms in international politics
	• Democratization and economic assistance

While they may slow the progress of weapons programs, supply-side strategies are unlikely to provide a lasting solution to the proliferation problem. The diffusion of technology, an increase in the number of supplier states, and the difficulties associated with bringing all potential suppliers into existing regimes will continue to undermine the effectiveness of supply-side constraints. Moreover, the implied "double standard" of the traditional nuclear non-proliferation regime, including export controls, may be increasingly untenable in the post-Cold War security environment. The continued reliance of the US and other states on nuclear weapons implies that these weapons have utility, and that their possession is legitimate, yet these same states insist that proliferation is illegitimate. Many developing countries are critical of this "dual standard." In their view, what is necessary and legitimate for advanced industrialized countries cannot be dangerous and illegitimate for developing nations. While the Northern position may have been defensible at the height of the Cold War, the dissolution of the Soviet Union and end of the East-West conflict have eliminated much of the traditional rationale for existing nuclear arsenals, raising serious questions about the future roles of mass destruction weapons in the national security policies of the United States and other nations. Thus in the post-cold war security environment, the legitimacy of the two-tier system is likely to come under increasing scrutiny, particularly as the 1995 review conference of the Nuclear Non-proliferation Treaty draws nearer. Unless there is progress toward transformation of non-proliferation into a truly global norm, the resistance of developing countries to what they perceive as discriminatory supply side controls is likely to continue.

"Demand" side approaches begin at the opposite end of the nuclear equation. The targets of these measures are not supplies of knowledge or materials, but the motivations that drive proliferation in the first place.[4] Demand-side approaches assume that countries perceive utility in weapons of mass destruction, either as valuable tools to counter security threats or to achieve political and economic objectives (see Table 15.2). The key to reducing demand thus is to change the calculus regarding the relative utility of nuclear and other mass destruction weapons as "solutions" to the problems that states face. If states or other groups are to foreswear nuclear, chemical and biological weapons, they must be convinced that their national interests can be more effectively secured through alternative means.

Attacking the motivations for proliferation demands a wide array of military, political, and economic measures:

- **Structural arms control agreements.** If states are seeking nuclear weapons as equalizers against the conventional superiority of a rival (as was the case for NATO), then conventional arms control agreements may diminish the perceived need for weapons of mass destruction.(An alternative supply-side measure might employ negotiated multilateral constraints on conventional arms transfers.)

- **Confidence-building measures.** When limitations on military forces are too ambitious, more modest precursors to structural arms control, such as confidence-building measures, may be feasible. In Europe, confidence-building measures were used to convey "credible evidence of the absence of feared threats," in order to dampen the military competition and enhance predictability, stability and trust in East-West relations.[5] The role of CBMs in non-proliferation efforts is considered in greater detail below.

- **Security assurances.** Pledges of international assistance to states facing the threat of nuclear blackmail or aggression may help to assuage concerns about a nuclear-armed adversary, and dissuade leaders from seeking an indigenous nuclear weapons capability. Such positive security assurances in the past have been both bilateral and multilateral. South Korea may have chosen to continue with its nuclear program had the United States not pledged its defense assistance; a similar logic may apply to the Japanese and German cases. Some have suggested the creation of a standing United Nations force, perhaps armed with nuclear weapons, in order to give more bite to the 1968 pledge by the United Nations Security Council that any threat of nuclear aggression against a non-nuclear state would lead to immediate action by the Security Council,[6] a pledge that was reaffirmed in separate declarations by the United States, the Soviet Union, and Britain.[7]

Table 15.2: Motivations for Proliferation

Category	Motivation
Military:	Deter nuclear attack
	Equalize conventional arms asymmetries with rivals
	Seek military superiority over rivals
	Anticipate or match nuclear weapons or rivals
	Intimidate rivals ("nuclear blackmail")
	Deter intervention by extra-regional powers
Political	Enhance regional or global political status
Domestic	National pride or morale
	Pressure from military groups
Economic	Scientific, technological or industrial benefits

Source: Adapted from OTA, p.100, and Stephen Meyer, *The Dynamics of Nuclear Proliferation* (Chicago: Univ. of Chicago Press, 1984), pp. 46-74.

Nuclear weapon states may also offer negative assurances that they will not use nuclear weapons against a non-nuclear state.

● **Regional or international security regimes.** The establishment of new multilateral mechanisms and institutions to address regional security concerns could also help to reduce demand for mass destruction weapons. Such regimes might facilitate the peaceful resolution of the root security problems that lead states to perceive utility in the possession of ever more powerful arsenals, as well as cultivating approaches to security, such as "cooperative" or "common" security.

● **New norms in international politics.** Reducing demand for nuclear weapons is linked to efforts to create and strengthen new norms in international politics. Some would argue that the only long-term solution to the problem of proliferation is to gradually delegitimize mass destruction weapons as instruments of international politics, and to sever the link between the possession of mass destruction weapons and political status and power. Reducing the roles of nuclear weapons in the national policies of the declared nuclear powers would be an important first step toward this end, and would help to address concerns about the present two-tier non-proliferation regime. Such steps to delegitimize proliferation might raise the perceived political costs of acquiring nuclear weapons, thus helping to change perceptions of utility. The case of Argentina may provide useful lessons in this regard.[8]

● **Democratization and economic development.** "Demand" side approaches may also involve measures intended to promote the forces of democratization and economic development. The reversal in the Argentinean and Brazilian nuclear programs followed the restoration of civilian power in both countries, a development that weakened the pressure from national militaries that had fueled the arms race. Similarly, South Africa's decision to admit possession of and dismantle its small nuclear arsenal followed radical political changes within the country. This suggests that efforts to reduce demand for mass destruction weapons must include development assistance or other "rewards" for nuclear forbearance, and support for democratic reforms.

The demand and supply sides of the proliferation equation of course are likely to be closely linked, and in some instances, particular policy instruments may target both supply and demand. For example, if the nuclear alternative becomes too costly because of tight export controls on certain supplies, then supply-side measures can change calculations of utility, and thus reduce demand for mass destruction weapons. In the Argentine case, export restrictions imposed by Western countries were perceived as hampering efforts to develop economically; a nuclear program partly intended to foster economic development in the final analysis proved counterproductive because of international restrictions.[9]

The Theory and Practice of Confidence-building: Lessons from Regional Applications

Originally designed as modest precursors to structural arms control, CBMs were employed originally in Europe to introduce greater openness or "transparency" into the military activities of the two alliances.[10] The first CBMs, codified in the 1975 Helsinki Final Act, were undertaken at a time when the state of political relations between East and West was such that limitations on military forces would have been too ambitious. Measures such as the pre-notification and observation of military exercises, secure communication lines, and exchanges of information on military forces or exercises were intended to reduce the incentives for military competition, and to introduce greater predictability and stability in East-West relations.[11]

Though theories of confidence-building were cast primarily in the language and objectives of operational arms control, the contribution of CBMs to the broader process of East-West conflict resolution was recognized implicitly. Beyond the specific function of greater military transparency, CBMs were intended, over time, to change perceptions of hostile intent. Confidence-building in the sense of greater certainty about miliary intentions was intended to build another type of confidence, that is, confidence as mutual trust. By requiring both sides to cooperate on minor military matters, CBMs could 'embody and project notions of shared interest -- a concept of common security." Specific military CBMs thus served a broader confidence-building process, whose purpose was to build an ethos of cooperation and a habit of trust between adversaries. The confidence-building process, like cooperation in the economic, cultural, or political sphere, was intended to reinforce the underlying forces for accommodation, encouraging states locked in conflict to intensify their cooperation, perhaps, over time, even contributing to a resolution of differences. In this sense, CBMs are "precursors" both to arms control and to conflict resolution; they are tools designed to move states toward the moment when a conflict has ripened, and to the "day when solution-oriented diplomacy can work."[12]

Confidence-Building Measures in the European Context

As originally conceived, CBMs clearly were designed to address the most salient security concerns of Central Europe.[13] Because any conflict in Europe could potentially escalate into nuclear conflagration, both sides shared a compelling interest in reducing the risks of inadvertent conflict and surprise attack. Measures such as the prenotification and observation of military exercises offered demonstrable proof that routine military activities were not being used as a subterfuge for surprise attack. Secure communication lines, it was hoped, would help to prevent the escalation of crises into war. The long-term objective of greater "transparency" was to reduce the secrecy surrounding military activities, thus enhancing mutual trust in East-West relations.[14]

The classification scheme developed by Richard Darilek provides a useful tool for categorizing the different types of CBMs introduced in the European context (see Appendix 1).[15] In this scheme, each category is defined in terms of its basic function. *Declaratory CBMs* involve commitments by states to undertake or to refrain from certain actions. *Communication* and *consultation CBMs* are both designed to provide more reliable means and routine procedures for the exchange of information and data. *Codes-of-conduct*, such as the 1972 Incidents at Sea agreement, commit the signatories to observe certain procedures or rules of behavior under specified conditions. *Prenotification CBMs* require states to inform other signatories of largescale military exercises, while *observation CBMs* obligate them to invite foreign observers. *Access CBMs* provide other states the opportunity to verify compliance with agreements, for example, through on-site inspections.

Two points are worth noting with regard to the evolution of confidence-building measures in the European context. First, efforts to build confidence with regard to the intentions of both military blocs were embedded in a broader strategy, and institutionalized in the Conference on Security and Cooperation in Europe (CSCE), that integrated political dialogue and economic cooperation, attention to human rights, and military CBMs. Second, CBMs evolved very slowly and incrementally. The first stage produced only "pre-CBMs," or what Alford has termed "subjective" CBMs.[16] "Subjective" or "pre-CBMs" were measures or actions, often taken unilaterally, whose primary objective was to "affect what people feel about a potential adversary." In the military realm, European "pre-CBMs" included the first Hotline Agreement, as well as agreements on naval "rules-of-the-road." Though not usually termed such, other non-military activities such as trade, sports and cultural exchanges, and informal contacts might also be counted as "pre-CBMs." Agreement on first generation CBMs, or "groundbreakers," signalled a small step toward agreements with very minor military significance. During phase III, the re-christening of CBMs as "confidence- and security-building measures" captured the progression toward activities that were militarily significant, politically binding, and verifiable, a trend sustained during phase IV.

Each phase corresponded to a different set of political pre-conditions and security needs. In Europe, this progression was reflected in the types of CBMs implemented or negotiated in each phase. Voluntary communication tools were followed by modest notification and information measures, which in turn gave way to obligatory prenotification and verification through on-site inspections. As East-West political relations improved, it gradually became possible to implement measures with more military "bite." Though the evolutionary process in other regions might spawn a different sequence of confidence-building tools, the basic point is that the phases of confidence-building are likely to involve different political preconditions. The more "bite" -- or "objective" content -- a CBM contains, the more difficult it will be to negotiate, and the more stringent the political pre-conditions. Each phase of confidence-building thus implies incremental progress toward the resolution of underlying differences, or the roots of conflict.

Regional Confidence-building

Though many have expressed skepticism about the application of CBMs to new regional contexts, in fact, confidence-building measures have proven remarkably adaptable. Certain security concerns, like border security or the fear of surprise attack, are fairly generic in nature, and are shared by many different states around the world, even as they are rooted in dissimilar historical, geographical, and political conditions. Parties to conflict in many other regions of the world have demonstrated an interest in the tools of European confidence-building, and have taken steps to devise CBMs uniquely suited to specific regional security concerns and conditions. In this process of regional adaptation, the confidence-building process has subsumed new tools and taken on new functions.

While a comprehensive review of regional confidence-building programs lies outside the scope of this paper, a brief summary of developments in four regions of past or present proliferation concern will serve to highlight the potential contribution of CBMs to "demand" side approaches to non-proliferation.

South Asia Though India and Pakistan have yet to resolve long-standing differences, particularly over the future of Kashmir, the two governments have succeeded in negotiating a number of agreements intended to diminish the risk of unintended war and to reduce tensions. In contrast to the European experience, CBMs negotiated between India and Pakistan often have not been worked out in detail, nor are they well publicized, attesting to the domestic difficulties of even limited accommodation between the two states. Most CBMs were negotiated in the aftermaths of wars (1947-48, 1965, 1971) and in the context of heightened military tensions (1986-91).[17]

The Indo-Pakistani agreements include a variety of tools employed in Europe, including: (i) communication measures designed to improve and facilitate the exchange of information between Indian and Pakistani military leaders, and for use during border incidents; (ii) notification measures requiring the pre-notification of military exercises involving ten thousand or more troops in specific locations, and proscribing maneuvers in close proximity of the border; (iii) transparency measures to confirm non-hostile intent during routine military exercises; (iv) border security measures, including "ground-rules" for the West Pakistan-India border, and regulations designed to prevent violation of airspace; (v) consultation measures to facilitate exchanges at the ministerial level; and (vi) a 1962 cooperative agreement for the management and sharing of rivers in the Indus basin.[18] The most significant CBM related to the two countries' nuclear activities was completed in December 1988. At that time, former Indian Prime Minister Rajiv Gandhi and Pakistani President Benazir Bhutto signed an agreement pledging that neither country would carry out a preemptive attack on the other's nuclear installations.

Though promising first steps, many of the measures have been implemented unevenly, undermining their effectiveness. Recurring border clashes in the contested regions of Jammu and Kashmir call into question the effectiveness of border security measures, while the "hotline" was apparently bypassed in 1986-87 and 1990, during a period of heightened tensions. Moreover, implementation of the nuclear installations agreement was slowed by a Pakistani decision to delay submission of the accord for ratification, thereby extending the deadline for the required exchange of information on each side's nuclear sites. The agreement was finally ratified in January 1992. Under its terms, both governments are required to exchange annual lists containing the location of all nuclear-related facilities. According to one source, each government reportedly left off one enrichment facility at the time of the initial exchange in 1992.[19]

Despite these discouraging setbacks, even such minor agreements are significant given the state of tension between the two rivals. The hotline connecting the respective military commanders on a number of occasions has been used to diffuse border skirmishes. If levels of tension along the border increase,[20] moreover, the Indo-Pakistani CBMs provide the two states an important "safety net" that may yet prevent crises from escalating into full-scale war.[21]

Middle East Despite the seemingly intractable nature of the Middle East conflict, Israel and its Arab neighbors have agreed to a modest program of confidence-building measures. Under the terms of the Sinai I Agreement, Israel and Egypt accepted the creation of a demilitarized buffer zone, controlled by the United Nations Emergency Force (UNEF), and agreed to verification inspections by UNEF. The Second Sinai Agreement expanded on the use of CBMS. Specifically, both states agreed to allow verification of the agreement by the United States through a combination of aerial inspections, unmanned sensors, and monitoring by civilian personnel.[22] In addition to these publicly acknowledged and formal agreements, under a series of more tacit agreements, Israel and Syria agreed to routine overflights, conducted by the United States, to confirm compliance with the limitations on military equipment and personnel in the designated thin-out zones.[23]

A variety of measures have been proposed to supplement this modest program of CBMs. One Israeli plan would establish contacts between the military leaders of Israel and Syria, and loosen restrictions on exchanges between the two countries' populations. These initial contacts could then be succeeded by bilateral talks on water management and joint development projects. Other proposals call for the creation of a nuclear-weapons-free zone or of a Conflict Prevention Center in the region.[24] The latter might serve as a clearing house for information on military budgets and exercises, and be responsible for sending observers to notifiable military activities. Further, the center could offer technical assistance for the conduct of aerial inspections, and house secure communications lines.[25]

Progress toward this more ambitious agenda of course depends on the evolution in political relations in the region, in particular, the negotiations between Israel and its Arab neighbors. As in the South Asian case, however, the fact that implacably hostile enemies have agreed to even minimal cooperative measures should be taken as an encouraging sign.

Latin America. The return of democratic rule to Argentina and Brazil paved the way for a series of confidence-building steps that promises to throttle the military competition between the two countries. Discussions between the two newly restored civilian governments began in 1984, and resulted the following year in the establishment of a Joint Committee on Nuclear Policy, which provided a forum for discussion of nuclear policy and technical cooperation in nuclear research.[26] After refusing for many years to open Argentine nuclear facilities to IAEA inspection, President Raul Alfonsín in March 1985 initiated a program of mutual inspections of the two countries' installations. The inspections were designed to build confidence that the other side was not seeking to acquire nuclear weapons. Cooperation in the nuclear sphere was supplemented with an agreement by both countries to join the Southern Cone Common Market (MERCOSUR).[27]

The turning point came in 1990 with the signing of the "Declaration on the Common Nuclear Policy of Brazil and Argentina." Under the terms of this bilateral agreement, the two countries agreed: (i) to establish a Common System of Accounting and Control of

Nuclear Materials, charged with verifying that all nuclear materials were being used for peaceful purposes; (ii) to negotiate a safeguards agreement between the IAEA and the Brazilian-Argentine Agency for Accounting and Control of Nuclear Materials (ABACC) (the Quadripartite Agreement); and (iii) to prepare for the two countries's full ratification of the Treaty for the Prohibition of Nuclear Weapons in Latin America (Treaty of Tlatelolco).[28] One of the most interesting aspects of the agreement is the creation of a *regional* body responsible for carrying out mutual inspections (the ABACC). This may prove an attractive alternative to countries in regions such as South Asia, where states would benefit from greater transparency into their respective nuclear activities but are loathe to join the NPT or open their facilities to international inspection.[29]

Confidence-building and Proliferation on the Korean Peninsula

The Korean peninsula is locked in a military face-off that has become a cause of increasing concern as uncertainties regarding North Korean nuclear intentions have multiplied. North Korea has over one million men under arms, and roughly 65 percent of its ground forces deployed within 15 to 20 miles of the Demilitarized Zone (DMZ). To the South, 750,000 South Korean and roughly 37,000 US troops are arrayed against them. Presumably not only the two Koreas, but Japan, China and Russia, and other states in North East Asia would benefit from measures to stabilize the Korean conflict, before the extreme hostility of the two states erupts once more into armed conflict.

Although the Korean conflict is in some respects similar to the military confrontation in Cold War Europe, two factors complicate the task of confidence-building: (i) the linkage to the reunification issue; and (iii) the basic asymmetry of the two states' confidence-building needs.

In the North, as in the South, relations with the other Korea have always been linked to the future of both states' respective political, economic, and social systems. Both governments, after all, claim reunification as their ultimate goal, and reunification, presumably, would lead to the triumph of one system over the other. The evolution of bilateral relations between the Republic of Korea and the DPRK, including their nascent confidence-building dialogue, thus can only be understood within the broader context of each side's reunification policy. Both Seoul and Pyongyang remain formally committed to achieving reunification, and initiatives to improve bilateral relations generally are in some way linked to this ultimate goal. A series of North Korean proposals to disarm the Korean peninsula, for example, has been coupled to the end goal of reunification. Similarly, South Korea's *Nordpolitik* was launched "in a wider context of improving inter-Korean relations, rather than just for the sake of normalizing relations with the northern countries."[30]

The reunification linkage, however, places a heavy burden on even the most "harmless" of CBMs.[31] The degree of animosity between the two Korean states may be mirrored in many other tension-laden regions of the world, but the national component of the conflict makes it unique. The tensions between India and Pakistan, for example, may - be no less dangerous than those between the two Koreas, but at least in South Asia the respective military commanders have been free to negotiate minor confidence-building measures away from the public eye, thus preventing the discussions from becoming overly politicized. In a divided Korea, and contacts between the states' civilian or military officials become politically charged because of the national issue. In the near-tenn, a confidence-building strategy would aim to reduce tensions on the peninsula, without prejudice to the form that reunification might take; in the long-term, the two issues clearly are linked. In this context, every proposal, no matter how minor, will be assessed not only on its own, perhaps minimal merit, but in light of its effect on domestic politics at home, and its impact on the legitimacy and stability of the national governments.

North Korea's nuclear ambitions must also be understood in light of the reunification issue. If the North Korean nuclear program is motivated in the first order by concern about the South Korean and the US military threat, then military transparency measures could weaken Pyongyang's interest in acquiring nuclear weapons status. On the other hand, if the North Korean nuclear program is driven in large measure by a sense of desperation regarding its continued existence as a state and a society, particularly after Kim Il Sung's death, then military CBMs may be only marginally relevant to North Korea's motives. If desperation is driving Pyongyang, the task of devising a mutually acceptable confidence-building regime becomes much harder. To succeed, the confidence-building process would have to provide assurances to North Korea that cooperation with the South would not lead to political instability, at least in the short term, and provide verifiable assurances to the South that North Korea's nuclear program had been stopped. Unless the North's sense of desperation can be defused, concerted pressure on Pyongyang to provide military assurances to South Korea could actually heighten Pyongyang's insecurities -- with unpredictable results. The reunification issue thus gives rise to asymmetrical confidence-building needs. Presumably both states and all regional powers would benefit from the implementation of a crisis stability regime. It is South Korea's need for military -- and particularly nuclear -- reassurances, and North Korea's need for reassurances regarding its economic and political viability that creates special challenges for confidence-building. Unless both needs are addressed, neither side may have sufficient incentive to cooperate with the other.

These are the delicate parameters within which confidencebuilding on the Korean peninsula must proceed. As long as the North Korean regime remains impervious to outside scrutiny, it will be difficult to assess the motives driving Kim's nuclear program, or to determine what combination of incentives or disincentives might elicit North Korean cooperation. If North Korean paranoia is so great that even minor economic assistance is perceived as a Trojan horse, or tied to unacceptable conditions, then the ambitious confidence-building agenda now on the table may be reduced to very marginal political and economic "pre-confidence building measures," and even minor inducements may be viewed as "poison carrots."[32] An even more pessimistic view would argue that it is too late for the incremental approach of confidence-building to contribute significantly to non-proliferation efforts.

The Korean Confidence-Building Agenda

Following decades of stalemate, the two Koreas in late 1991 launched an ambitious confidence-building program with a comprehensive menu of military, political, and economic measures. The "Agreement on Reconciliation, Nonaggression, Exchange, and Cooperation," is a comprehensive framework agreement for cooperation. Under the terms of the accord, Seoul and Pyongyang each promised to respect the other's political system, and to refrain from acts of terrorism, slander, or aggressive actions against the other state. Additionally, the two governments pledged to allow exchanges of radio and television broadcasts, newspapers and other publications; to reestablish regular communication and transport links; to permit correspondence and visits between the two populations; and to facilitate the reunification of divided families. The accord further called for both governments to develop trade in goods and to invest jointly in industrial projects, and envisioned exchanges and cooperation in science, technology, education, literature, the arts, health, sports, the environment, and publishing. Finally, in the military realm, the two states agreed to establish a communications "hotline" between their respective military commanders, to offer prior notification of major military movements, and to create a joint military committee charged with carrying out "steps to build military confidence and realize arms reductions."[33] The second agreement addressed proliferation concerns directly. The "Joint Declaration on the Denuclearization of the Korean Peninsula" prohibits both states from the testing, production, possession, storage, deployment or use of nuclear weapons.[34] The agreement called for the creation of a North-South Nuclear Control Commission which would be tasked with the design of a bilateral inspection regime to verify compliance with the accord.[35]

Progress toward implementation of this ambitious confidence - building program has been slowed, however, by the state of political tension on the peninsula and North Korea's continued intransigence regarding nuclear inspections. After months of vacillation, North Korean representatives on January 30, 1992 signed a nuclear safeguards agreement with the IAEA, paving the way for the first nuclear inspections in mid-May 1992 of its Yongbyon nuclear complex.[36] A subsequent reversal of course, however, has revived fears that Pyongyang is using the North-South dialogue and international diplomacy to "buy time" until its nuclear weapons program is a fait accompli.

At this writing, there is room for considerable doubt regarding North Korea's intentions to fulfill its commitments under the IAEA agreement or the North-South nonaggression and denuclearization declarations.[37] The bilateral agreements could collapse if the North remains intransigent on the issue of nuclear inspections or reprocessing. A cynical view would argue that the North has manipulated negotiations on international inspections in the hope of easing Western pressure on its nuclear program, to further raise expectations in the South, and in the hope that the accord will persuade Japan to provide much needed economic aid and investment; Pyongyang may have no intention, however, of allowing intrusive bilateral or international inspections.

CBMs as Non-proliferation Tools

Though CBMs have been viewed primarily as a component of arms control, this brief review of regional confidence-building efforts suggests that CBMs may serve a number of useful functions in areas of proliferation concern (see Table 15.3):

(i) **Where proliferation has already occurred, CBMs can help to diminish the chances of inadvertent or accidental war and thus reduce the chances that mass destruction weapons will be used.** Where non-proliferation efforts have failed, CBMs may help to reduce the chances of nuclear use. For example, if implemented consistently, the CBMs negotiated by India and Pakistan may help prevent border incursions or other incidents from plunging the two countries' into war once again, with the inestimable risk of nuclear conflict. If pessimistic assessments of the North Korean nuclear program are correct, then CBMs may be relegated to a similar function in East Asia.

In a proliferated regional context, crisis stability CBMs would seem to be the most appropriate tools. Like Europe in the coldest period of the Cold War, states could benefit from consultation and communication measures, codes or conduct, or agreements on the prenotification and observation of major military exercises.

(ii) **CBMs can help to verify nuclear "roll-back."** When would-be proliferants reverse course, confidence-building measures can be useful in locking in positive changes and maintaining trust in the other's intentions. The three prominent cases of "nuclear forbearance" in the 1980s -- Argentina, Brazil, and South Africa -- are undergoing important internal political transitions. Mutual inspections of nuclear facilities, and other transparency measures could help to sustain mutual confidence and cooperation in the nuclear sphere during a crucial period of transformation in which political setbacks cannot be excluded. In such instances, CBMs would serve to enhance "nuclear transparency."[38]

(iii) **In the long term, CBMs may contribute to efforts to manage and resolve conflicts, thereby reducing "demand" for mass destruction weapons.** By offering small tests of trust, CBMs work over time to change the perceptions that adversaries hold of their rivals' intentions. Operating at the margins of the proliferation equation, CBMs may contribute to creating a climate in which the resolution of underlying differences becomes possible, and the acquisition of mass destruction weapons is therefore perceived as unnecessary. Confidencebuilding measures of course will not be able to perform this third function in every instance, as the Korean case demonstrates. Improving the chances for success will require a better understanding of the confidence-building process, both as it functions in non-European contexts and as a non-proliferation tool.

Though definitive conclusions await more systematic and comprehensive analyses of regional confidence-building measures, particularly when employed as non-proliferation tools, some tentative observations are possible. CBMs seem more likely to function effectively in a non-proliferation context, if three conditions are met: (i) The political pre-conditions for confidence-building are extant; (ii) the confidence-building package is tailored to address the motivations that are driving proliferation in a particular region, and integrated with other supply- and demand-side measures; and (iii) CBMs are given sufficient time to work at reducing demand.

The pre-conditions for confidence-building. As the European and other regional experiences demonstrate, CBMs can only be as ambitious as political relations will allow. Though the preconditions for confidence-building may not be as demanding as those for conflict resolution, a minimum degree of trust is necessary. In Europe, certain historical, cultural, societal and political aspects of the East-West conflict facilitated the negotiation and implementation of CBMs.[39] In other regions, the conditions under which CBMs have been negotiated varies significantly from the European pattern; it would be unwise therefore to extrapolate general lessons regarding the preconditions of successful confidence-building on the basis of one, perhaps unique historical success story. Systematic and comprehensive treatments of regional confidence-building will doubtless enhance our understanding of how, and under what political, economic, or cultural circumstances, CBMs do or do not work, particularly when they are implemented in regions of proliferation concern.

Table 15.3: CBMs as Non-proliferation Tools

Region	Type of CBM
Proliferated	Crisis stability measures: • Communication • Consultation • Pre-notification • Observation • Information exchange
Nuclear "roll-back"	"Nuclear" transparency measures: • Information exchange • Access (inspections)
Non-nuclear	CBM strategies tailored to regional security needs: • Economic • Cultural • Political dialogue • Military

Tailored confidence-building programs. Second, CBMs must be tailored to the motivations driving proliferation in a particular region. A basic understanding of how states perceive their security in a regional context, and the role of nuclear weapons in achieving national objectives, is essential to designing more effective CBM packages.

For example, in the Korean case, the motivations for proliferation likely are linked to the reunification issue. A more multilateral approach to confidence-building might help to diffuse the national question that has burdened the bilateral efforts of the two Korean states. Though unpopular in the past, initiatives to create new institutions for security cooperation in the North Pacific could provide additional, indirect support to the confidence-building efforts of the two Koreas.[40] To allow consideration of economic, political, and military security issues, the mandate of the group might be broadly conceived, as was that of the CSCE. Former CSBM negotiator James Goodby has suggested as a logical starting point the multilateral application of two Soviet-American accords designed to deal with incidents and accidents at sea, with the Korean peninsula providing the focal point for the new agreement. Further, the regional powers might use the new forum to provide indirect support to bilateral negotiations between Seoul and Pyongyang, perhaps offering commitments to non-aggression, or to prohibitions on the transfer of nuclear technology to the peninsula. By creating additional avenues of communication and negotiation, multilateral security discussions could not only defuse pressure on the inter-Korean dialogue, but -- in the most optimistic of scenarios -might ensure that the process of Korean unification is embedded in a broader regional framework.[41]

Timing. Finally, in order to perform in a non-proliferation function, there must be sufficient time for the incremental process of confidence-building to work. The Korean experience suggests that it would be wise to adjust our expectations of what CBMs can accomplish in regional conflicts where the time to prevent proliferation is short. If the threat of proliferation is a matter of months rather than years, then it may be too late for CBMs to make any significant contribution to non-proliferation efforts. In the European context, negotiations on first-generation CBMs were preceded by two decades of "small tests of trust," and were embedded in a broader strategy of economic, political, and military dialogue. On the Korean peninsula, CBMs have been among the very first ventures in trust between bitterly divided enemies and, moreover, have lacked the supporting infrastructure present in the European context. The two Korean states launched a program of confidence-building that was unprecedented in its timetable and ambitious in scope. In contrast, the confidence-building process in Europe was designed to achieve only incremental progress, and often operated at the margins of conflict. This suggests that the process of engagement and confidence-building on the Korean Peninsula may have begun too late *to address proliferation concerns*. This is not to suggest, however, that CBMs cannot perform useful functions in the Korean context, just that they may be ineffective non-proliferation tools given the urgency of the problem. Even under the best of political circumstances, CBMs offer no short-term solutions to the problem of proliferation.

Designing Integrated Strategies for Non-proliferation Supply- and demand-side approaches both have a role to play in combatting the spread of mass destruction weapons. Supply side instruments may buy valuable time, but do not always change the perceptions of utility that lead states to acquire weapons of mass destruction. The processes of conflict resolution, democratization and economic development may be more effective non-proliferation tools in the long term, but their effects are likely to be felt only very slowly and after many setbacks.

The most effective approach to non-proliferation may lie in crafting "integrated strategies" that work at both ends of the proliferation equation. Designing such strategies, however, will require a more complete understanding of why states acquire, choose not to acquire, or change their minds about acquiring nuclear weapons. What are the principle motivations behind the Iraqi and North Korean nuclear programs? What utility do India and Pakistan perceive in the possession of mass destruction weapons? Just as important is an understanding of the examples of nuclear forbearance. A number of states have chosen to discontinue programs to develop nuclear weapons, including Sweden in the 1950s, Taiwan and South Korea in the 1970s, and Argentina, Brazil, and South Africa in the late 1980s. In the southern cone, for example, supply side constraints, domestic political and economic changes, and other demand-side incentives appeared to work together to change perceptions of the utility of nuclear arsenals. A close comparison of these cases may wield valuable lessons about changes in perceptions of utility, and the relative effectiveness of supply and demand-side strategies.

Combining supply- and demand-side tools, however, raises a number of issues. Two are addressed below: (i) the compatibility of demand- and supply-side tools; and (ii) the coordination demands placed on national and international decision-makers.

Though directed toward a common goal, demand and supply-side approaches rest on contradictory premises. Supply-side measures, in the final analysis, are coercive tools of statecraft; confidence-building measures, in contrast, aim at creating and maintaining an ethos of cooperation among states. Technology denial through export controls assumes that the target state is adversarial in nature, while the confidence-building process relies on a (minimal) degree of mutual trust.

Combining punitive or coercive instruments with cooperative "demand" side strategies at times may require a diplomatic balancing act, and a recognition that conflict between competing strands of policy sometimes may be unavoidable. Squaring the circle may be complicated by the fact that suppliers' groups may not be identical to those most interested in regional confidence-building. Moreover, within these two groups, there may be diverse opinions on the appropriate mix and timing of incentives and punishment. Differences between the United States and its allies in the early 1980s over the relative emphasis on Western defense efforts versus cooperation with the Soviet Union are instructive in this respect.

Managing this delicate balance will place heavy demands on leadership at the national and international levels. Integration of such supply and demands-side tools may be logical from the perspective of non-proliferation objectives; in the real world, achieving policy coherence presents a daunting task.

If non-proliferation efforts are to succeed, however, there may be little alternative to more broadly-conceived strategies, despite the attendant complications. National and multinational export controls would serve to "buy time" until the utility and value that proliferant leaders attach to the possession of these weapons had been sufficiently reduced through incremental "demand-side tools." Confidence-building measures may make a small, but valuable, contribution to "demand"-side strategies for non-proliferation.

Appendix 15.1: Stages in East-West Confidence-Building[1]

STAGE/ CHARACTERISTICS	AGREEMENT (YEAR)	PROVISIONS	TYPE OF CBM/CSBM
I **Pre-CBMs**	Hotline Agreement (1963)	• Created direct communications link	Communication
• informal or voluntary	Agreement to Reduce Risks of Nuclear War (1971)	• Commitment to improving national safeguards against accidental or unauthorized launch	Declaratory
• no military significance		• Notification of accidental or unauthorized nuclear incident	Prenotification
• not verifiable		• Prenotification of missile launches beyond national territory	
• impact is "subjective"	Incidents at Sea Agreement (1972)	• Regulation of dangerous maneuvers	Code-of-Conduct
		• Restrictions on harassment	Information exchange
		• Signaling guidelines	Consultation mechanisms
		• Prenotification of dangerous activities on the high seas	
		• Consultations between naval attaches	

STAGE/ CHARACTERISTICS	AGREEMENT (YEAR)	PROVISIONS	TYPE OF CBM/CSBM
II **1st Generation CBMs-- "Groundbreakers"** • voluntary or politically binding • minor military significance • impact is primarily "subjective" but may have "objective" component	Helsinki Final Act (1975)	• Obligatory prenotification of maneuvers with 25,000+ troops, 21 days in advance • Voluntary prenotification of other military maneuvers • Voluntary invitations to send observers • Voluntary prenotification of major military movements	Notification Access
III **2nd Generation CBMs -- Security-Building Measures** • militarily significant • politically binding • verifiable • impact effect is primarily "objective"	Stockholm Agreement (1986)	• Obligatory prenotification of maneuvers with 13,000+ troops or 300 battle tanks • Obligatory information exchange on notifiable military activities • Obligatory invitations to send observers • Exchange of annual calendars of military activities • Verification through on-site inspections	Prenotification Information Observation Access

STAGE/CHARACTERISTICS	AGREEMENT (YEAR)	PROVISIONS	TYPE OF CBM/CSBM
III (cont'd)	Agreement to Establish Nuclear Risk Reduction Centers (NRRC) (1987)	• High-speed data links	Communication Information Exchange
	Agreement on Prevention of Dangerous Military Activities (1989)	• Regulation of dangerous military activities • Guidelines for unintended entry into national territory • Exchange of information on dangerous activities or incidents • Establishment of Joint Military Commission	Code-of-Conduct Prenotification Communication and consultation mechanisms
	Agreement on Notification of Strategic Exercises (1989)	• Prenotification of 14 days through NRRC • Consultations on implementation	Prenotification Consultation mechanisms

STAGE/ CHARACTERISTICS	AGREEMENT (YEAR)	PROVISIONS	TYPE OF CBM/CSBM
IV 3rd Generation CSBMs	Vienna Agreement (1990)	• Annual exchange of information on military forces, major weapons deployments, & military budgets	Information exchange
		• Consultation mechanisms on unusual military activities	Consultation
		• Visits to air bases, military contacts	Access
		• Obligatory prenotification of certain military activities	Prenotification
		• Obligatory invitations to observers for notifiable military activities	Observation
		• Exchange on annual calendars	
		• Verification through on-site inspections	
		• Creation of communications network	Communications
		• Annual implementation assessment meeting at Conflict Prevention Center	
	CFE Treaty (1990) (CSBM provisions)	• Annual exchange of information on artillery, main battle tanks, APCs, combat aircraft, and combat helicopters	Information
		• Notification and exchange of information	Notification
		• On-site inspections during three-phased reductions of equipment and personnel; verification and inspection to monitor holdings and reductions	Access
		• Establishment of Joint Consultative Group	Declaratory
		• Agreement to move destroyed equipment east of Urals prior to treaty signature	Consultation

STAGE/ CHARACTERISTICS	AGREEMENT (YEAR)	PROVISIONS	TYPE OF CBM/CSBM
IV (cont'd)	Open Skies Treaty (1992)	• Mandatory overflights	Access
		• No restricted areas except for overflight; use of cameras, infra-red, and synthetic aperture radars	*Information exchange
		• Data available to all parties	
	Vienna Document (1992) (CSBM provisions only)	• Obligatory prenotification of certain military activities involving 9,000+ troops or 250+ tanks	Information exchange
			Notification
		• Obligatory invitations to observers for notifiable activities involving 13,000 troops, 300 tanks, or 3,500 amphibious or airborne paratroopers	Access
		• Obligatory annual exchange of detailed technical data on military forces, weapons, equipment, and personnel strength	
		• Voluntary invitations to observers for notifiable military activities within CBM Zone of Application	
		• Verification by multinational inspection teams	
		• Voluntary aerial inspections	

STAGE/ CHARACTERISTICS	AGREEMENT (YEAR)	PROVISIONS	TYPE OF CBM/CSBM
IV (cont'd)	CFE 1A Agreement (1992) (CSBM provisions only)	• Obligatory prenotification of any permanent increase in personnel strength, wing/air regiment or equivalent level, 42 days in advance	Notification
		• Obligatory prenotification of any call-up of army reserve personnel 42 days in advance	Access
		• Exchange of annual calendars for strength of individual units at or above brigade/regiment level	Information exchange
		• Inspection of CFE weapons	
		• Obligatory access to information on personnel serving at inspection sites	
		• Consultative Commission composed of participating states for treaty verification	
		• Voluntary aerial inspections	

1. Adapted from Fisher, pp. 42-45.

Notes

1. For an assessment of the nuclear proliferation threat, see Leonard S. Spector *Nuclear Ambitions: The Spread of Nuclear Weapons 1989-90* (Boulder: Westview Press, 1990), pp. 3-55. See also U.S. Congress, Office of Technology Assessment, United States Congress *Proliferation of Weapons of Mass Destruction: Assessing the Risks* OTA-ISC-558 (Washington, D.C.: U.S. Government Printing Office, August 1993), pp. 46-50.

2. See, for example, OTA, 107; see also Kosta Tsipis and Philip Morrison, "Arming for Peace," *The Bulletin of Atomic Scientists* March/April 1994, pp. 38-43; and Kathleen Bailey, *Strengthening Nuclear Non-proliferation* (Boulder, Colo.: Westview, 1993), pp. 17-26.

3. Under the 1968 Nuclear Non-proliferation Treaty, nuclear weapon states agree to provide civilian nuclear materials to NPT signatories, subject to full IAEA safeguards, in exchange for an agreement from non-nuclear weapons states to renounce the manufacture or possession of nuclear weapons. Export controls, similarly, seek to constrain the supply of weapons-related technologies. If other measures fail, states or international organizations may increasingly choose the option of military action in order to destroy suspected nuclear, chemical or biological weapon programs. On supply-side measures, see Spector, pp. 293-300; OTA, pp. 18-25, 83-98; and Bailey, pp. 3-26.

4. More a complete discussion of demand-side calculations, see Stephen Meyer, *The Dynamics of Nuclear Proliferation* (Chicago: Univ. of Chicago Press, 1984), pp. 46-74. See also OTA, pp. 104-9; and Bailey, p. 24.

5. Johan Jorgen Holst and Karen Alette Melander, "European Security and Confidence-building Measures," *Survival* 19, no. 4 (July/August 1977), P. 147.

6. Tsipis and Morrison, pp. 42-3.

7. OTA, p. 104.

8. While Argentina's return to democracy appears to have been decisive in President Menem's decision to renounce the country's nuclear program, the political cost of acquiring nuclear weapons had also become evident to the country's leaders, as seen in the remarks of a senior Argentine official: "We found we were blacklisted by the international community for our aggressive policies and in the end found we had to cooperate with the netherworld of third-

312   *Nonproliferation Export Controls*

world countries." Quoted in "Sequel to an Old Fraud: Argentina's Powerful Nuclear Program," *Washington Post*, 18 January 1994, A10. See also David Albright, "Confidence-building on Nuclear Related-Issues Between Argentina and Brazil: A Chronology," in *A Handbook of Confidence-building Measures for Regional Security*, eds. Michael Krepon, Dominique M. McCoy, and Matthew C.J. Rudolph (Washington, D.C.: The Henry L. Stimson Center, September 1993), pp. 11-15; and Abraham Itty, *Argentina-Brazil and India-Pakistan: Stepping Back from the Nuclear Threshold?*, Occasional Paper Series (Washington, D.C.: The Henry L. Stimson Center, 1993).

9. Albright.

10. On confidence-building,see Jonathan Alford, *Confidence-buildingMeasures in Europe: the MilitaryAspects*, Adelphi Paper no. 149 (London: International Institute for Strategic Studies, 1979); Rolf Berg and Adam-Daniel Rotfeld, *Building Securityin Europe: Confidence-buildingMeasuresand the CSCE* (New York: Institute for East-West Security Studies, 1986); R.B. Byers, F. Stephen Larrabee, and Allen Lynch, *Confidence-building Measures and International Security*,Institute for East-West Monograph Series no. 4 (New York: Institute for East-West Security Studies, 1987); Brian J. Gillian, Alan Crawford and Kornel Buczel, *Compendium of Confidence-building Proposals*, 2d ed., Department of National Defence, Canada, Operational Research and Analysis Establishment, Extra-mural Paper no. 45 (Ottawa, 1987); Johan Jorgen Hoist, "Confidence-building Measures: A Conceptual Framework," Survival 25, no. I (January/February 1983), pp. 2-15; Johan Jorgen Hoist and Karen Alette Melander, "European Security and Confidence-buildingMeasures,"Survival 19, no. 4 (July/August 1977), pp. 146-54; Karl Kaiser, ed., *Confidence-building Measures*, Forschungsinstitut der Deutschen Gesellschaft fuer Auswaertige Politik, no. 28, proceedings of an international symposium in Bonn, 24-27 May 1983 (Bonn: Europa Union Verlag, 1983); and Stephen Larrabee and Dietrich Stobbe, eds., *Confidence-buildingMeasuresin Europe* (New York: Institute for East-West Security Studies, 1983).

11. Hoist and Melander, "European Security," P. 147.

12. Richard N. Haass, *Conflict Unending: The United States and Regional Conflicts* (New Haven: Yale University Press, 1990), p. 29. On the notion of "ripeness," see Haass; 1. William Zartman, *Ripe for Resolution: Conflict and Interventionin Africa* (New York: Oxford Univ. Press, 1986), chaps. 1, 6; and ibid., "Ripening Conflict, Ripe Moment, Formula, and Mediation," in *Perspectives on Negotiation*, eds. Diane B. Bendahmane and John W. McDonald (Washington: Center for the Study of Foreign Affairs, Foreign Service Institute (Washington, D.C.: US Dept. of State, 1986), pp. 205-227.

13. The discussion builds on the author's previous work on confidence-building measures in the European context. See Cathleen S. Fisher, "The Preconditions of Confidence-building: Lessons from the European Experience," in *A Handbook of Confidence-Building Measures for Regional Security*, The Henry L. Stimson Center (Washington, D.C.: September 1993), pp. 31-45.

14. On the theory of European confidence-building measures, see Alford, *The Future of Arms Control*; Hoist and Melander, "European Security and Confidence-building Measures," pp. 146-54; Hoist, "Confidence-building Measures: A Conceptual Framework," pp. 2-15; and Byers, et al.

15. Richard E. Darilek, "East-West Confidence-building: Defusing the Cold War in Europe," in *A Handbook of Confidence-Building Measures*, pp. 25-6.

16. Alford, P. 6.

17. Matthew C.J. Rudolph, "Confidence-building Measures between Pakistan and India," *A Handbook of Confidence-building Measures*, pp. 46-48.

18. *Ibid.*

19. *Ibid.*, p. 48.

20. Concern about rising tensions in the region has prompted the Clinton Administration to propose a series of bilateral and multilateral confidence-building measures to supplement those already in place. The American program includes proposals for an agreement. banning the deployment of surface-to-surface missiles, and a halt to the production of nuclear weapons materials, to be verified through international inspections. In addition, the US has suggested the establishment of a multinational forum to consider confidence-building measures for the region, a step that would pave the way for inclusion of China in regional discussions. On the American proposals, see "South Asian Lands Pressed on Arms," *New York Times*, 23 March 23 1994, A5.

21. Michael Krepon, "The Decade for Confidence-Building Measures," in *A Handbook of Confidence-Building Measures*, p. 3.

22. On confidence-building in the Middle East, see Trevor Findlay, "Sinai and Contadora: Non-European Models for Asia/Pacific Confidence-Building," Peace Research Centre, Australian National University, working paper no. 79 (Canberra: April 1990), pp. 2-6. On the implementation of aerial inspections in the Middle East, see also Michael Krepon and Peter Constable, "The Role of

314   *Nonproliferation Export Controls*

Cooperative Aerial Inspections in Confidence Building and Peacemaking," in *Arms Control and Confidence Building in the Middle East* ed. Alan Platt (Washington, D.C.: U.S. Institute of Peace, 1992), pp. 43-64. See also United Nations General Assembly, forty-fifth session, "Establishment of a Nuclear-Weapon-Free Zone in the Region of the Middle East," report of the Secretary-General in pursuance of resolution 43/65, A/43/435, 1990; and James E. Goodby, "Transparency in the Middle East," *Arms Control Today* (May 1991), pp. 8-11.

23. Krepon, p. 2.

24. United Nations General Assembly, forty-fifth session, "Establishment of a Nuclear-Weapon-Free Zone in the Region of the Middle East," report of the Secretary-General in pursuance of resolution 43/65, A/43/435, 1990.

25. Goodby, pp. 8-11.

26. John Redick, "Latin America's Emerging Non-Proliferation Consensus," *Arms Control Today*, p. 5.

27. Spector, pp. 223-25.

28. Jose Goldemberg and Harold A. Feiveson, "Denuclearization in Argentina and Brazil," *Arms Control Today* (March 1994), pp. 10-14.

29. *Ibid.*, p. 14.

30. "Sports, Youth Minister Assesses Northern Policy," FBIS-EAS, 13 March 1991.

31. Bracken refers to reunification as the underlying "second game" being played out on the Peninsula. See Paul Bracken, "Nuclear Weapons and State Survival in North Korea," *Survival*, vol. 35, no. 3 (Autumn 1993), pp. 147-8.

32. The phrase is Paul Bracken's. See "North Korea: Warning and Assessment," testimony prepared for the Armed Services Committee of the U.S. House of Representatives, Hearing on the Situation on the Korean Peninsula, March 24, 1994.

33. "2 Koreas Resume Ministerial Talks," *New York Times*, 23 October 1991; *New York Times*, 25 October 199 1; "North and South Korea Agree to Draw Up Accord," *Financial Times*, 24 October 1991; Paul Blustein, "Two Koreas Pledge to End Aggression," *Washington Post*, 13 December 1991; David E. Sanger,

"Koreas Sign Pact Renouncing Force in Step to Unity," *New York Times*, 13 December 1991; John Ridding, "Korean Accord Eases 40-Year Tension," *Financial Times* ' 13 December 1991; "Korea's Historic Accord Masks Long Road to Unity," *Financial Times*, 13 December 1991.

34. See the text of the declaration in "South and North Initial Nuclear Agreement," *Korea News/Views*, no. 91-63 (Washington, D.C.: Korean Information Office, Embassy of Korea), 31 December 1991. See also "South Korea Tries, Again, for Close Look at North," *New York Times*, 19 February 1992.

35. These bilateral measures have been accompanied by unilateral "confidence-building" steps by the United States. In October 1991, President Bush announced the global withdrawal of all American land- and sea-based tactical nuclear weapons. The announcement in December 1991 that South Korea was "nuclear free" removed a long-standing point of contention in relations between the two Koreas. In attempting to persuade North Korea to accede to IAEA inspections of its nuclear facilities, Washington has also held out the promise of elevated political relations and economic assistance. In a series of low-profile meetings with North Korean officials begun in 1988, the United States has indicated its willingness to upgrade relations with the North if it were to accede to full IAEA safeguards. Further, the United States reaffirmed its negative security assurance, under which it pledges to refrain from using nuclear weapons against any non-nuclear state party to the NPT, except in the case of an attack on the US or its allies by a non-nuclear state allied with a nuclear-weapon state. On US initiatives, see Don Oberdorfer, "Baker Vows Constancy On Asian Security Ties," *Washington Post*, II November 1991; Thomas L. Friedman, "Baker Asks Japan to Broaden Role," *New York Times* 12 November 1991; John Lancaster, "U.S. Troop Cut to Halt Over N. Korea Arms," *Washington Post*, 21 November 1991; David E. Sanger, "U.S. Officials Step Up Warnings to North Korea on Nuclear Arms," *New York Times* 21 November 1991; David E. Sanger, "Seoul to Permit Nuclear Inspections," *New York Times*, 12 December 1991; Paul Blustein, "U.S. Nuclear Arms All Withdrawn," *Washington Post* 12 December 1991; "N. Korea Nuclear Inspection Begins," *Washington Post*, March 4, 1994, A1.

36. "North Korea Signs Accord on Atom Plant Inspections," *New York Times*, 31 January 1992.

37. South Korea is determined to achieve an accord that would allow more intrusive inspections than those currently allowed under the IAEA regime. At meetings of the Joint Nuclear Commission, Pyongyang has demanded the right to inspect virtually all US facilities in the ROK but, in return, offered only one

site in the North for inspection.   See "Kleiner Fortschritt in Korea,"
Sueddeutsche Zeitung, 14 May 1992.

38. For more on the function of CBMs as tools of "nuclear transparency," see
Lisbeth Gronlund, *From Nuclear Deterrence to Reassurance: The Role of
Confidence-Building Measures and Restrictions on Military Development*,
Center for International Security Studies at Maryland, School of Public Affairs,
Project on Rethinking Arms Control, Paper no. 8, December 1993.

39. Analysts of European CBMs commonly refer to several "contextual" factors
as having contributed to the negotiation and implementation of confidence-
building measures, including shared cultural and religious affinities, the bipolar
structure of Europe that resulted in a fairly stable system of states, civilian
control over the military, well developed societal and political infrastructures,
and the presence of nuclear weapons. See Fisher, pp. 35-7.

40. A 1991 Canadian proposal to convene a North Pacific Cooperative Security
Dialogue provoked a cool response from both the United States and Japan, as
did an Australian plan to create a Conference on Security and Cooperation in
Asia (CSCA). Washington has insisted that existing multilateral organizations
and bilateral channels are sufficient to address the security problems and needs
of the region, while Japan has argued that the needs and perceptions of the
region are far too diverse to be discussed fruitfully in a CSCA. The Chinese
leadership, too, has voiced a preference for bilateral confidence-building, while
South Korea has been less than enthusiastic about region-wide security
initiatives. See Trevor Findlay, "Attitudes toward CSBMs in the Asia-Pacific
Region," *Confidence-buildingMeasures in the Asia-PacificRegionDisarmament*
United Nations Department for Disarmament Affairs, Topical Papers, no. @
(New York: 1991), p. 71. In the same volume, see also Ain Huasun, "An
Approach to Confidence-building in the Asia-Pacific Region," pp. 78-84; "North
East Asian Security and Confidence-Building," pp. 85-97.

41.   James Goodby, "The Application of Confidence-building Techniques to
North-East Asia and the Middle East," *Confidence and Security-building
Measures: From Europe to Other Regions, Disarmament*, United Nations
Department of Disarmament Affairs Topical Papers no. 7 (New York: 1991),
77.

Chapter 16

Missile Technology Transfer in Asia

Shuji Kurokawa

The Missile Technology Transfer Issue

Missile technology is one of the most imminent items for export control in the 1990s. A growing list of nations now produce ballistic missiles with indigenous technology and are increasingly less dependent on imported materials. These new supplier states have shaped cooperative relationships with other developing nations seeking to develop or purchase their own missiles.

In the 1970s and 1980s, the USSR exported its Scud and SS-21 missiles; the United States exported its MGM-52 Lance systems; China exported its SS-2's, and North Korea sold abroad a version of the Soviet Scud. Argentina, Egypt, and Iraq were jointly developing their own ballistic missile, the Condor-II. India also was developing the *Agni* (Fire) missile, it's range: 2,500 kilometers, capable of reaching inland China or Teheran, and a short-range surface-to-surface missile, the *Prithvi* (Earth). Pakistan, its chief adversary was developing the *Haft* I and 2 systems, their range: 80 to 600 kilometers.

Of the five cases of missile deployment since 1945, three have been cases of employment during Third World conflicts: The Yom Kippur War of 1973, the Iran-Iraq War of 1980-1988, and the war in Afghanistan of the late 1980s and early 1990s.

Any country with nuclear, chemical and biological weapons capabilities will dramatically increase its military strength after acquiring the ability to deliver these fearful weapons over a great distance. As Peter Van Ham states, the main hazard of this spread of missile technology is the - "multiplier effect."[1]

The Missile Technology Control Regime (MTCR)

In April 1987 MTCR (Missile Technology Control Regime) was established composing the Group of Seven countries: the United Kingdom, France, West Germany, Italy, Canada, Japan, and the United States. They announced that they would restrict exports that could advance the proliferation of nuclear missile technologies (with a range of 300 kilometers or more, and a payload of 500 kilogram or more). The regime consists of common export policy guidelines - referred to as the Guidelines - applied to a common list of controlled items called the Annex.

The Guidelines deal with controlling technology and equipment that could make a contribution to nuclear weapons delivery systems. The Guidelines are not designed to impede non-military national space programs or international cooperation in such programs as long as these programs do not contribute to nuclear weapons delivery

The Annex consists of two categories of equipment and technology to be controlled. Category I consists of complete rocket systems (including ballistic missile systems, space launch vehicles, and sounding rockets) and unmanned air vehicle systems (including cruise missile systems, target and reconnaissance drones) and subsystems, as well as the specially designed production facilities for these systems. Category II consists of goods and technology such as propellants and propulsion systems, certain structural materials, instruments, flight control systems and avionics equipment, launch and ground support equipment and facilities, certain types of computers and software, test equipment, stealth technology, radiation hardened devices, and related production equipment and technology.

At the Oslo Plenary Meeting of the MTCR (June 29-July 2, 1992) Greece, Ireland, Portugal, and Switzerland attended for the first time. As the MTCR has no such thing as an observer status, it was not possible for China, Israel and Russia to attend. In 1992, missiles capable maximum range equal or superior to 300 kilometers were included in a new item 19 under category II of the Equipment and Technology Annex. This extension in the coverage of the MTCR guidelines has been implemented in national legislation by all members as of January 7, 1993.

The twenty-five nations of the MTCR have adopted revised guidelines to extend the scope of the regime to missiles capable of delivering biological and chemical weapons as well as nuclear weapons.[2] The guidelines also called for particular restraint and the presumption to deny transfers of any missiles (whether or not they are included in the annex) and any items of the annex if the government judges that they are intended to be used for the delivery of weapons of mass destruction. The government judgement on the likely use of the missile items will be made, 'on the basis of all available, persuasive information, evaluated according to factors including:

a) concerns about the proliferation of weapons of mass destruction;
b) the capabilities and objectives of the missiles and space programs of the recipient state;
c) the significance of the transfer in terms of the potential development of delivery systems (other than manned aircraft) for weapons of mass destruction;
d) the assessment of the end-use of the transfers, including relevant assurances of the recipient state; and
e) the applicability of relevant multilateral agreements."[3]

These measures will further strengthen the MTCR and be will be important factors in countering the proliferation of missile systems. In addition, a number of countries, although not members of the Regime, have publicly announced their commitment to adhering to the MTCR guidelines. In May 1990, the USSR revealed that it would observe the spirit as well as the guidelines of the MTCR, and it was willing to take the measures to restrict the proliferation of missile technology. In 1991, Argentina announced in the termination of its Condor II ballistic missile program and its intention to adopt the Guidelines, and Israel proclaimed and took steps to implement its adherence to the regime guidelines. In keeping with an agreement reached during US Secretary of State James Baker's November 1991 visit to Beijing, China announced on February 1992, that it would be following MTCR guidelines in return for the lifting of US missile sanctions imposed on it in June 1991. The sanction was imposed on two Chinese companies for transferring missile items to Pakistan and Syria. However, the commitment of major missile producers like China and North Korea, is still in considerable doubt, as will be discussed in the case studies.

The MTCR does not capture all types of cruise missile systems, and arms control agreements ignore many types of these cruise missiles as well. The United States promotes the export of short-range anti -ship missiles such as the Harpoon class. In addition, The United States does not oppose the transfer of every technology that could be used in the development of cruise missiles or systems that utilize cruise missile technology. The US policy is an ambivalence that reflects an important reality: cruise missiles and cruise missile systems however play an increasingly significant role in the military forces friendly to the United States. In President Bill Clinton's address to the United Nations General Assembly on September 27, 1993 he stated that:

> We will maintain our strong support of the Missile Technology Control Regime. We will promote the principles of the MTCR Guidelines as a global missile nonproliferation norm and seek to use the MTCR as a mechanism for tasking joint action to combat missile proliferation. We will support prudent expansion to the MTCR's membership to include additional countries that subscribe to international nonproliferation standards, enforce export controls and abandon effective ballistic missile programs. The United States will also promote regional efforts to reduce demand for missile capabilities....For MTCR member countries, we will not encourage new space launch vehicle programs, which raise questions on both nonproliferation and economic viability grounds. The United States will, however, consider exports of MTCR-controlled items to MTCR member countries for peaceful space launch programs on a case-by-case basis.

The MTCR as a Regime

As the MTCR is neither based upon a treaty or upon an official agreement, it is also lacks an international executive body that monitors the exporters of missile-related technologies on a permanent basis. Moreover, it has no verification provisions and, no formal mechanisms to enforce its guidelines. Furthermore it can not apply sanctions to members which violate them. Accordingly, by these factors we could call MTCR a 'typical' regime. Stephen Krasner offers an apt definition, "'regimes' can be defined as sets of implicit or explicit principles, norms, rules, and decision-making procedures around which actor's expectations converge in a given area of international relations."[4]

The major weaknesses of the MTCR are as follows: First, the MTCR has a limited number of states as members. Many non-member Third World nations including those of Egypt, India, Iran, Iraq, Pakistan, and the two Koreas are capable of attaining physical elements necessary to construct ballistic missiles. And many private corporations of the advanced industrial nations want to export products, parts and technical know-how to these developing countries. On June 20, 1993, the US executed sanctions on the Indian Space Research Organization (ISRO) and the Russian space company, Glavkosmos, following India's purchase of three cryogenic liquid-fueled rockets and associated technology. India and Russia both protested the imposition of the sanctions. India claimed that it had provided adequate end-use assurances that the engines were to be used for peaceful purposes only, and that the technology was not suitable for military applications. Russian officials expressed their belief that the sanctions were imposed to keep Russia from competing with US companies in the commercial space launch market. The American judgement was based on their assertion that the sale was a violation of MTCR Guidelines. India's ballistic missile program continued in spite of American sanctions. Previously, India had conducted its second test of the intermediate range 'Agni' missile, which it referred to as a 'technology demonstrator' in May 1992 at the missile test range at Balasore.

Second, there is the problem of securing the cooperation of non-member states, even with assurances of 'adherence' to regime guidelines. Russia and the People's Republic of China (PRC) are key players in curbing missile proliferation because of their diplomatic influence and status as major suppliers of missiles and related technology. Russia will continue to cooperate in the area of export control because it needs the resources to establish a stable government and economy. The real threat to the MTCR will be China and North Korea who, in spite of promises to the contrary, continue to supply missiles and related technology to other countries.

Third, the restriction categories are difficult to enforce and could be easily circumvented by a determined proliferator. In the past, much of these controlled technologies were easily exported to those nations that assured the exporting government that their use was intended for civilian space launch systems. This is a gray area of the MTCR's restrictions. For example, the US Titan II served as a booster rocket for the American civilian Gemini space program, but as the same time it remained a mainstay of the US ICBM forces.

Fourth, technology thresholds are difficult to enforce. The technology needed to produce a cruise missile capable of reaching a target at 1,000 kilometers is not inherently different from that required to produce a missile system with a range of only 150 kilometers. The range of a cruise missile can be extended considerable distances merely by reducing the size and weight of the warhead and by adding additional fuel.

Fifth, as W. Seth Carus contends, the effective range of a missile is that of the weapon and delivery vehicle carrying it.[5] This presents a strategic military, as well a proliferation concern because cruise missiles can be launched from aircraft with relatively little difficulty. For example, the ASMP strategic cruise missile has a maximum range of only 250 kilometers, the French military believes that it has a strategic role because the ASMP is launched from long-range aircraft with a radius of up to 4,000 kilometers. The US ALCM cruise missile may have the range of 2,500 kilometers, but the bomber launching it can be based 10,000 kilometers from the launch site.

Despite these faults, the MTCR will continue to exist because nonproliferation regimes supply a kind of 'public good'. Once MTCR guidelines were established, their utilization by one country does not diminish the use by others (non-rivalry), and no nation can be excluded from enjoying their benefits (non-excludability). As long as the MTCR function as a regime, there is no way to avoid the 'free rider' problem. The MTCR is perceived by many developing nations as a discriminatory cartel of industrialized country interests conflicting with their sovereignty and independence. They contend, the regime it the primary instrument to prevent developing countries from acquiring cruise missiles and technologies necessary for space programs.

The 'Catch-All' Export Control

Because of the Gulf War, the United States took quite a different approach to export control. COCOM, the MTCR and the Australia Group, each make their respective control lists. But a new method could regulate and control the export of sensitive goods and technologies even though they are not on the regulation lists, if the exporter knew the items would be used in connection with or could form part of weapons system. This "know" regulation or "catch-all" control was announced by President George Bush on December 13, 1990 as a component of the Enhanced Proliferation Control Initiative (EPCI). During 1991, the US, the United Kingdom and Germany adopted the 'know' regulation. This regulation targets the nations that are suspected of developing weapons of mass destruction, but there is no internationally agreed upon list. These nations applied this regulation against China, North Korea, Libya, Iraq and Iran. If the new nonproliferation export control system adopts the 'catch-all' control policy, it would be a heavy burden for private industry. The "burden of proof" should not be on the private companies, but on the government that controls the export.

Case Study I: China

China is the largest supplier of military and dual-use equipment to the developing world. In 1979, the Central Committee of the Chinese Communist Party decided that as a part of "Economic Reform," China would give priority to defense production. In 1980 every military agency received the right to export military weapons. The most notorious example was the export of the HY-2 'Silkworm' anti-ship missile cruise missiles to both sides during the Iran-Iraq War. And tens of thousands of land-based intermediate ballistic missiles were exported to Saudi Arabia.[6] These were a mobile and liquid-style missile whose range was 2,800 kilometers. China named it 'Dong Feng 3A' (East Wind), but the US calls it 'CSS-2' (Chinese Surface-to-Surface 2). On June 22, 1988, The US published a statement alleging that Syria wanted to import Chinese M-9 missiles, and warned the missile export was dangerous because they could carry tactical nuclear warheads. The M-9 is a highly accurate (CEP is estimated to be 650 meters), mobile, surface-to-surface missile with a range of 600 kilometers.Production of the missile began in 1987. Syria had contracted an order for importing the missile with China before the flight tests in 1986.

On June 25, 1991, the US took economic sanctions against China. The reason was that two Chinese companies were engaged in less-than-prudent transfer of missiles and missile technology. One of the companies, CPMIEC exported M-11 missiles to Pakistan. The range is estimated to be over 300 kilometers, with a payload of 500 kilograms. These characteristics exceeded the MTCR guidelines. In November 1991, China pledged to accede to the Nuclear Nonproliferation Treaty

(NPT), and to abide by the MTCR guidelines; it further promised to cancel controversial missile sales to both Pakistan (M-11's) and Syria (M-9's). But after the US presidential elections of 1992, the Central Intelligence Agency (CIA) found that China had imported the components and technologies to Pakistan, not the missile itself. Finally on August 25, 1993, after several rounds of negotiations between the US and PRC, the two giants clashed. The US levelled economic sanctions against Pakistan and China for a period of two years. Washington took China's export activities with Pakistan as a clear violation to the MTCR guidelines. But the Chinese government denied the violations and strongly criticized the American actions. The Pakistani government acknowledged the importation of the M-11 missiles from China. The most serious aspect of the economic sanctions was the embargo on satellites which an American company wanted to export to China. It was estimated that the American economic loss would be $500 million a year. Considering the trade volume between the US and China ($17 billion in 1992) the sanction would not inflict serious harm to China. Arguably, the sanction was not designed to punish China, but to persuade China to join the MTCR. The 1994 defense budget of China exceeded 50 billion yuan, and the growth rate was over twenty percent. Although commodity prices rose 14.7 percent, this growth in military expenditures might create a 'Chinese military threat' in East Asia. A potential flashpoint in the region rose when China declared possession over the Paracel and Spratley Islands in 1992. There was a regional military conflict over the Paracel's in 1982 between Vietnam and the PRC. Furthermore, Vietnam, Malaysia, Taiwan and the Philippines have all claimed the territory of the Spratly Islands.

Case Study II: North Korea

North Korea is the country in East Asia that causes the most anxiety over strategic and proliferation matters. North Korea, long thought to be a potential nuclear weapon state, signed a comprehensive safeguard agreement with the International Atomic Energy Agency (IAEA) on January 30, 1992. The agreement was ratified by the North Korean Parliament on April 9, and was entered into force on April 10, 1992. This step, which came six and a half years after North Korea acceded to the NPT, was a result of concerted efforts by the international community to persuade North Korea to abandon its alleged nuclear intentions and fully comply with its NPT obligations to accept comprehensive IAEA safeguards.

In its declaration to the IAEA delivered on May 4, 1992, North Korea acknowledged the possession of a 5 megawatt gas-cooled, graphite-moderated research reactor at Yongbyon, which had begun operation in 1986. Additionally, after years of denying its existence, North Korea acknowledged it was building a 'radioisotope laboratory' capable of reprocessing plutonium, a key nuclear weapon ingredient.[7] But on February 9, 1992, IAEA Director General Hans Blix requested a special inspection of the two sites because of discrepancies in North Korean declarations to the IAEA and information provided by Western intelligence sources. The plutonium separation facility in Yongbyon became to main focus of debate. In 1992, North Korea produced a reverse-engineered Scud-B missile with a range of 500 kilometers, as well as a Scud-C missile (also called the 'Nodong' or 'Rodong'), with a range of 1,000 kilometers. North Korea exported ballistic missiles to Iran and Syria. On June 11, 1993, a high ranking officer of the Japanese government leaked to the press that in May, the North Koreans test launched three Nodong-I missiles successful. As North Korea announced its departure from the IAEA, the world was left wondering whether they had already developed a nuclear weapons capability. Combined missile technology, which could reach Japan and nuclear weapon production capability, caused grave concern in the Japanese government. *Jane's Defence Weekly* reported on March 9, 1994, that North Korea was developing a new type of missile that could reach Southeast Asia and Guam. In February 1994, US satellites identified new types of missiles, and gave them code names 'Tepodom-1', with a range of 1,900 kilometers and 'Tepodom-2', with a range of 3,500 kilometers. The Japanese Defense Agency concurred with the findings.[8]

There was a crime that would cast dark shadows over the effectiveness of the Japanese export control system. The Japanese police investigated 'Yokohama Machine Trade' and 'Anritu', communication equipment maker, on January 14, 1994, for illegal shipment of a spectrum analyzer to North Korea. The April 1989 issue of *Jane's Defence Weekly* reported that North Korea received a spectrum analyzer from Japan and from some NATO countries for ballistic missile development. Yokohama Machine Trade shipped three spectrum analyzers to North Korea via China in 1989. These were allegedly used to improve the missile's capability in targeting.

To avoid international sanction, Pyongyang finally accepted inspection by the IAEA. But on March 16, 1994, the IAEA complained that the investigation was not thorough enough to prove the non-transfer of nuclear materials to military applications. The US proposed to create a working group for the production of a Theater Missile Defense (TMD) in 1993 as a counter-measure against North Korea's 'Nodong- I'. The first meeting of the working group was held in December 1993.

A Demand Side Approach

The MTCR can slow but not stop missile proliferation. The MTCR has been effective in delaying a missile program and raising the costs of the acquisition of missile-related items and technologies. However, it is unable to halt the politically determined threshold state from pursuing and obtaining the required components for its missile program. As this 'supply-side' approach has inherent limitations, we need another approach, i.e., a 'demand-side' approach. As a starting point, confidence-building measures (CBM's) would lessen the need for missiles.

As Lewis and Joyner state, the US has tended to concentrate its energies on four basic arms limitations strategies.[9] 1) Supply-side restraints are intended to restrict military capabilities of Third World countries by denying them access to technologies and materials likely to produce weapons of mass destruction; 2) Demand-side strategies are intended to eliminate or temper political and economic disputes that might serve as catalysts for armed conflicts; 3) Confidence-building measures seek to encourage cooperation between adversaries in order to reduce the risks of war, or to limit the scope of violence should war erupt; 4) Deterrence involves measures (mainly military) taken to persuade an opponent not to initiate aggressive actions by convincing the latter that the costs and risks of doing so would outweigh anticipated gains. Understanding the reasons why countries desire to possess weapons of mass destruction is critical in formulating nonproliferation strategies. On the demand side, three factors are important: 1) acute threat perceptions; 2) general national security concerns; and 3) political prestige. On the supply side, the issue of the availability of sensitive materials, technology, equipment and know-how is of critical importance.

Notes

1. Peter Van Ham, "Other Non-Conventional Control Regimes" paper presented before the Joint Project of the Royal Institute of International Affairs (London) and the International Institute for Global Peace (Tokyo), June 22-24, 1993, Tokyo, Japan. P. 15.

2. As of February 1995, there were 25 members of the MTCR. The original membership was comprised of France, Germany, Italy, the UK and US. They were later joined by Canada and Japan. Since then, membership has expanded to the present number. The additional members are Argentina, Australia, Austria, Belgium, Denmark, Finland, Greece, Hungary, Iceland, Ireland, Luxembourg, Netherlands, New Zealand, Norway, Portugal, Spain, Sweden and Switzerland. Some other states, including Brazil, China, Israel, Romania, Russia, Slovakia, South Africa and Ukraine have pledged to abide by the MTCR guidelines.

3. *Nonproliferation Regimes: Policies to Control the Spread of Nuclear, Chemical and Biological Weapons and Missiles,* a report prepared for the Committee on Foreign Affairs, U.S. House of Representatives by the Congressional Research Service. Library of Congress, 103d Congress, 1st Session, March 1993, 45.

4. Stephen D. Krasner, "Structural Causes and Regime Consequences: Regimes as Intervening Variables," *International Organization,* 36:2, (1982) 186.

5. W. Seth Carus, "Cruise Missile Proliferation in the 1990s." *The Washington Papers,* No 159, (1992), 94.

6. See an authoritative article by John W. Lewis and Hua Di, "China's Ballistic Missile Programs: Technologies, Strategies, Goals," *InternationalSecurity,* 17:2 (1992) 5-40.

7. Dunbar Lockwood and Jon Brook Wolfsthal, "Nuclear Weapons Developments and Proliferation", *SIPRI Yearbook 1993,* (Oxford: Oxford University Press, 1993) 244-245.

8. *Yomiuri shinbun* (in Japanese), March 11, 1994.

9. William H. Lewis and Christopher C. Joyner, "Proliferation of Unconventional Weapons: The Case for Coercive Arms Control," *Comparative Strategy,* 10, (1991), 301.

Chapter 17

Trade Implications of Future Nuclear Energy Programs

Roger G. Loasby

The driving force for nuclear power has always been the provision of energy once fissile fuel supplies have been exhausted. There remains no substitute for fission reactors when this takes place, but the continuing supply of low cost oil and natural gas has obscured this inevitability. At present, nuclear power is neither needed nor is it an economic prospect. Attention has tended, therefore, to concentrate on its demerits, particularly the environmental risks of reactor waste and the potential for use of the fissionable by-products in nuclear weapons.

Governmental reactions to the public pressures on these problems have varied from withdrawal from the nuclear power arena to a restructuring of nuclear power programs, which has included intensive research to minimize the problems. Several nations, including Japan and Russia, have carefully designed their future nuclear power programs to balance the demand for nuclear fuels with production, so as to avoid the accumulation of uranium and plutonium. Such programs will serve the energy needs of these nations well, but potential problems could arise when other nations move towards nuclear power to meet their own energy needs. The widening use of nuclear power will threaten the materials balance, and hence increase the risks of the use of these materials in weapons.

One question, therefore, relates to policy regarding exporting technologies that will lead to exacerbation of the materials issues. The powers of organizations like the IAEA do not extend to imposing technologies that will lead to exacerbation of the materials issues. The powers of organizations like the IAEA do not extend to imposing conditions on export policies at source, but some kind of internationally supervised management may be necessary to prevent the uncontrolled dissemination of nuclear material.

A second question relates to the trade relationships between the haves and the have nots in reactor technology. There will be an increasing gap between those who have advanced reactor technology to offer the world market, and those who opted out of the field, and hence out of the competition. This situation could lead to trade tensions, notably between the United States and Japan, where the disparity in capability threatens to be large.

Given the long time scales involved in nuclear power technologies and reactor construction times, the US may have to take steps within the next decade to preempt the problems it may have with its trade relationship with Japan, and with the global control of nuclear materials. Possible steps to achieving these objectives include forming joint programs with other nations in nuclear technology, promoting common export policies between the future supplier nations, and supporting an increase in the authority of the IAEA to enable it to maintain control over the global nuclear material stockpile.

Since the introduction of nuclear power in the 1950s, major differences in policy have emerged between nations contemplating its use. Most nations, including the United Kingdom and the United States, saw it as the future source of their energy, but allowed its development to proceed solely on a commercial basis. This led to a major mismatch between supply and demand for the materials produced in these programs. Large quantities of reactor waste, containing considerable quantities of plutonium and uranium have accumulated. In proportion, public concern has grown on two issues; the environmental risks associated with the disposal of the waste, and the threat that the fissile and fissionable material content in the waste could be diverted to nuclear weapon use.

The policies in these countries have essentially led to the abandonment of nuclear power technology, policies readily acceptable in the light of abundant supplies of low cost oil and gas. This approach has, however, done no more than buy time, as these countries will have to respond to the exhaustion of oil and gas supplies, whenever that occurs. The later this is left the greater will be the economic burden, as power stations are heavy consumers of capital and take considerable time to build. Of course, nations like the United States have the capability to recover their position, but the time for beginning this recovery is fast running out, and there is bound to be a period of dependence on those possessing modern technologies. By contrast to this approach, some nations planned, from the outset, for 'closed cycle' nuclear power programs; that is, programs based on a balance of supply and demand of nuclear materials, and on a systematic research program to provide for the safe disposal of active waste. Originally, as in the case of the former Soviet Union, the reasoning was economic rather than social concern, but, more recently, both France and Japan have based their programs on the future needs for socially acceptable energy sources which will be able to replace oil and gas at reasonable cost.

The combination of these two situations; exports which have potential risks, and the disparities between nations in their abilities to effectively compete, could result in political tension as trade opportunities develop in the wake of increasing fissile fuel costs. This paper examines these issues.

Issues of Energy Supply

For the foreseeable future, there are few options for energy supply. Currently, there are three major sources, coal, oil and gas, and nuclear power. Wind and water power may be long term options for some nations, but both the engineering and economics of such sources have yet to be resolved, and they are therefore, relatively unknown quantities. Certainly, they will not be significant options for many nations, particularly those with high energy requirements or strong environmental concerns. Characteristically, neither wind nor water power systems have high energy or power densities: they would thus cover large areas in producing useful amounts of energy. Some nations have large reserves of coal and may return to this source as oil and gas supplies decline. Coal does, however, have major environmental and social disadvantages; in the handling of the by products of its use, and the health of those exposed to both its production and use. Where coal is abundant these problems will, no doubt, be adequately dealt with, and thus the concerns associated with nuclear power avoided.

Most advanced nations do not have this option, however, and will have to consider the alternatives. Although in the distant future new sources may emerge, in the time scale of concern the alternatives reduce to one, nuclear fission power. No other source is a viable option now, and the demands on resources of developing one will prevent their being available when needed.

Nuclear Power Programs

In nuclear power terms, there are essentially two groups of nations; those which have terminated their programs, and those which are embarking on expansion, with the intention of developing a coherent energy policy to minimize the impact of the inevitable rise in oil and gas costs. Many of the early enthusiasts for nuclear power have allowed their programs to languish in the face of declining need and increasing public concern regarding the by products of nuclear power generation. The United Kingdom, having begun an ambitious program in the 1950s to replace its declining coal supplies, acquired its own oil and gas in the 1960s and has all but abandoned its nuclear power generation program. The UK continues to operate a waste reprocessing program, on a commercial basis. Others, including Sweden and the United States, had the same need, and originally, similar programs, but have foregone their programs under unrelenting anti nuclear campaigns. The US does not reprocess any of its waste: this is stored awaiting agreement on its disposal.

Several nations have coherent programs that address each of these concerns. The (then) Soviet Union envisaged a balanced program when it entered the nuclear power era in the 1950s, the rationale being the economic use of the materials produced. Despite the increased use of oil since that time, this policy remains.[1] The Russian projection is that the demand for electricity will increase by a factor of four by the year 2010 and that this 'cannot be supported without jeopardizing the environment unless nuclear power is used.'[2] Initially based on thermal reactors utilizing enriched uranium, the Soviet program included fast breeder reactors burning uranium, of which the USSR had a good supply. The delays in the fast reactor program are now projected to lead to a surplus of some 86te of plutonium, and new fuel compositions are now planned to consume the excess metal.

Mixed plutonium and uranium oxide (MOX) fuels are being developed for use in the current generation of light water reactors

(LWR's) and will also be used in future designs of both thermal and fast reactors. These steps will help reduce the plutonium excess ahead of the availability of the advanced fast reactor generation, and allow for the material balance to be positively managed. Recent events in the former Soviet Union have served to disturb this optimum progression, but it is still the intention to stay with the program as resources allow. An adjunct to this program is the processing of reactor waste: along with several other nations, Russia is studying vitrification as a long term solution to the storage problem.

The French example is intermediate between those of Russia and Japan. Although France imports most (96 percent) of its oil, it can meet nearly half (47 percent) of its energy requirements, mostly from coal and hydroelectric sources. The drive to insulate itself from any repetition of the quadrupling of oil prices in the early 1970s led to a nuclear program which now supplies 73 percent of the nation's electricity needs. France stands third (after Russia and Japan) in nuclear capacity under construction[3]: it also plans to process all its waste. France has plans to introduce MOX burning reactors to reduce its plutonium stockpile, which it hopes will begin to shrink after the year 2000.

Japan is, perhaps, the most interesting of the nations with coherent nuclear policies. It has the highest dependence on imports for its energy (84 percent of its energy; 100 percent of its oil), and the highest dependence on exports for its economic survival. its modem industrial base and economic strength enables it to undertake a comprehensive nuclear power program but it is having to pay particular attention to the waste and weapon issues in the face of a vociferous and powerful anti nuclear faction. As a consequence of these combined pressures, Japan has balanced short, medium and long term elements in its nuclear program and plans to have its own fuel cycle in position by early in the next century. As elsewhere, the initial reactor type will be LWR'S, which will be operating by the mid 1990's with 25 percent mixed uranium/plutonium oxide (MOX) fuel.[4] This will provide for take up of some of the existing excess plutonium. An Advanced Thermal Reactor (ATR), designed to have flexibility in fuel type, will be introduced to fill the gap until the long term generation, of fast breeder reactors, is introduced.

Two important features characterize the Japanese program. First, reactor choices and the program funding are designed for balanced plutonium utilization from the mid 1990's onwards: second, 'efforts are being directed at stimulating and supporting industrialization in the private sector, which is accumulating considerable expertise.'[5] Thus, Japan is establishing policies that will optimally satisfy its social and economic needs, whilst setting up its industry for exploitation of these capabilities.

Repercussions of Nuclear Policies

The contrasts between these various nuclear power policies are striking. Where programs have been summarily terminated, immediate problems have been created. Ironically, termination has exacerbated the social problems: the reactors these nations still have in operation are producing waste that is either accumulating unprocessed (United States) or is being processed (United Kingdom), with the resulting accumulation of valuable nuclear materials for which there is no planned application. In both cases storage and security costs are considerable. As the storage problem increases, the time for response once the need for new reactors is recognized grows shorter. The later new programs are begun the greater will be the economic burden, as energy supplies are heavy consumers of capital and take considerable time to install. By diverting resources on a major scale nations like the United States have the capability to recover, but the time for beginning this recovery is fast running out, and there is bound to be a period of dependence on those nations that possess the technologies in the interim.

By contrast, the programs of those nations with coherent policies will enable them to avoid all but the short term problems. Opposition to nuclear power remains strong in most countries, and will no doubt remain so until standards of living are threatened. As this begins to impact on them, however, the investment in a long term, coherent, program will pay off, in economic stability terms and in export potential.

The Russian program should result, sometime between 2010 and 2030, in it having expertise in the technology and the operating experience in three reactor types, along with some experience in waste handling.

As an export oriented industrialized nation, France will be in the forefront of exploitation of these technologies as demand rises. Japan, likewise, will have experience in a comprehensive range of reactor technologies; three modem reactor types, waste processing and fuel production, and waste disposal.

Impact on External Relations

These programs for nuclear power utilization appear very satisfying. They will meet internal needs and relieve some of the pressures on fissile fuels, which will indirectly benefit non participant nations. For the next two decades or so, few problems are anticipated with these coherent nuclear power policies.

From the global standpoint, however, there are important flaws in the logic of these closed cycle programs, which will emerge as the plans mature. The carefully contrived materials balance is based on national needs: once these are satisfied and the mature reactor industries begin to expand beyond national borders, several potential problems will arise.

First, as fissile fuels decline, the world economy will be obliged to increasingly depend on nuclear power and, as it does so, the balance of the closed cycle on a global scale will be disturbed. Not all users will be as concerned with the waste and weapon issues as are the suppliers. As a consequence, global concerns regarding waste and weapon material production will resurface. Further, many of the countries that will need to invest in a nuclear power program, or who are in the process of modernizing, are in the militarily suspect category with respect to nuclear weapon possession. Second, ahead of these problems concerning nuclear materials, there will be potential problems in the trade relationships between the haves and the have nots in reactor technology. Those nations possessing a mature expertise will have a high value, advanced, technology to export, virtually to the world, as the oil and gas decline will strike fairly evenly. These technologies can neither be developed nor applied rapidly and hence those without this expertise will be both out of the competition and obliged to import the technologies for their own use.

Multilateral Export Control Issues

It is of interest to consider whether any changes in export control policies and mechanisms seem necessary to cover the specific problems that widespread trading in nuclear reactor technology and materials will introduce. At present, a fair degree of international control exists on the dissemination of nuclear materials, due partly to the dominant control the United States exerts, through trade controls, but also to the effectiveness of the monitoring regime operated by the IAEA. Both of these may be weakened by the introduction of new generations of efficient reactors, and the build up of an export trade. The United States, if it continues to be a non participant in the field, will lose its particular leverage, and may have to initiate new control approaches. At the international level, the authority of the IAEA at present extends only to the monitoring of materials in situ, and it has that authority only by the grace of the nations concerned. Its role is essentially passive and does not extend to the preemptive type of control that may be required in the future.

As matters stand, therefore, there is probably only adequate control for such trade to proceed between the committed signatories of the Non Proliferation Treaty (NPT). On the global scale there may well be risk, and there may be a need for more controls. Against this there are, however, trends in world trade that may mitigate the obvious risks and act to reduce the need for new control mechanisms. First, there is an international awareness of the risks which should at least ensure that there will be wide cooperation in fora such as the UN. Second, the nations principally concerned with reactor technology export have a responsible concern for international security in addition to their self interests and it is unlikely that there will be any unregulated activity ahead of international agreement. Third, and perhaps most importantly, there is an increasing global trade interdependence between nations which covers everything from raw materials, particularly those related to energy, through to the commodities on which modem societies depend. Modernization increases this interdependence and, at the same time, the responsibility to conform to global concerns and norms. A good example of a nation in the process of such change is the PRC, now moving from a cavalier phase in its nuclear dealings, to more concerned policies, as it becomes heavily dependent on Western nations for trade to fuel its growth.

The PRC is also going to be influenced by its need for modem reactor technology as its energy demands grow: a practice of responsible behavior will pave the way for acquiring this when the need arises.

None of these considerations decreases the need for a global non proliferation regime, internationally supervised, but the implication is that the growing global interdependence may itself serve to dilute the problems that international trading in nuclear power technologies might otherwise bring.

Non-Proliferation Mechanisms

It is not difficult to speculate on the form additional export control regulations might take. All three of the current potential exporters, France, Japan, and Russia, will have reprocessing facilities and would be in a position to make the return of reactor waste part of export agreements. This type of arrangement would need to be supported by some form of redress, and this would have to be internationally based to be effective. Sanctions as currently operated through the UN are one obvious form of redress, and these are likely to become more effective as trade interdependence increases.

Changes in export control regimes of this kind may appear necessary, even obvious, but problems can be visualized in their acceptance. In the first place, giving any external body influence and a degree of control over nations' export activities is unlikely to **find** ready support internationally, as it represents involvement in a nation's internal affairs. Second, attempts to impose controls on sales of further reactor technology would be unlikely to find favor with exporter nations and, given the number of competing nations in the field, might also be ineffective. As an observation, the Iraq sanctions were quite difficult to achieve, even though virtually all the members of the UN had a direct interest in holding down the price of oil.

Despite these foreseeable difficulties, it is apparent that, once nuclear reactor technologies become major export commodities, clear and significant enhancement of export controls will have to be in place, and enhanced power will have to be given to some international body, such as the IAEA, to positively manage the world inventory of nuclear materials.

Bilateral Export Control Issues

There are likely to be a number of problems at the bilateral level which may complicate export control policies. Of particular concern may be the US - Japan trade relationship. At the present time, there is a broad equality between the two nations at both the low and high end of the technology spectrum, and this gives both nations satisfaction in dealing both with each other and with the export activities between either one and the rest of the world. The contrasting nuclear power policies of the two nations, however, could lead to major trade asymmetries in the future. As matters stand, Japan will be able to command the trade in reactor technology, both with the rest of the world, and with the US. The US will have virtually no recourse on this issue, particularly as it is complicated by the parallel involvement of France and Russia. The US will have little leverage on the issue of approving recipient nations for reactor technology, and hence of proliferation control.

It is probably none too early for the US to begin minimizing these potential problems, perhaps by exploring some of the options already discussed. Confidencebuilding measures, such as joint programs in reactor technologies, and steps toward the formation of a consensus on policies between the future producer nations are possibilities.

Observations

There are likely to be at least three nations actively involved in the export trade of reactor materials and technologies; France, Japan, and Russia. The potential for widespread dissemination of nuclear materials and the acquisition of expertise and nuclear materials by unreliable or unstable nations is, therefore, real. In the long run it is likely that several nations in this category will acquire expertise and nuclear materials, which they will be prepared to share with their allies. It may be desirable, therefore, to strengthen the export control regime to include three features; 1) an extension of the 'closed cycle' principle to cover exports of both equipment and technologies, 2) a strengthening of the active role of the IAEA to enable it to positively manage the world inventory of nuclear materials; and 3) the achievement of some agreement on forms of effective redress.

Notes

1. Yu. K. Bibilashvilli and F.G. Reshetnikov, "Russia's Nuclear Fuel Cycle: An Industrial Perspective", *IAEA Bulletin*, Vol.35, No.3, p.28-33, 1993

2. B.A. Semenov and N. Oi, "Nuclear Fuel Cycles: Adjusting to New Realities", *IAEA Bulletin*, Vol.35, No.3, p.2-7, 1993

3. International Datafile Information, *IAEA Bulletin*, Vol.35, No.3, p.52, 1993

4. National Reports, "Nuclear Energy and its Fuel Cycle in Japan: Closing the Circle", *IAEA Bulletin*, Vol.35, No.3, p.34-37, 1993

5. *Ibid.*

Chapter 18

Nonproliferation Export Controls: U.S.-Japanese Interests and Initiatives

Gary K. Bertsch, Richard T. Cupitt and Takehiko Yamamoto

U.S.-Japanese Export Control Cooperation

The need for cooperation between the United States and Japan on nonproliferation export controls is at a premium. In addition to their mutual efforts to enhance multilateral cooperation within other export control arrangements, including the Missile Technology Control Regime (MTCR), the Australia Group (AG), and the Nuclear Suppliers Group (NSG), both countries are at the forefront of the movement to design a new multilateral export control arrangement to replace COCOM (the Coordinating Committee for Multilateral Export Controls).

For over forty years, the United States and Japan, along with other key members of the Western alliance, worked together in COCOM to control the export of munitions, nuclear items, and militarily critical industrial goods and technologies to the Soviet Union and other communist destinations. Cooperation between the United States and Japan within these multilateral regimes demonstrates both countries' commitment to export controls as a tool of nonproliferation policy, and their broader commitment to global peace and security.

This chapter summarizes the key findings and recommendations made in two workshops related to the project. The first workshop was held at The University of Georgia in Athens, Georgia on March 29-30, 1993. The second workshop took place at Waseda University in Tokyo, Japan on April 5-6, 1994.

The Need for a New Rationale

FINDING: *The governments of Japan and the United States are shifting the rationale for their export control policies from containment to nonproliferation.* In the United States, the revisions of the Export Administration Act will formalize nonproliferation as the primary objective of the export control system, while bureaucratic changes, including re-organizing responsibilities in the Departments of Commerce, Defense, Energy, and State, the Arms Control and Disarmament Agency and the Central Intelligence Agency, continue to shift the focus of the executive to nonproliferation, while restrictions on trade with the post-communist and residual communist countries are liberalized.

In Japan, amendments to Cabinet and Ministerial orders continue to relax controls on trade with the post-communist countries, while increasing restrictions for nonproliferation reasons, a process likely to continue with the new law on export controls.   Bureaucratic re-organization in the Ministry of Foreign Affairs and the Ministry of International Trade and Industry also increases the importance of administering nonproliferation export controls.

FINDING: *The determinants of Japanese and US. export control policy appear to be converging.* Some evidence indicates that internally - motivated security interests, not US pressure or fear of U.S. economic retaliation, now shape Japanese nonproliferation export control policy. At the same time, concerns over US economic interests appear to contribute to US efforts to make controls multilateral and to emphasize verifiable end-use rather than country of destination as a control criteria. Divergent views on dual-use controls mainly exist on tactics towards a few countries (including the People's Republic of China, Iran, and Russia), and on the link between dual-use and arms export controls.

Many difficulties persist in implementing nonproliferation export controls, however, causing important and legitimate concerns in the business communities of both countries.   Indeed, many of the issues raised by the US and Japanese business communities parallel each other. In both countries, businesses are concerned that a broad interpretation of the "catch-all" controls to proscribed end-users or end-uses will be inefficient, ineffective, and generally damaging to any interest in promoting exports.   In both countries, how to share critical information, such as which projects are associated with proscribed end--uses, between governments, within governments, and between business and government remains problematic. In both countries, what items constitute truly strategic goods or "chokepoints" remain ill-defined. In both countries there is continuing interest in streamlining the export licensing process, and in improving internal compliance programs (ICPs) among small and medium size businesses.

FINDING: *Both countries are adopting new control criteria, distancing policy from strategies of delay or denial* Much more sophisticated export control systems are evolving in both the United States and Japan, and more complex ratios between the costs and benefits of controls are emerging. In the next decade, the benefits from nonproliferation export controls may not be as great as the benefits from containment. The new criteria focus on the end-use and end-user, more than the country of destination. Ideally, under this new approach, controls on exports for civil end-use (with the appropriate safeguards) should be more liberal, while controls on exports for suspect end-uses or end-users will be stricter.

Some reforms, however, particularly that implementing the "know" standard, promise to add significant compliance costs for enterprises in both Japan and the United States. Japanese and US industries express very similar concerns about the implementation of nonproliferation controls. As dual-use technologies increasingly permeate the commercial sector, the volume and complexity of controls are likely to rise and the opportunity costs for abiding by the controls will increase. While suppliers need to know their customers, firms typically do not have access to the range of intelligence available to governments, nor the resources to acquire or analyze such information. Without new criteria, the costs of nonproliferation controls may exceed that of containment controls.

FINDING: *Many of these problems stem from the lack of a firm rationale for nonproliferation export controls in a broader, common framework of nonproliferation.* Without the relatively integrated threat posed by Soviet communism and without a broad framework on how to address proliferation issues, multilateral cooperation on nonproliferation export controls will require much greater effort to reach consensus on which targets are threatening, the level of threat, and the "choke-points" and other control mechanisms that might best apply. A realistic assessment of threat depends on evaluations of both capabilities and intent. Containment export controls targeted a group of countries that not only had the capability to harm US and Japanese interests, they also had relatively common ideological (communism) values that were in conflict with the basic security, economic, and political values of the United States and Japan. While the targets of nonproliferation export controls will have some capability to harm US and Japanese interests, their intentions, common interests in opposing the United States and Japan, and their capabilities will vary much more widely making threat assessment much more difficult.

Generally, cooperation on nonproliferation export controls should continue to advance incrementally within existing arrangements, with an emphasis on flexibility. While a grand strategy for export controls would help address methodological and technical issues more clearly, including how to integrate regional and global export control efforts, which items should be controlled, and how catch-all end-user controls should evolve, such a strategy depends on agreement on a broader framework of nonproliferation which does not yet exist.

RECOMMENDATION: *Encourage further multilateral cooperation on nonproliferation export controls by developing of a broader framework of common nonproliferation policies and practices.* Without a more developed overall nonproliferation framework which places export controls into a context of other means for stemming proliferation (such as embargoes, conditional foreign assistance, military action to counter proliferation, or confidence building measures to reduce regional security tensions), many of the disputes over methodological and technical issues will hamper cooperation. As the United States used Mutual Defense Assistance agreements in the 1950s to build cooperation on export controls outside of COCOM with some success, nonproliferation goals could be integrated into the broader framework of foreign policy. Bilateral and multilateral assistance might be used to assist countries in creating or complying with export safeguards, non-proliferation impact statements might be part of development assistance decision-making for individual projects in countries that do not participate in export control arrangements, and market access could be used to reward or punish proliferators, among other possibilities. The costs of implementing these programs should be more diffuse than the current focus on industry compliance, though the latter should remain an important objective.

RECOMMENDATION: *Improve multilateral cooperation on nonproliferation export controls by articulating a more compelling, more complete nonproliferation rationale.* Among other issues, a compelling nonproliferation rationale must establish the relationship between export controls on arms and dual-use items, between export controls and other supply and demand-side policy options, and between nonproliferation and other objectives, especially global and national economic security. This will assist efforts to convince government and business leaders that adhering to nonproliferation norms is not merely Western moral imperialism or an attempt by industrialized countries to maintain market shares for their economic interest. This will allow greater harmonization in licensing and enforcement among countries and regimes. A better rationale will allow the construction of a more coherent set of nonproliferation policies, and where export controls fit within that set. In turn this will allow for better understanding of what can be expected of export controls compared to other policy tools and when they need to be relaxed, tightened, or otherwise modified concerning particular items and targets.

RECOMMENDATION: *Lists of controlled items should be kept relatively short and be indexed on the basis of technological advances and uncontrolled foreign availability.* By minimizing the costs of compliance, cooperation should become more attractive. This will also help policy-makers assess the specific economic costs of controls in the licensing process. If coupled with a license-free zone among participating states, however, pressures for item liberalization may be further reduced, while the incentives for adopting nonproliferation export controls will increase.

RECOMMENDATION: *Most importantly, the norm that exports should be governed by nonproliferation considerations requires a high-level political commitment of an enduring nature from the United States, Japan, and other countries.* With leadership, and the provision of sufficient information, being labelled "soft on proliferation" could be the most effective sanction available. At the same time, an open discussion of the costs of nonproliferation export controls could help develop more effective and efficient means of countering proliferation. In particular, the expectation of policy stability --- which clear and consistent support from political leaders generates --- would attract greater support for the policy from industry by reducing the degree of uncertainty facing the business community.

Reforming Multilateral Export Control Arrangements

FINDING: *Both the US. and Japanese governments are playing key roles in creating a nonproliferation arrangement for arms and dual-use items to replace the late Coordinating Committee for Multilateral Export Controls (COCOM), and are taking the lead in tightening controls in the other export control arrangements.* In a major shift in policy by the United States, both countries are now in agreement that a post-COCOM arrangement should include controls on both arms and dual-use items in the name of nonproliferation and regional stability. Japan and the United States have cooperated closely in reforming rules and procedures in the Australia Group, the Missile Technology Control Regime, and the Nuclear Suppliers Group. Japan also undertakes important leadership responsibilities in multilateral export control arrangements. Since the Toshiba affair, Japan has become more active and committed in various multilateral export control fora, as evidenced by its agreement to provide a point of contact for the NSG. As a key supplier of most dual-use technologies, the Japanese government now views its cooperation and leadership in the area of nonproliferation export controls as an important means of contributing to global peace and prosperity.

FINDING: *Though much can be done to harmonize the existing export control policies on a multilateral basis, full consolidation of all export control arrangements is not likely to succeed in the near future.* Despite many commonalities, critical differences exist between the multilateral arrangements. The arrangements differ significantly in the amount of global production controlled by the supplier states, the total number of suppliers and consumers of controlled items, the costs of compliance, monitoring and enforcement, the importance of controlled items for national and global commerce, besides the many differences in item lists, target lists, norms, rules, and procedures. This differences will not prove trivial. Even in COCOM member states never harmonized fully crucial elements of export control policies and programs after forty years of effort. The current level of national discretion and interpretation for the non-proliferation arrangements exceeds that of COCOM, suggesting that full harmonization within these arrangements will be difficult to achieve in the near future.

FINDING: *The cost-to-benefit ratio of existing export control arrangements continues to worsen, however, making additional reform imperative.* The global diffusion of dual-use technologies, the emergence of the commercial sector as the primary source for dual-use technologies, and broader and deeper integration among national economies all suggest that the costs of existing export control arrangements are likely to increase. The growth in the number of multinational companies and production processes alone creates pressures for greater harmonization of various national export control systems, if they are to be effective. At the same time, no specific military threat is likely to evolve in the next decade that equals that once posed by the Soviet Union.

RECOMMENDATION: *The United States, Japan, and cooperating states should encourage further multilateral cooperation on nonproliferation export controls by incrementally reforming the existing institutional framework.* Working within existing institutions will provide some protection against proliferation (as well as allow government and business officials more practical experience), and prevent *ad hoc* dismantlement of export controls. Creating a more compelling nonproliferation rationale and developing appropriate policies will take considerable time. As the threats from proliferation have not abated, abandoning existing export control arrangements would not be prudent.

RECOMMENDATION: *A broader framework for export control incentives and sanctions should fortify existing enforcement efforts, the weakest aspect of current multilateral export control arrangements.*
As with many international agreements, the multilateral export control arrangements rely almost exclusively on national enforcement programs. Differences in enforcement practices and legal systems, difficulties in sharing intelligence, and the relative scarcity of resources for export

controls mean that some suppliers can avoid sanctions altogether, and that sanctions against individuals or firms, if applied, are too late or are otherwise ineffective in stopping specific transactions. This exacerbates tensions among the participating states.

RECOMMENDATION: *Cooperating states should create a multilateral council that will consolidate parts of the various export control arrangements on a trial basis.* Despite the many problems, additional reform is necessary. There is general agreement on some items and targets among the key supplier countries. Participants in this arrangement might agree that, for a period of twenty-five years after its creation, they would meet regularly to share licensing and enforcement information and otherwise harmonize their export control systems. Members of the Council could:

• maintain a license-free zone with other members; o prohibit any exports of proscribed items, and apply "prior notification" and "no-undercut" rules for the export of controlled items to non-members of the Council;
• develop explicit criteria for membership, based on acceptance of export control standards and nonproliferation performance; o share resources for multilateral monitoring and verification of safeguards, enforcement, and gathering and analyzing information on the potential impact of emerging dual-use technologies on nonproliferation; and
• develop a secure electronic network to share information on suspect end-users or suppliers, with at least some access, however restricted, for industry (public input, including the opportunity to challenge data, could be incorporated into database procedures).

Addressing Regional Problems

FINDING: *The collapse of Soviet communism not only did not resolve crucial security issues in the region, it made some proliferation problems even worse.* Though the threats differ in nature and degree, the role of North Korea and China in the proliferation of weapons of mass destruction (advanced conventional and unconventional) and their means of delivery and production weapons continue to be of vital, immediate concern to Japan and the United States. In addition, current and potential proliferation of sensitive goods, technologies, and personnel from the newly independent states of the former Soviet Union poses even more danger for the global and regional interests of Japan and the United States.

FINDING: *While Russian and Chinese declared nonproliferation policy increasingly conforms to US. and Japanese policies, their intentions and abilities to implement those policies remain a matter of concern.* Not only does the gap between declared and actual policy diminish efforts to promote nonproliferation, these gaps will become an increasing source of tension between these two countries and the United States and Japan. If the Chinese view Japanese plutonium policy from a worst case perspective, for example, China may pursue a policy of noncompliance despite nominal adherence to various export control arrangements. The possibility that the United States and Japan will disagree over how to respond, however, will diminish to the extent that a post-Cold War common framework for proliferation controls can be expanded.

FINDING: *In a particularly difficult case, the North Korean nuclear program appears to be closely associated with the legitimacy of the current North Korean government, so incentives and disincentives based only on tangible economic or military security interests will not prove effective.* North Korean leaders would like to reduce the degree of economic isolation, avoid the costs of an arms race, and reduce the security threats they perceive from the United States and Japan. The nuclear program, however, is also tied to the legitimacy or illegitimacy of the current leadership. Without continued gestures from Western states that permit the current leadership to save face, it is unlikely to comply fully to the 1994 agreement to dismantle its potential for developing nuclear weapons.

RECOMMENDATION: *New criteria for evaluating export control policy must be developed with a special emphasis on regional conflicts.* During the Cold War, success was measured largely by the impact export controls had on the Soviet strategic threat. In the post-Cold War era, policy evaluation must include a broader assessment of the impact of controls on mutual economic development, political reform in recipient countries, and on military stability. Any new criteria will first depend on the creation of a new global security framework, which will help determine the role of export control policy in overall efforts to manage the proliferation of dual-use technologies. Nonetheless, it is clear that governments must enhance the coordination of national and multilateral export control systems to reduce regional conflicts, which are likely to pose the greatest security threats in the next few decade.

RECOMMENDATION: *Encourage further multilateral cooperation on nonproliferation export controls by modifying the institutional framework to better address Asian-Pacific issues.* Through multiple channels, formal and informal, government and non-government, Japan and the United States should expand on their efforts to raise the importance of nonproliferation export controls among states as they become producers, consumers, or transit points for proscribed items. Since current human and financial resources for institutional efforts are limited, care must be taken to increase or redirect assets to avoid diluting the overall nonproliferation effort.

RECOMMENDATION: *Begin efforts to assist China in developing its controls on exports for economic development to link its less formal system of nonproliferation export controls.* As the declared nonproliferation policy of China increasingly conforms with US and Japanese policies, holding the Ministry of Foreign Affairs more accountable, engaging the Ministry of Foreign Economic Relations and the People's Liberation Army more directly in the process, and perhaps providing assistance similar to that promised the newly independent states of the former Soviet Union may help China participate in and comply more **fully** with the overall nonproliferation effort.

RECOMMENDATION: *Follow promises of assistance for export controls and nonproliferation policies to the newly independent states of the former Soviet Union with actual assistance befitting the needs of the particular state, and increase assistance where it proves effective.* While both the United States and Japan have provided some assistance, many officials in the newly independent states feel that very little has actually been dispensed. While taking care to evaluate the impact of these funds, these funds are a relatively inexpensive preventative measure against proliferation.

RECOMMENDATION: *Develop model corporate strategies for Nonproliferation Export Controls implementing nonproliferation export controls through close cooperation between business, government, and academia.* Through corporate strategies depend on the direction and leadership provided by government, developing some model strategies along with a new nonproliferation rationale should make policy implementation easier and compliance more likely. Model strategies may also help governments understand the special problems facing industry in implementing nonproliferation export controls. Developing model strategies will also promote the norm of nonproliferation in critical social institutions.

Conclusion

In recent testimony before U. S. Senate, Undersecretary of State for International Security Affairs Dr. Lynn E. Davis testified that the proliferation "of weapons of mass destruction and sophisticated conventional arms is perhaps the single most important security threat" to the United States and its allies.[1] Reports by the Office of Technology Assessment of the US Congress, the Security Export Control Committee of the Industrial Structure Council of the Ministry of International Trade and Industry (MITI), the US National Academy of Sciences, and other institutions, however, have demonstrated the difficulties in finding effective policies to stem the proliferation without creating unwarranted barriers to economic security.[2]

Although a variety of arms control techniques are necessary to solve this problem, export controls have an important role to play in slowing the rate of proliferation, and even stemming the flow of certain types of weaponry and weapons technology. As nonproliferation export controls are emerging as a critical item on the global political agenda, the G-7 leaders noted in the political declaration from their July 1992 meeting that "[a] major element of this effort is the informal exchange of information to improve and harmonize ... export controls."[3]

Since the 1950s, military technologies have become ever more enmeshed with dual-use items (goods and technologies that have both military and civil uses). How Japan and the United States resolve the balance between military and economic security will have a significant impact on multilateral efforts to improve and harmonize export controls. These two countries produce virtually every dual-use item now subject to controls, or that might be subject to controls. Moreover, they have had many difficulties coordinating their dual-use export control policies. As both countries forge new overall foreign policies for the post-Cold War era, however, cooperation on export controls now has the potential to create a balanced and durable global partnership. Certainly, without the cooperation of these countries, no multilateral export control arrangement can be sustained.

Notes

1. Statement by Undersecretary Davis before the Senate Committee on Banking, Housing, and Urban Affairs Subcommittee on International Finance and Monetary Policy, February 24, 1994.

2. See, for example, Security Export Control Committee, *The Future of Security Export Controls* (Tokyo: MITI, March 1993), mimeo; Panel on the Future Design and Implementation of U.S. National Security Export Controls, *Finding Common Ground & U.S. Export Controls in a Changed Global Environment* (Washington, DC: National Academy Press, 1991); and U.S. Congress, Office of Technology Assessment, *Proliferation of Weapons of Mass Destruction: Assessing the Risks,* OTA-ISC-559 (Washington, DC: USGPO, August 1993).

3. "Full text of the political declaration issued at the Munich summit," *The Japan Times,* July 8, 1992: 19.

Index

About the Contributors

Dr. Gary K. Bertsch is Co-Director and Professor of Political Science, Center for International Trade and Security (CITS), University of Georgia, Athens, Georgia

Dr. Richard T. Cupitt is Associate Director of Research and Adjunct Professor of Political Science, Center for International Trade and Security (CITS), University of Georgia, Athens, Georgia

Dr. Takehiko Yamamoto is Associate Dean and Professor of International Politics, School of Political Science and Economics, Waseda University, Tokyo, Japan

Dr. Beverly Crawford is Associate Director of the Institute for International Studies, and Associate Professor of Political Science, University of California, Berkeley, California

Dr. Zachary S. Davis is a Senior Researcher in the International Nuclear Policy Division of the Congressional Research Service at the Library of Congress, Washington, D.C.

Dr. Cathleen S. Fisher is a Senior Associate with the Henry L. Stimson Center in Washington, D.C. and is the Director of the Center's Project on Eliminating Weapons of Mass Destruction

Dr. Glennon J. Harrison is Specialist in International Trade and Finance in the Economics division of the Congressional Research Service at the Library of Congress, Washington, D.C.

Dr. Hajime Izumi is Professor of International Relations, University of Shizuoka, Tokyo, Japan

Dr. Shuji Kurokawa is Professor of International Politics, School of Liberal Arts & Sciences, Yokohama City University, Japan

Dr. Roger Loasby is a Defense Analyst with York Research Associates, Carnesville, Georgia

Dr. William J. Long is Associate Director and Associate Professor of International Affairs, School of International Affairs, Georgia Institute of Technology, Atlanta, Georgia

Dr. Yuzo Murayama is Associate Professor, Osaka University of Foreign Studies, Osaka, Japan

Mr. Jun-ichi Ozawa and **Mr. Takeshi Ito** are Senior Research Fellows with the International Institute of Policy Studies (IIPS), Tokyo, Japan

Dr. Han S. Park is Director, Center for the Study of Global Issues (GLOBIS), and Professor of Political Science, University of Georgia, Athens, Georgia

Dr. Thomas J. Schoenbaum is Academic Director, School of Law and Professor of Political Science, University of Georgia, Athens, Georgia

Dr. Yoko Yasuhara is Associate Professor, College of International Relations, Nihon University, Shizuoka, Japan

Mr. Michio Yoneta is Director-General of the Research Department, Center for Information on Security Trade Control (CISTEC), Tokyo, Japan